ICSA Study Text

# Academy Governance

ICSA Study Text

# Academy Governance

**Katie Paxton-Doggett**

The Governance
Institute

First published 2018
Published by ICSA Publishing Ltd
Saffron House
6–10 Kirby Street
London EC1N 8TS

Typeset by Patricia Briggs

British Cataloguing in Publication Data
A catalogue record for this book is available from the British Library.

ISBN  9781860727276

# Contents

# How to use this study text

This study text has been developed to support ICSA's Level 4 Certificate in Academy Governance and includes a range of navigational, self-testing and illustrative features to help you get the most out of the support materials.

The text is divided into three main sections:

◆ introductory material
◆ the text itself
◆ additional reference information.

The sections below show you how to find your way around the text and make the most of its features.

## Introductory material

The introductory section includes a full contents list and the aims and learning outcomes of the qualification, as well as a list of acronyms and abbreviations.

## The text itself

Each part opens with a list of the chapters to follow, an overview of what will be covered and learning outcomes for the part.

Every chapter opens with a list of the topics covered and an introduction specific to that chapter.

Chapters are structured to allow students to break the content down into manageable sections for study. Each chapter ends with a summary of key content to reinforce understanding.

## Features

The text is enhanced by a range of illustrative and self-testing features to assist understanding and to help you prepare for the examination. You will find answers to the 'Test Yourself' questions towards the end of this text. Each feature is presented in a standard format, so that you will become familiar with how to use them in your study.

These features are identified by a series of icons.

The text also includes tables, figures and other illustrations as relevant.

## Reference material

The text ends with a range of additional guidance and reference material, including a glossary of key terms, a directory of web resources and a comprehensive index.

Stop and think

Test yourself

Making it work

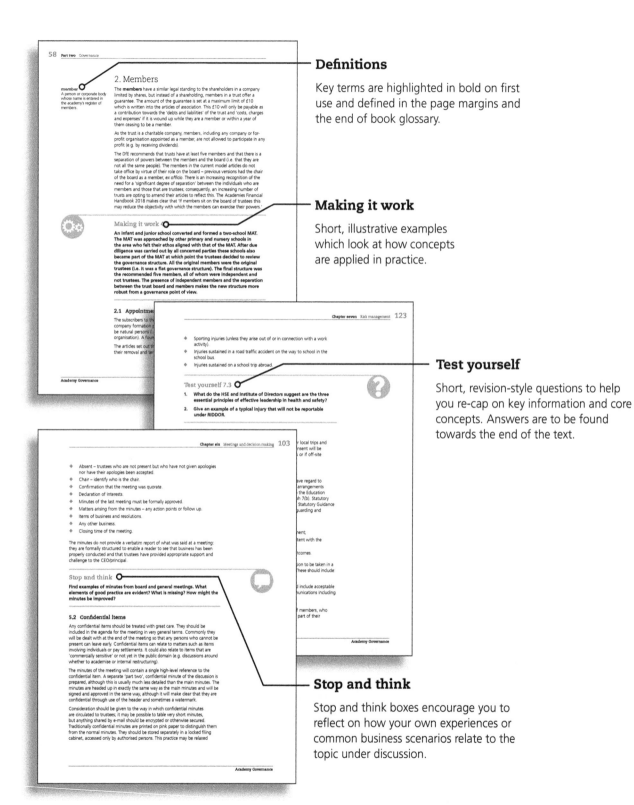

## Definitions

Key terms are highlighted in bold on first use and defined in the page margins and the end of book glossary.

## Making it work

Short, illustrative examples which look at how concepts are applied in practice.

## Test yourself

Short, revision-style questions to help you re-cap on key information and core concepts. Answers are to be found towards the end of the text.

## Stop and think

Stop and think boxes encourage you to reflect on how your own experiences or common business scenarios relate to the topic under discussion.

# Syllabus outline

## Qualification outline and aims

The Level 4 Certificate in Academy Governance has been designed to help students learn the skills required to develop good governance practices in academy schools. In particular, the course focuses on the governance requirements of multi-academy trusts (MATs) and the roles and responsibilities of key officers including the board of trustees, clerk and company secretary.

## Part one: Legislative and Regulatory Framework – 15%

### Overview

This part explores the nature of governance and the legislative and regulatory framework which shapes it. It examines the impact of regulators and the constitution as a charitable company and subsequent requirement to comply with charity and company law.

Students will gain a broad understanding of the legal framework within which the governance of academies is set.

### Learning outcomes

In this part you will:

1 Understand how the principles of good governance are applied by academies in the UK.
2 Know about the legal and regulatory framework for academies and the role of regulators in academy governance.
3 Know about the roles and responsibilities of the Department for Education (DfE) and the Education and Skills Funding Agency (ESFA).
4 Understand how compliance with charity and company law impacts on academies.

# Part two: Governance – 35%

## Overview

This part explains the different types of governance structures that are available for academies. It outlines the nature of an academy's constitution as set out in its articles, how the roles and responsibilities of the officers are delineated and how responsibility is delegated through an academy. The roles of clerk and company secretary are explored in detail.

Students will gain a broad understanding of the different governance structures and a more detailed understanding of the roles and responsibilities of officers and delegation of authority.

## Learning outcomes

In this module you will:

1 Understand how the legal structures of academies impact on governance.
2 Understand the roles and responsibilities of the board of trustees, board committees and members.
3 Understand the roles and responsibilities of the clerk and the company secretary.

# Part three: Risk, Compliance and Policies – 35%

## Overview

This part examines the process of risk management, looking at how different types of risk are identified, managed and tolerated, and the factors that influence the treatment of risk. It considers statutory and regulatory compliance and how information, especially electronic data, should be managed. It also explains the types of reviews that can be used to ensure robust governance practices.

Students will gain a broad understanding of the legal and regulatory requirements for academies as well as best practice around risk management and reviews that can be put in place.

## Learning outcomes

In this module you will:

1 Understand the importance of assessing and managing risk in academies.
2 Understand how to comply with legal and regulatory requirements for academies.
3 Know how legal requirements for information management are met.
4 Know the procedures around performance management and internal and external reviews.

# Part four: Financial Management – 15%

## Overview

This part explores the main sources of income for academies as well as the legal and governance issues that relate to the proper application and management of funds. It also examines the need for financial compliance to legal requirements as well as the need for robust financial controls.

Students will gain a broad understanding of the key principles affecting financial management in an academy and how they affect the trustees and office holders as they seek to discharge their legal duties and responsibilities in practice.

## Learning outcomes

In this module you will:

1    Understand the main sources of income for academies and restrictions imposed on their management.
2    Understand regulatory and legal requirements for financial planning, reporting and control.
3    Understand the importance of financial planning and how it relates to strategic planning.

# Acronyms and abbreviations

| | |
|---|---|
| ACAS | Advisory, Conciliation and Arbitration Service. |
| AFCS | Armed Forces Compensation Scheme. |
| AGM | Annual General Meeting. |
| AP | Alternative provision academies. |
| ARD | Accounting reference date. |
| ASP | Analyse School Performance. |
| AWPU | Age-weighted pupil unit. |
| CA 2006 | Companies Act 2006. |
| CBI | Confederation of British Industry. |
| CEO | Chief Executive Officer (in a MAT). |
| CFO | Chief Financial Officer. |
| CIF | Condition Improvement Fund. |
| CPD | Continuing professional development. |
| DBE | Diocesan Board of Education. |
| DBS | Disclosure and Barring Service. |
| DfE | Department for Education. |
| DPO | Data protection officer. |
| EAL | English as an additional language. |
| EEF | Education Endowment Foundation. |
| EFA | Education Funding Agency. |
| EHCP | Education, Health and Care Plan. |
| ERG | External review of governance. |
| ESFA | Education & Skills Funding Agency. |
| ESG | Education Services Grant. |
| EYFS | Early Years Foundation Stage. |
| FE | Form Entry (as in 2FE). |
| FE | Further Education. |
| FMGS | Financial Management and Governance Self-Assessment. |
| FNtI | Financial Notice to Improve. |

| | |
|---|---|
| FOI | Freedom of Information. |
| FS | Foundation stage. |
| FSM | Free school meals. |
| GAG | General annual grant. |
| GASDS | Gift Aid Small Donations Scheme. |
| GDPR | General Data Protection Regulation |
| GIAS | Get information about schools. |
| HMRC | HM Revenue and Customs. |
| HPCF | Healthy Pupils Capital Fund. |
| HSE | Health and Safety Executive. |
| ICO | Information Commissioner's Office. |
| ICSA | The Institute of Chartered Secretaries and Administrators. |
| IDACI | Income deprivation affecting children index. |
| ISO | International Organization for Standardization. |
| KPI | Key Performance Indicator. |
| KS1 | Key Stage 1. |
| KS2 | Key Stage 2. |
| KS3 | Key Stage 3. |
| KS4 | Key Stage 4. |
| LA | Local Authority. |
| LAAP | Local Authority Associated Persons. |
| LAC/CLA | Looked after children. |
| LADO | Local Authority Designated Officer. |
| LGB | Local Governing Body (in a MAT). |
| LSCB | Local Safeguarding Children Board. |
| MAT | Multi-academy trust. |
| NED | Non-executive director. |
| NFF | National funding formula. |
| NGA | National Governance Association. |
| NLE | National Leader of Education. |
| NLG | National Leader of Governance. |
| NSS | National Support School. |
| OFSTED | Office for Standards in Education. |
| PFI | Private Finance Initiative. |
| PP/PPG | Pupil premium grant. |
| PPA | Planning, preparation and assessment. |
| PROOF | 'Protected online filing'. |
| PSC | Persons of significant control. |

| | |
|---|---|
| PSHE | Personal, social, health and economic education. |
| PTA | Parent Teacher Association. |
| RAG | Red, Amber, Green. |
| RIDDOR | Reporting of Injuries, Diseases and Dangerous Occurrences Regulations. |
| RPA | Risk Protection Arrangement. |
| RSC | Regional Schools Commissioner. |
| SAIL | Single alternative inspection location. |
| SAR | Subject access request. |
| SARA | Sector annual report and accounts. |
| SAT | Single academy trust. |
| SCA | School condition allowance. |
| SEF | Self evaluation form. |
| SEN | Special educational needs. |
| SENCo | Special educational needs coordinator. |
| SEND | Special educational needs and disability. |
| SFA | Skills funding agency. |
| SIC | Standard industrial classification. |
| SIP | School improvement plan. |
| SORP | Statement of Recommended Practice. |
| UIFSM | Universal infant free school meals. |
| URN | Unique reference number. |
| UTC | University Technical College. |
| VA | Voluntary aided. |
| VAT | Value added tax. |
| VC | Voluntary controlled. |
| VLE | Virtual learning environment. |
| WGA | Whole of Government Accounts. |
| WPS | War pensions scheme. |
| WRAP | Workshop to Raise Awareness of Prevent. |

# Part one

# Legislative and Regulatory Framework

**Overview**

This part explores the nature of governance and the legislative and regulatory framework which shapes it. It examines the impact of regulators and the constitution as a charitable company and subsequent requirement to comply with charity and company law.

Students will gain a broad understanding of the legal framework within which the governance of academies is set.

## Learning outcomes

In this part you will:

◆ Understand how the principles of good governance are applied by academies in the UK.
◆ Know about the legal and regulatory framework for academies and the role of regulators in academy governance.

◆ Know about the roles and responsibilities of the Department for Education (DfE) and the Education and Skills Funding Agency (ESFA).

◆ Understand how compliance with charity and company law impacts on academies.

# Chapter one
# Introduction to governance and the academies landscape

**CONTENTS**

1. Introduction
2. Defining good governance
3. Strategic versus operational
4. Background to academisation
5. Legal structure of academies
6. Independent trustees
7. Academy freedoms
8. The role of governance in school improvement
9. Principles of good governance
10. Collaboration

## 1. Introduction

This chapter outlines what makes good governance and provides details of the UK Corporate Governance Code. The expectations on academy trusts to secure effective governance stem from several different sources including the legislative framework, their articles of association and funding agreements, guidance produced by the Department for Education (DfE) such as the Academies Financial Handbook and accountability through Ofsted (the Office for Standards in Education) and Regional School Commissioners (RSCs).

## 2. Defining good governance

Corporate governance is the system of rules, practices and processes by which a company is directed and controlled. It is about the way that organisations establish an infrastructure that improves the quality of decision making by the board and management by ensuring that processes and monitoring controls are in place. Good corporate governance creates a structure with clear levels of accountability and communication which allows a trust to operate smoothly and staff to understand their roles and responsibilities. This will, ultimately, enable the trust to work efficiently and effectively and will support improvements in pupil outcomes.

*Financial Aspects of Corporate Governance* was published in 1992 in response to a series of major scandals that had taken place in the corporate world. Produced by a committee chaired by Sir Adrian Cadbury and known as the 'Cadbury Report', it covered financial, auditing and corporate governance matters and made specific recommendations on the arrangements of company boards and accounting systems to mitigate risks and failures.

**remuneration**
Payments and benefits that an employee is entitled to in respect of services provided by the employee to an academy.

The UK Corporate Governance Code (originally known as the Combined Code) was subsequently published. The Code sets 'standards of good practice in relation to board leadership and effectiveness, **remuneration**, accountability and relations with shareholders'. The purpose of corporate governance is to 'facilitate effective, entrepreneurial and prudent management that can deliver the long-term success of the company'. Although the Code is aimed primarily at listed companies, non-listed public and private companies are encouraged to comply.

In July 2018, the Financial Reporting Council published a revised Code. The revised Code has five sections:

**1.**   Board leadership and company purpose

> **A.**   A successful company is led by an effective and entrepreneurial board, whose role is to promote the long-term sustainable success of the company, generating value for shareholders and contributing to wider society.
>
> **B.**   The board should establish the company's purpose, values and strategy, and satisfy itself that these and its culture are aligned. All directors must act with integrity, lead by example and promote the desired culture.
>
> **C.**   The board should ensure that the necessary resources are in place for the company to meet its objectives and measure performance against them. The board should also establish a framework of prudent and effective controls, which enable risk to be assessed and managed.

**stakeholder**
A person or group of persons with an interest in an academy or who are in some way affected by an academy's activities

> **D.**   In order for the company to meet its responsibilities to shareholders and **stakeholders**, the board should ensure effective engagement with, and encourage participation from, these parties.
>
> **E.**   The board should ensure that workforce policies and practices are consistent with the company's values and support its long-term sustainable success. The workforce should be able to raise any matters of concern.

**2.**   Division of responsibilities

> **F.**   The chair leads the board and is responsible for its overall effectiveness in directing the company. They should demonstrate

objective judgement throughout their tenure and promote a culture of openness and debate. In addition, the chair facilitates constructive board relations and the effective contribution of all **non-executive directors**, and ensures that directors receive accurate, timely and clear information.

G.  The board should include an appropriate combination of executive and non-executive (and, in particular, independent non-executive) directors, such that no one individual or small group of individuals dominates the board's decision-making. There should be a clear division of responsibilities between the leadership of the board and the executive leadership of the company's business.

H.  Non-executive directors should have sufficient time to meet their board responsibilities. They should provide constructive challenge, strategic guidance, offer specialist advice and hold management to account.

I.  The board, supported by the **company secretary**, should ensure that it has the policies, processes, information, time and resources it needs in order to function effectively and efficiently.

3.  Composition, succession and evaluation

J.  Appointments to the board should be subject to a formal, rigorous and transparent procedure, and an effective succession plan should be maintained for board and senior management. Both appointments and succession plans should be based on merit and objective criteria and, within this context, should promote diversity of gender, social and ethnic backgrounds, cognitive and personal strengths.

K.  The board and its committees should have a combination of skills, experience and knowledge. Consideration should be given to the length of service of the board as a whole and membership regularly refreshed.

L.  Annual evaluation of the board should consider its composition, diversity and how effectively members work together to achieve objectives. Individual evaluation should demonstrate whether each director continues to contribute effectively.

4.  Audit, risk and internal control

M.  The board should establish formal and transparent policies and procedures to ensure the independence and effectiveness of internal and external audit functions and satisfy itself on the integrity of financial and narrative statements.

N.  The board should present a fair, balanced and understandable assessment of the company's position and prospects.

O.  The board should establish procedures to manage risk, oversee the internal control framework, and determine the nature and extent of the principal risks the company is willing to take in order to achieve its long-term strategic objectives.

**non-executive director**
A director who is not a full-time employee involved in the management of the academy.

**company secretary**
An officer of a company with no legally defined role but who generally has responsibilities with regard to the administrative, governance and compliance aspects of a company's affairs.

5. Remuneration

   **P.** Remuneration policies and practices should be designed to support strategy and promote long-term sustainable success. Executive remuneration should be aligned to company purpose and values, and be clearly linked to the successful delivery of the company's long-term strategy.

   **Q.** A formal and transparent procedure for developing policy on executive remuneration and determining director and senior management10 remuneration should be established. No director should be involved in deciding their own remuneration outcome.

   **R.** Directors should exercise independent judgement and discretion when authorising remuneration outcomes, taking account of company and individual performance, and wider circumstances.

Trusts should take into consideration the principles set out in the Code, not least those relating to the operation of the board.

The DfE's *Governance Handbook* sets out the government's 'vision and priorities for effective governance' and should be read alongside the DfE's *Competency Framework for Governance* and the *Clerking Competency Framework*.

The *Governance Handbook* states that the purpose of governance 'to provide confident, strategic leadership and to create robust accountability, oversight and assurance for educational and financial performance'. It is clear that all boards, no matter what types of school or how many schools they govern, have three core functions:

◆ ensuring clarity of vision, ethos and strategic direction;

◆ holding executive leaders to account for the educational performance of the organisation and its pupils, and the performance management of staff; and

◆ overseeing the financial performance of the organisation and making sure its money is well spent.

The handbook also sets out the six key features necessary for effective governance:

1. Strategic leadership that sets and champions vision, ethos and strategy.
2. Accountability that drives up educational standards and financial performance.
3. People with the right skills, experience, qualities and capacity.
4. Structures that reinforce clearly defined roles and responsibilities.
5. Compliance with statutory and contractual requirements.
6. Evaluation to monitor and improve the quality and impact of governance.

The DfE's guidance on Schools Causing Concern also includes expectations about effective governance and provides powers for the Regional Schools Commissioners to intervene in schools and trusts which give cause for concern, including where 'leadership and governance has broken down'. This guidance re-affirms the three core strategic roles of governance mentioned above and states that evidence that governors may be failing to deliver on one or more of these strategic roles could include, but is not restricted to:

◆ high governor turnover;

◆ a significant, unexplained change to their constitution;

◆ the governing body having an excessive involvement in the day-to-day running of the school;

◆ lack of appropriate engagement with data. This might include, but is not limited to, data on pupil learning and progress or staff recruitment;

◆ not sufficiently managing risks associated with strategic priorities and school improvement plans; and/or

◆ evidence of poor financial management and oversight, such as through consistent overspending the school's budget beyond agreed thresholds.

In such circumstances, a trust could be issued with a warning notice and will be held to account by the RSC.

# 3. Strategic versus operational

The *Governance Handbook* states that one of the board's core functions is strategic leadership, which, it states, 'involves setting the organisation's overall strategic framework, including its vision and strategic priorities. It also includes responsibility for setting and modelling its culture, values and ethos'. This means that the trustees are responsible for the high-level aims of the trust and the strategy involved in meeting them: the chief executive officer/principal is responsible for the day-to-day operational matters involved in realising the strategic vision.

Ensuring that the focus of the board remains strategic is not always easy and there is often a temptation for trustees to venture into operational territory. The *Governance Handbook* makes clear that the trustees' role is to provide strategic oversight, hold the executive leaders to account for educational performance and to oversee the finances. There is an increasing recognition of the need for 'clear separation between strategic non-executive oversight and operational executive leadership' – not only does this mean that executive leaders or other staff should not sit as members of the board, but it also recognises that trustees should not be participating in the practical running of the school.

To ignore this distinction risks undermining the board and is a potential indicator of concern for the RSC. Put simply, it is impossible to hold yourself to account for the operational responsibilities that you have taken on. This principle is in line with the Charity Commission's approach to trustees and the practice for Chief Executive Officers of charities not to be appointed to the board.

# 4. Background to academisation

The first publicly funded state schools, independent of local authority control, were introduced by the Conservative government. In 1988, the Education

**sponsor**
A body responsible for the performance and finances of an academy.

Reform Act allowed for the establishment of City Technology Colleges (CTCs). CTCs are secondary-level schools, independent of local authority control, which specialise in mainly technology-based subjects such as science, mathematics and technology. One-fifth of capital costs were to be met by private business **sponsors** who owned or leased the buildings.

The aim was to base CTCs in the middle of urban areas. However, local authorities failed to support the initiative and refused to identify suitable school sites. Fifteen CTCs were built, largely on the outskirts of cities. The programme proved much more expensive than anticipated and was eventually abandoned.

The legislation for CTCs was amended by the Learning and Skills Act 2000 to introduce City Academies. The programme was intended to improve pupil performance at failing schools. It required a financial contribution from a sponsor, but the level of commitment was half that under the CTC scheme. The majority of CTCs converted to city academies.

In 2002, the Education Act amended the name of City Academies to 'Academies'. Retrospectively, these 'Mark 1' academies have become known as 'sponsored academies'.

**maintained school**
A school funded by central government via the local authority.

The academies programme was significantly expanded by the Coalition government's Academies Act 2010. For the first time, any excellent **maintained school**, primary or secondary, could choose to become an academy and take on greater autonomy. Only schools assessed as 'Outstanding' by Ofsted could choose to convert to academy status, thereby redefining academisation as an indicator of quality.

The programme was expanded further following the comprehensive spending review in October 2010. Schools assessed as 'Good' with one or more Outstanding features could convert. Other schools were also eligible if they worked in partnership with a 'Good' or 'Outstanding' school which had committed to assist them in improvement. The policy was amended to allow 'Outstanding' special schools to convert in January 2011.

In March 2016, the Conservative government's white paper 'Education Excellence Everywhere' stated that all maintained schools would be required to convert or be in the process of converting to academy status by 2022. However, the white paper received a huge backlash and the proposal to bring in compulsory academisation was withdrawn.

**multi-academy trust**
A single legal entity formed by a number of schools combining to form a single academy.

The Education and Adoption Act 2016, together with the statutory guidance from Schools Causing Concern, identify those schools which have failed to 'support its pupils to fulfil their potential'. If a school falls within the criteria and is defined as 'coasting', the guidance states that Regional Schools Commissioners (RSCs) will engage with the school to consider whether additional support is required. Ultimately, this could lead to the school becoming a sponsored academy or for a coasting academy to move to a new **multi-academy trust** (MAT). However, this is rare in practice.

# 5. Legal structure of academies

A trust is a single or group of state-funded independent schools that is constituted as a **charitable company limited by guarantee**.

As a company, every trust must register with **Companies House** and comply with company law.

Trusts are also governed by charity law. Trusts do not need to register with the Charity Commission as they are exempt charities: the Secretary of State for Education is the '**principal regulator**'.

A funding agreement is signed by the trust and the Secretary of State which forms a contract between the two parties. In a multi-academy trust, this is replaced by a master funding agreement between the trust and the Secretary of State, as well as a supplemental funding agreement with each individual academy. In return for ongoing public funding, the trust agrees to comply with the requirements set out in the funding agreement. These requirements extend to ongoing guidance produced by ESFA/DfE and explicit reference is made to the *Academies Financial Handbook*. The articles of association are also included as an appendix to the funding agreement.

## 5.1  Charity status

The Charities Act 2011 states that a charity must:

◆ be established for charitable purposes only; and

◆ have a purpose that is for the public benefit.

For trusts, the charitable purpose is 'the advancement of education' which is set out in the objects clause of the articles of association as 'to advance for the public benefit education in the United Kingdom'.

Charities must be independent of outside control.

However, trusts do not need to apply for charity status as they are automatically classified as exempt charities (Academies Act 2010, s 12(4)). Trusts formed before August 2011 had to stop using their charity number and apply to be removed from the Charity Commission register.

Trusts are not directly regulated by the Charity Commission. Instead, the Secretary of State for Education is the principal regulator and, therefore, responsible for ensuring compliance by trustees with 'their legal obligations in exercising control and management of the administration' of the trust (Charities Act 2011, s. 26(3)). In practice, the role is undertaken by the **Education & Skills Funding Agency** (ESFA). Information about specific charity law requirements are provided to trusts and their advisors by ESFA. It can use existing monitoring and oversight to check compliance but will have no additional powers by virtue of its role as principal regulator and can involve the Charity Commission if there are concerns. There is a memorandum of understanding between the DfE and the Charity Commission which sets out the working arrangements around co-ordinating regulatory operations and formulates the framework within which they work. This

**charitable company**
A company set up and run solely for non-profit making purposes with the proceeds only to be used for the purpose of the charity.

**company limited by guarantee**
A company where the liability of the members is limited to a fixed amount that each member agrees to contribute to the assets of the company in the event of a winding up.

**Companies House**
An executive agency of the Department for Business Innovation and Skills, Companies House is the registry for companies incorporated in the UK.

**principal regulator**
Responsible for overseeing the compliance of exempt charities with charity law. For academies, the principal regulator is the Secretary of State for Education.

**Education & and Skills Funding Agency**
An executive agency of the DfE (formerly EFA, Education Funding Agency)

clarifies their respective roles and responsibilities and the circumstances in which the Secretary of State will invite the Charity Commission to use its powers of intervention and investigation.

If the trust has an endowment or other charitable fund, that too may benefit from the exempt status. The fund must be a charity itself, controlled by the trust and established for one or more of its purposes. The funds should also be included in the trust's accounts.

For tax purposes, trusts must make a formal application to HMRC via Government Gateway for recognition as a charity. This will mean that the trust will not pay tax on most types of income and can reclaim tax that has been paid such as bank interest or via Gift Aid. The trust will need to complete tax returns if it does not hold recognition as a charity for tax purposes or if it receives income that does not qualify for tax relief.

Charity status imposes additional restrictions on the operation of the trust such as restrictions around non-charitable trading.

Parent Teacher Associations (PTAs) are separate legal entities and must register with the Charity Commission if appropriate. Some PTAs choose to operate as a committee or club.

## 5.2 The shift from the stakeholder model

**model articles**
The standard form articles for academies prescribed by the Secretary of State under powers granted by the Companies Act.

Early converter academies had articles which provided for stakeholder representation particularly at board level – the **model articles** had trustees appointed by the members, elected parent and staff trustees and the headteacher/principal. The idea is that the board will act in the best interests of all stakeholders (parents on behalf of pupils, staff, community, etc.) if they are represented. Of course, in practice, the efficacy of board dynamics is not that simple!

The DfE's preference has now shifted from the stakeholder model. The emphasis is now on making the right trustee appointments; consideration should focus on best fit and individual skills rather than simply which sector of the community the potential trustee is drawn from!

Careful consideration must be given to building and maintaining a board which has a balance of skills, experience and capacity that will provide effective direction and governance for the trust.

The move away from a representative appointment system helps to ensure that the focus remains on the provision of the best education for all pupils irrespective of the cohort or academy (in a MAT setting) and without the personal agenda sometimes brought by individual stakeholders.

The *Governance Handbook 2017* explains how membership of the board should focus on skills:

'the primary consideration in appointment decisions should be acquiring the skills and experience the board needs to be effective. Boards should therefore develop a skills-based set of recruitment criteria which they should share with any third parties, such as academy trust Members or a foundation or sponsor, that has a role in appointing people to the board.'

In some trusts, particularly the 'early adopters' of academy status, there is often a high crossover of membership, with the same individuals involved at member, board and in MATs at local governance level. Whilst this is normally acceptable within the articles of association there is now a preference from the DfE for greater degrees of separation. The *Academies Financial Handbook 2018* states:

'the Department's view is that there should be a significant degree of separation between the individuals who are members and those who are trustees. If members sit on the board of trustees this may reduce the objectivity with which the members can exercise their powers. The Department's strong preference is for a majority of members to be independent of the board of trustees'.

There is also an increasing preference for a separation between the membership of MAT boards and those serving on local governing bodies.

## Stop and think 1.1

**Thinking about the role of elected governors, consider how the board can emphasise the importance of skills which each governor is expected to bring to it.**

# 6. Independent trustees

The corporate sector has seen an increasing prominence of the role of the non-executive director (NED). The Higgs Report in 2003 called them 'custodians of the governance process'. The objective viewpoint of the independent trustee enables robust governance and an impartial viewpoint from which to oversee the development of strategy that is truly in the best interests of the trust and all pupils and staff. Unlike NEDs in the corporate world, trustees receive no payment or financial benefit as trusts are charitable structures in receipt of public funding.

There has now been a distinct shift by the DfE away from the stakeholder model of governance representation and there is a particular emphasis on not appointing trust staff to the board. As well as retaining 'clear lines of accountability through the trust's single senior executive leader', this also supports the creation of an independent board. Although the current model articles permit the trust's CEO to be appointed as a trustee, it will be through a member resolution (who could choose not to appoint) and is subject to the CEO's approval. In any event, there is distinct move away from this model with some RSCs advocating a separation of powers. The Charity Commission has long been concerned about the potential for conflicts to arise from any employees holding a position on the board and most CEOs in the charitable and third sector are not trustees.

Trustees may still have other commitments which mean that their independence may be compromised on particular issues. It is essential that declarations of interests and potential conflicts of loyalty are made and reviewed regularly and that any conflicts of interest are handled appropriately.

Lord Agnew, Parliamentary Under-Secretary of State for the School System, wrote to auditors in June 2018 about the issue:

> The role of the chair and non-execs on a trust. At departmental level, we have increased the level of engagement with chairs. There are training courses run by some audit firms aimed at non-exec board members. We would encourage you to think about this as an added service if you are not already doing it.

# 7. Academy freedoms

Historically, much emphasis was placed by the DfE on the freedoms that academisation offered:

- freedom from local authority control;
- the ability to set pay and conditions for staff;
- freedom not to follow the national curriculum;
- the ability to set the length of terms and school days.

It was claimed that these freedoms allowed academies to innovate and raise academic standards.

All staff that previously worked for a school that became a Single Academy Trust (SAT) or formed or joined a MAT will would be protected by the Transfer of Undertakings (Protection of Employment) Regulations 2006 (TUPE). These employees will transfer to their new trust employer on the same terms and conditions. Of course, the trust is free to consult with transferred staff and their union representatives to subsequently change terms and conditions. Typically, changes will relate to increased rates of pay to attract and retain high-quality staff or changes to the working day. The trust can set its own pay and conditions that are not aligned to the nationally agreed terms and conditions for any new members of staff.

As publicly funded independent schools, trusts receive their funding direct from the government and not via the local authority. The trust can choose how to allocate the budget and, in a MAT, may decide on the level of funding allocation per academy. The trust is not restricted in its choice of suppliers and can shop around for best value. However, most local authorities now offer their services on a traded basis to all schools,

Whether these really represent freedoms that offer any value to trusts or their academies is a moot point and the DfE has largely discontinued referring to them. Interestingly, in a letter to auditors in the academies community sent in June 2018, Lord Agnew, Parliamentary Under-Secretary of State for the School System, identified general annual grant (GAG) pooling as 'one of the greatest freedoms a MAT has. The opportunity to pool GAG is particularly valuable, in particular to simplify the provision of support to weaker schools in a MAT until they can grow their pupil numbers.'

### Making it work 1.1

**The Harris Federation in London takes advantage of the academy freedoms. It has a generous salary and benefits package which exceeds the levels set out by the National Terms and Conditions and has an additional Harris Allowance for teachers. The Harris academies are able to make changes to the standard school day (e.g. Harris Academy Riverside has an early finish day on a Friday where school ends at 1.35pm).**

# 8. The role of governance in school improvement

The *Governance Handbook* states that one of the purposes of governance is to 'create robust accountability, oversight and assurance for educational and financial performance'. In addition to setting the strategic vision, the governing board's core functions are to hold executive leaders to account for 'the educational performance of the organisation and its pupils, and the performance management of staff' as well as to oversee the financial performance of the organisation, making sure its money is well spent. Good governance is about more than just compliance with statutory requirements; the governing board is responsible, and accountable, for securing educational standards in the trust. Good governance not only underpins the success of a trust but is essential for it.

Trustees, and members of local governing boards with delegated responsibility, must always recognise the distinction between strategic and operational and their role in terms of oversight. This may not always be easy. Whilst it is essential that trustees are able to understand and analyse pupil performance data, both live and historic, they are not responsible for that data or its use – they must be able to identify trends or pick up any potential concerns from the data which they should question the executive leadership about and may be able to triangulate through the use of third-party reports or their own visits or learning walks. The same is true of the financial affairs of the trust: the board should not be involved in their preparation but should be suitably conversant with financial reports to enable robust questioning and monitoring as well as oversight of a suitable programme of internal controls and external audit.

Trustees and governors must be extremely wary of over-reliance on the executive to draw attention to areas that require consideration. All must be proactive in ensuring that they understand the workings of the trust and the data that is presented to them and independently seek information or verification so far as this is possible.

The *Governance Competency Framework*, introduced in January 2017, sets out what is expected of trustees. It explains the principles and personal attributes which all trustees should have: committed, confident, curious, challenging, collaborative, critical and creative. These, together with the 'commitment of time and energy to the role', underpin effective governance. It specifically states that trustees should 'understand the impact of effective governance on the quality of education and on outcomes for all children and young people'. The *Competency Framework* details the specific knowledge and skills required which are split into what is essential for everyone, what is required of the chair and what is required by at least one person on the board.

In a letter to auditors in June 2018, Lord Agnew, Parliamentary Under-Secretary of State for the School System, included a series of questions that should be considered around simple changes of operation that could yield 'impressive results':

◆ Are your clients using a standard employment contract for all teaching staff so that they can be cross-deployed to different schools?

◆ Are they using the same exam boards in all their schools to enable cross-school marking and also to optimise the point above?

◆ Do they have a central electronic purchase order system to ensure strong controls on expenditure?

◆ Do they have a central bank account that simplifies bank reconciliations and ensures that there is constant, easy visibility of the cash position?

◆ Are they benchmarking their supply costs and, if over a number of years the level is constant, have they considered employing permanent staff to fill some of this requirement thereby improving the quality and removing agency charges?

◆ Are they accessing the Department's procurement arrangements if they are providing better value than they can achieve on their own?

# 9. Principles of good governance

Effective governance is not imposed by the government or external body but must be put in place by the trust. As a result, an increasing number of trusts are engaging the services of governance professionals to advise the board on appropriate structures and processes. The importance of professional support for the board is recognised in the *Clerking Competency Framework* and in the provision of support via the programme to establish national leaders of Governance. However, there has been considerable focus on governance by the corporate and charity sectors which trusts can rely on. As well as the UK Corporate Governance Code, some guiding principles have been established which should be adopted.

## 9.1 The Nolan Principles

The Committee on Standards in Public Life chaired by Lord Nolan was formed in October 1994 following the 'Cash for Questions' affair in the House of

Commons. The remit of the Committee was to examine the concerns about standards of conduct of holders of public office and to make recommendations as to any changes in present arrangements which might be required 'to ensure the highest standards of propriety in public life'.

The Committee established the Seven Principles of Public Life often known as the 'Nolan Principles'. They apply to anyone who works in education and are explicitly referred to in the *Governance Handbook*, the *Academies Financial Handbook*.

1. *Selflessness* – Holders of public office should act solely in terms of the public interest. They should not do so to gain financial or other benefits for themselves, their family or their friends.

2. *Integrity* – Holders of public office should not place themselves under any financial or other obligation to outside individuals or organisations that might seek to influence them in the performance of their official duties. They should not act or take decisions in order to gain financial or other material benefits for themselves, their family or their friends. They must declare and resolve any interests and relationships.

3. *Objectivity* – Holders of public office must act and take decisions impartially, fairly and on merit, using the best evidence and without discrimination or bias.

4. *Accountability* – Holders of public office are accountable to the public for their decisions and actions and must submit themselves to whatever scrutiny is appropriate to their office.

5. *Openness* – Holders of public office should act and take decisions in an open and transparent manner. They should give reasons for their decisions and withhold information from the public only when there are clear and lawful reasons for so doing.

6. *Honesty* – Holders of public office have a duty to declare any private interests relating to their public duties and to take steps to resolve any conflicts arising in a way that protects the public interest.

7. *Leadership* – Holders of public office should actively promote and robustly support these principles by leadership, exhibiting the principles in their own behaviour. They should be willing to challenge poor behaviour wherever it occurs.

## Test yourself 1.1

1. **Why were the Nolan Principles introduced?**

2. **What are the Seven Principles?**

## 9.2 Code of governance

The Charity Governance Code is intended to be a practical tool to help trustees to develop high standards of governance. It 'sets the principles and recommended practice for good governance and is deliberately aspirational'. This, it explains, is intentional, so that all charities will use the Code as a tool for continuous improvement.

- *Organisational purpose.* The board is clear about the charity's aims and ensures that these are being delivered effectively and sustainably.
- *Leadership.* Every charity is led by an effective board that provides strategic leadership in line with the charity's aims and values.
- *Integrity.* The board acts with integrity, adopting values and creating a culture which help achieve the organisation's charitable purposes. The board is aware of the importance of the public's confidence and trust in charities, and trustees undertake their duties accordingly.
- *Decision making, risk and control.* The board makes sure that its decision-making processes are informed, rigorous and timely and that effective delegation, control and **risk assessment** and management systems are set up and monitored.
- *Board effectiveness.* The board works as an effective team, using the appropriate balance of skills, experience, backgrounds and knowledge to make informed decisions.
- *Diversity.* The board's approach to diversity supports its effectiveness, leadership and decision making.
- *Openness and accountability.* The board leads the organisation in being transparent and accountable. The charity is open in its work, unless there is good reason for it not to be.

**risk assessment**
The process of identifying risks, the persons affected by them, the severity of the likely injuries or loss that might result from them, whether the control measures in place are adequate and any further measures needed to control them.

Although the Code is not a regulatory requirement, it is expected that all charities 'apply or explain' the approach that they are taking to applying the code to ensure transparency. It is suggested that charities include a brief statement in their annual report explaining the use of the Code or whether an alternative governance code is followed.

Whilst there is no absolute obligation on trusts to adhere to the Code or other recommendations, trusts are recipients of public funding and free of local authority control so must demonstrate a greater regard for effective, accountable and independent governance.

The seven principles apply directly to anyone who works as a public office-holder. This includes anyone who works in academies and any appointed or elected as a trustee or member.

# 10. Collaboration

The government's emphasis is on the creation of a sustainable, self-improving school system. One of the key elements is through school-to-school support and collaborative arrangements. Although not formally monitored by the DfE, RSCs take into consideration the collaborative arrangements in place and support provided when looking at vulnerable or underperforming schools. Collaborative arrangements enable pooling of resources which can be used to improve school performance, expand the curriculum or get better value for money.

Schools often have long histories of working with other local schools in their cluster or partnership to offer opportunities for pupils or provide a forum for headteachers to share experiences and best practice. Informal collaborative arrangements like this can be expanded to enable more structured school improvement work to take place between academies, maintained schools and independent schools. Although there is no shared governance, it is possible to agree a memorandum of understanding which sets out the details around the arrangements.

This type of collaborative arrangement would be regarded in law as a partnership. This would pose a high risk: all parties in a partnership have 'joint and several' liability which means that every individual party is liable to the full extent of an obligation in respect of a liability. One of the schools in the partnership could find themselves liable to pay the full extent of a claim to a claimant – it would then need to take action against the other partners for a contribution. This makes it more difficult to employ staff centrally or make large joint purchases: an individual school or trust will need to employ staff or procure goods or services which will then be sold to the other partners.

The Education Act 2002 (ss 11–13) permit maintained schools and trusts to collaborate through a 'school company':

◆ to provide services or facilities for any schools;

◆ to exercise relevant LA functions; or

◆ to contract for goods or services from third parties on behalf of member schools.

## Stop and think 1.2

**Thinking about the rise of multi-academy trusts, especially the larger ones, consider how individual schools and MATs can collaborate with each other and how this can benefit pupils and staff.**

### 10.1 The rise of the multi-academy trust

The most formalised collaborative structure is the MAT. Every school that joins a MAT ceases to exist as a separate legal entity. Instead, the MAT offers a single legal structure where the future success or failure of every academy is interlinked. Whilst support for school improvement can be secured through more informal collaborative routes, in a MAT the trust is responsible and accountable.

All staff working at all of the academies as well as those employed centrally are employees of the MAT. This facilitates the sharing and transfer of employees across the trust to wherever the need is greatest (subject to individual terms and conditions of staff who have be transferred under TUPE). The MAT model offers an ideal structure to provide effective support in a cost efficient and timely way to any academy that needs it.

The MAT structure also offers flexibility around the use of funding. Although funding for individual academies is largely calculated on the basis of pupil numbers, the *Academies Financial Handbook 2018* allows MATs to pool General Annual Grant (GAG) to form a central fund which can be applied in accordance with the trustees' wishes.

The MAT structure is favoured by the DfE and RSCs will encourage forming or joining a MAT for schools contemplating academisation. Whilst technically the SAT model is still available for excellent schools, RSCs will often look for suitable arrangements so that a MAT can be formed with other vulnerable schools. Support will be sought for schools that are underperforming with the vast majority of sponsors being MATs.

# Chapter summary

- Good governance is based on an infrastructure of processes and monitoring controls which improves the quality of board decisions. Corporate governance is shaped by the UK Corporate Governance Code and, for trusts, the DfE's *Governance Handbook*. One of the board's key core functions is strategic leadership.

- The concept of state-funded schools independent of local authority control was introduced in 1988 and has been developed by successive governments. A trust is a charitable company limited by guarantee and must comply with company and charity law.

- Trusts are regulated by the Secretary of State for Education, who acts via ESFA, as the principal regulator. A formal application must be made to HMRC for recognition as a charity for tax purposes.

- There has been a shift from the stakeholder model of representation on the board to a skills-based emphasis. There is also an emphasis on not appointing trust staff to the board and for appropriate degrees of separation in the tiers of governance. The current model articles do allow for the members to appoint the CEO to the board if they agree to act.

- Good governance is essential to the success of trusts. It must provide robust accountability, oversight and assurance for educational and financial performance. Trustees should recognise and adopt guiding principles including the Nolan Principles and other codes for the charity sector.

- The creation of a sustainable, self-improving school system will require school-to-school support and collaborative arrangements. The most formalised collaborative structure is the MAT which is a single legal entity.

# Chapter two
# Legislation and regulation

**CONTENTS**

## 1. Introduction

This chapter outlines the legislative framework within which all trusts must operate and the regulations with which they must comply. Trusts are charitable companies limited by guarantee which means that they are regulated and controlled via a mixture of charity and company law.

The chapter also outlines the oversight and governance framework established by the DfE and the specific guidance and regulation produced in relation to trusts.

# 2. The legislative framework

Trusts must comply with the general law relating to companies and charities as well as dedicated legislation.

## 2.1  Academies Act 2010

The Academies Act was a watershed moment in the shift towards an independent, state-funded education system. Prior to this, the academy programme related only to underperforming schools and the Act enabled more schools to become academies. The government expected a significant number of academies to open and for the number to continue to grow.

The key areas of the Act were to:

◆ enable all maintained schools to apply to become academies, with schools rated 'outstanding' by Ofsted being pre-approved;

◆ allow maintained primary and special schools to apply to become academies in their own right;

◆ give the Secretary of State the power to issue an academy order requiring the local authority to cease to maintain the school;

◆ remove the requirement to consult the local authority before opening an academy;

◆ require the consent of any existing foundation (mainly churches) before a school applies to become an academy (and prohibit the religious character changing during the conversion to academy); and

◆ deem academy trusts to be exempt charities.

## 2.2  Companies Act 2006

The Companies Act 2006 consolidated and codified company law for the United Kingdom, bringing it together for the first time. As companies, trusts must comply with the requirements of the Act. There are detailed provisions covering all aspects of a company's life span, many of which relate to academies including company formation, execution of documents, **written resolutions**, notice for meetings and filing of accounts.

**written resolution**
A document setting out one or more proposed resolutions that is circulated to an academy's members for approval as an alternative to holding a general meeting.

The legislation was intended to simplify the regime for small privately held companies (i.e. not public companies). This means that academies benefit from a number of the relaxations such as the removal of the requirement to appoint a company secretary, the need to hold Annual General Meetings (though this is often included in trusts' articles making it compulsory to hold them), convening meetings on short notice and the abolition of the requirement for unanimity in members' written resolutions.

The Act contains detailed provisions in relation to directors which replace and codify the main common law and equitable duties of directors into:

◆ to act within their powers;

◆ to promote the success of the company;

- to exercise independent judgment;
- to exercise reasonable care, skill and diligence;
- to avoid conflicts of interest;
- not to accept benefits from third parties; and
- to declare any interest in a proposed transaction with the company.

The Act also gives shareholders/members a statutory right to pursue a derivative action against the directors for misfeasance on behalf of the company. In addition, at least one director on the board must be a natural person and must be at least 16 years old. Directors can provide a **service address** to Companies House so that their home address can be held on a separate register with restricted access.

**service address**
An address for correspondence that directors must provide to Companies House which can, and ideally should, be different from their residential address. Generally, this is the academy's registered office address.

## 2.3 Charity law

Trusts are charitable companies and so must comply with charity law, in particular the Charities Act 2011 which repealed and simplified earlier legislation.

### Stop and think 2.1

**Consider how the legal structure of trusts might impact on the way that trustees approach governance. How might this be different if a different structure was used?**

However, as trusts are exempt charities, there is no need to register with the Charity Commission. Instead, trusts are regulated by the Secretary of State for Education who is the Principal Regulator and who has a duty to 'promote compliance' by trustees with their 'legal obligations in exercising control and management of the administration of the charity'. Although the Principal Regulator can provide information about charity law requirements and check whether trusts are complying using existing monitoring arrangements, they have no additional powers as a result of their role. It is possible to involve the Charity Commission if the Principal Regulator has concerns about the way that a trust is operating, although it is difficult to envisage a situation where the DfE would wish to exercise this opportunity.

# 3. Academies Financial Handbook

The funding agreement contains the requirement that trusts must abide by the requirements of the *Academies Financial Handbook*. It is updated annually with changes intended to strengthen financial stewardship arrangements. Any changes come into effect on 1 September – at the start of each financial year.

The *Academies Financial Handbook* sets out the requirements relating to financial management, control and reporting. However, it focuses on principles and best practice guidance rather than detailed specifications for trusts to follow balancing 'requirements for effective financial governance and management of funds, with the freedoms that trusts need over their day-to-day business'.

The *Academies Financial Handbook 2018* contains provisions allowing the Secretary of State to require a trust to remove a member or trustee or to prohibit an individual from taking part in academy trust management (i.e. effectively barring them from acting as a member, trustee or executive leader of a trust).

In addition, where there has been 'non-compliance with legal or regulatory requirements or misconduct or mismanagement in the administration' of the trust, ESFA can refer it to the Charity Commission which could use its regulatory powers.

### 3.1 Letters to accounting officers

In addition to the *Academies Financial Handbook*, trusts must read and comply with letters sent to trust accounting officers from the chief executive and accounting officer of ESFA. These highlight key responsibilities on financial management and governance.

The ESFA's accounting officer sends an annual letter to trusts' accounting officers about the accountability framework. This covers issues pertinent to the trusts' role such as developments in the accountability framework or findings from ESFA's work with trusts. The annual letter (and other letters where required) must be shared with members, trustees, the chief financial officer and other members of the senior leadership team. The letters must be specifically discussed by the board and action taken 'if necessary to strengthen financial controls'.

# 4. Academies Accounts Direction

The Academies Accounts Direction sets out the direction and guidance around preparing and auditing the financial statements which, together with the Companies Act 2006 and the Charities' Statement of Recommended Practice (SORP) 2015, as amended by Charities SORP (FRS102) Update Bulletin 1 (together defined as SORP 2015), and Financial Reporting Standard [FRS] 102, is used by trusts and their auditors. It is reissued annually. It makes clear that trusts are not permitted to claim small company exemptions and must report as a 'larger' charity in the context of SORP 2015.

The Academies Accounts Direction outlines the requirements for trusts to:

- Prepare an annual report and financial statements to 31 August.
- Have these accounts audited annually by independent registered auditors.
- Produce a statement of regularity, propriety and compliance and obtain a regularity assurance report on this statement from the auditor.
- Submit the audited accounts and auditor's regularity assurance report to ESFA by 31 December.
- File the accounts with the Companies Registrar as required under the Companies Act 2006.
- Publish the audited accounts on the trust's website by 31 January.

The Accounts Direction provides quite a detailed level of guidance around the elements that must be included in the annual report and financial statements, setting out the specific accounting treatments required. A model format for the report and financial statements, the Coketown Academy Trust, is included which ensures a consistent approach by trusts.

# 5. Department for Education (DfE)

The DfE is the ministerial department responsible for children's services and education. It publishes statutory guidance on a wide range of issues that sets out what trusts must do to comply with the law. Some of the guidance must be followed strictly and without exception but trustees should be familiar with all the guidance and follow it unless there are very good reasons not to.

It is supported by 18 agencies and public bodies including Ofqual, Ofsted and ESFA. The DfE is responsible for:

- teaching and learning for children in the early years and in primary schools;
- teaching and learning for young people under the age of 19 years in secondary schools and in further education;
- supporting professionals who work with children and young people;
- helping disadvantaged children and young people to achieve more; and
- making sure that local services protect and support children.

# 6. Education and Skills Funding Agency (ESFA)

ESFA is an executive agency sponsored by DfE which is accountable for funding education and skills for children, young people and adults. It brings together the two separate agencies of the Education Funding Agency (EFA) and the Skills Funding Agency (SFA).

ESFA is responsible for:

- providing assurance that public funds are properly spent, achieves value for money for the tax payer and delivers the policies and priorities set by the Secretary of State;
- regulating academies, further education and sixth-form colleges, and training providers, intervening where there is risk of failure or where there is evidence of mismanagement of public funds; and
- delivering major projects and operating key services in the education and skills sector, such as school capital programmes, the National Careers Service, the National Apprenticeship Service and the Learning Records Service.

ESFA's accounting officer is accountable to Parliament for how ESFA uses its funds and for the 'regularity and propriety' of expenditure and 'ensuring value for money'. Consequently, ESFA seeks confirmation that trusts have 'appropriate arrangements for sound governance, financial management and securing value for money and accounting, and that the way trusts use public funds is consistent with the purposes for which the funds were voted by Parliament'.

The *Academies Financial Handbook* explains that ESFA 'exercises the rights, powers and remedies in this handbook on behalf of the Secretary of State'; any failure or delay in using any right, power or remedy will not prevent it from doing so later!

# 7. Governance Handbook

The DfE's *Governance Handbook* is a primary resource for trustees and governors in trusts as well as maintained schools. It states the three core functions of the board:

◆ Ensuring clarity of vision, ethos and strategic direction.

◆ Holding executive leaders to account for the educational performance of the organisation and its pupils, and the performance management of staff.

◆ Overseeing the financial performance of the organisation and making sure its money is well spent.

The contents are structured around the DfE's 'six features of Effective Governance' which are described in the *Competency Framework for Governance*. It sets out boards' roles and functions, where they can find support and the main features of effective governance.

The *Handbook* sets out the role of both members and trustees and emphasises the need for separation of roles. Useful example questions are included to help boards to challenge school leaders in relation to financial accountability and educational performance.

# 8. Competency frameworks

The DfE has produced guides on governance and clerking which make clear the level of competency required from those individuals involved in these roles. These apply to boards of trustees as well as sponsors, foundations and dioceses, organisations that are involved in supporting governing boards or anyone providing clerking services. The frameworks also apply to maintained schools.

### 8.1  Competency Framework for Governance

The framework sets out the 'knowledge, skills and behaviours' that trustees need to be effective. It is structured around 16 competencies which are grouped into the 'six features of effective governance:

**1**    Strategic leadership

Effective boards provide strategic leadership; these competencies relate to the function of the board to set vision, ethos and strategic direction.

◆ Setting direction

- Culture, values and ethos
- Decision making
- Collaborative working with stakeholders and partners
- Risk management.

**2** Accountability

The board must hold the executive leaders to account for the educational and financial performance of the trust.

- Education improvement
- Rigorous analysis of data
- Financial frameworks and accountability
- Financial management and monitoring
- Staffing and performance management
- External accountability.

**3** People

Trustees need to form positive working relationships to function well as part of a team. They will also need to relate to staff, students, parents and the community as well as connecting with the wider education system.

- Building an effective team

**4** Structures

Trustees must understand and design the governance structures in which they operate to ensure they are effective.

- Roles and responsibilities

**5** Compliance

Trustees and all those involved in governance must understand the legal frameworks and context, as well as the requirements with which the trust must comply.

- Statutory and contractual requirements.

**6** Evaluation

The board must assess its effectiveness and efficiency to ensure 'ongoing compliance with its statutory and legal duties under review'. Individual trustees should reflect on their own contribution helping to create a stronger and more motivated board.

- Managing self-review and personal skills
- Managing and developing the boards effectiveness.

Within each of the competencies is a list of knowledge and skills and effective behaviours and whether these should be held by everyone on the board, the chair or just someone on the board.

Underpinning the competencies is a foundation of principles and personal attributes that the trustees bring to the board. These qualities enable them to use their skills and knowledge to operate effectively as part of a team and make an active contribution to effective governance:

♦   *Committed*. Devoting the required time and energy to the role and ambitious to achieve best possible outcomes for young people. Prepared to give time, skills and knowledge to developing themselves and others to create highly effective governance.

♦   *Confident*. Of an independent mind, able to lead and contribute to courageous conversations, to express their opinion and to play an active role on the board.

♦   *Curious*. Possessing an enquiring mind and an analytical approach and understanding the value of meaningful questioning.

♦   *Challenging*. Providing appropriate challenge to the status quo, not taking information or data at face value and always driving for improvement.

♦   *Collaborative*. Prepared to listen to and work in partnership with others and understanding the importance of building strong working relationships within the board and with executive leaders, staff, parents and carers, pupils/students, the local community and employers.

♦   *Critical*. Understanding the value of critical friendship which enables both challenge and support, and self-reflective, pursuing learning and development opportunities to improve their own and whole board effectiveness.

♦   *Creative*. Able to challenge conventional wisdom and be open-minded about new approaches to problem-solving; recognising the value of innovation and creative thinking to organisational development and success.

### Test yourself 2.1

**What are the six features of effective governance identified in the Competency Framework for Governance?**

### 8.2  Clerking Competency Framework

The framework sets out the 'knowledge, skills and behaviours' required to provide professional clerking to the trust board. The trust's articles require that the board appoint a clerk; the framework defines the functions and duties of a clerk who must ensure the efficient functioning of the board by:

♦   administrative and organisational support;

♦   guidance to ensure that the board works in compliance with the appropriate legal and regulatory framework, and understands the potential consequences for non-compliance; and

♦   advice on procedural matters relating to the operation of the board.

Clerks have an important role in supporting the six features of effective governance, as set out in the *Competency Framework for Governance*.

The framework sets out four key competencies for clerks:

**1.** Understanding governance

The clerk needs a 'sound understanding of the board's duties and responsibilities; governance legislation and procedures; and the wider context in which the board is operating'. The clerk will support effective governance since it will enable:

◆ Better quality advice on legal and procedural matters

◆ More accurate recording of discussions and decisions

◆ More efficient use of the board's time.

**2.** Administration

The clerk will ensure that the processes and procedures are administered efficiently enabling the chair and board to focus on strategic matters. Professional clerking involves developing a forward plan with the chair so that there is proper preparation for meetings and high-quality paperwork available.

**3.** Advice and guidance

The clerk provides timely and accurate advice and guidance to the board. This will contribute to better and more efficient decision making, helps the board manage the risk of non-compliance with legal and regulatory frameworks and remain focused on its strategic functions. A professional clerk will be proactive in keeping knowledge current and is aware of relevant and reliable sources of information. They will also be clear when they need to recommend external or specialist advice.

**4.** People and relationships

The clerk builds and maintains professional working relationships with the board, plays an important role in ensuring that accurate records of the board members and their skills are kept and contributes to the induction and training of new board members.

**Test yourself 2.2**

**What are the four key competencies set out in the Clerking Competency Framework?**

# 9. Schools Commissioners Group

The Schools Commissioners Group is part of the DfE and comprises of a National Schools Commissioner and Regional Schools Commissioners (RSC). It works with school leaders to take action in underperforming schools.

There are eight regions across the country: East of England and North-East London; East Midlands and the Humber; Lancashire and West Yorkshire; North of England; North-West London and South-Central England; South-East England and South London; South-West England; and West Midlands. Each region has its own Regional Schools Commissioner who acts on behalf of the Secretary of State for Education and who is accountable to the National Schools Commissioner.

The main responsibilities of the RSCs include:

◆ taking action where academies and free schools are underperforming;

◆ intervening in academies where governance is inadequate;

◆ deciding on applications from local-authority-maintained schools to convert to academy status;

◆ improving under-performing maintained schools by providing them with support from a strong sponsor;

◆ encouraging and deciding on applications from sponsors to operate in a region;

◆ taking action to improve poorly performing sponsors;

◆ advising on proposals for new free schools;

◆ advising on whether to cancel, defer or enter into funding agreements with **free school** projects; and

◆ deciding on applications to make significant changes to academies and free schools.

**free school**
An academy set up by a 'proposer group' such as parents, teachers, charities or other groups.

### 9.1  Headteacher board

Each RSC is supported by a headteacher board (HTB) which is responsible for advice and challenge to support its RSC. The HTB can be involved in assessing school performance data, reviewing the governance structure of a new MAT or challenging a school's improvement plan. Their role is to contribute 'local knowledge' and 'professional expertise' to aid in the decision-making of the RSC.

Headteacher boards generally meet once or twice a month. They are made up of between four and eight members who are generally headteachers, former headteachers, trustees or business leaders. Four members of each HTB are elected by local academy headteachers and two may be appointed by the RSC.

RSCs and HTBs also make use of local networks to gather information.

# 10. Companies House

Trusts, whether SATs or multi-academy trusts (MATs), are limited companies and must be registered at Companies House.

Companies House is an executive agency, sponsored by the Department for Business, Energy and Industrial Strategy. It is responsible for incorporating and dissolving limited companies, registering company information and making it available to the public. The Registrar of Companies (England and Wales) is based in Cardiff and there is also a London office and information centre.

Companies House is headed by the Registrar of Companies who is responsible for its operation. Filing obligations are set out in the Companies Act 2006 in terms of delivering the required information to the Registrar. In reality, the duties and powers of the Registrar are delegated to a large staff body.

Trusts are registered with Companies House on **incorporation** and filing requirements must be met until that trust ceases to exist. Details held must be updated any time there is a change, as well as an annual Confirmation Statement confirming the information on record. Most documents can be filed using the online WebFiling service. Some documents such as the annual report and accounts must be delivered in hard copy.

**incorporation**
The process by which a company is created, also referred to as 'formation' and 'registration'.

Some filings including the confirmation statement attract a fee.

Although there are timescales within which filings must be made, only a few attract a fine. The failure to deliver accounts on time is a criminal offence and will attract a fine on a rising scale; ultimately all the directors of the company could also face prosecution and an unlimited fine!

The basic information that must be provided includes:

◆ the confirmation statement;
◆ the annual accounts;
◆ notification of any change in the company's officers or in their personal details;
◆ notification of a change to the company's **registered office**; and
◆ notification of any change in the company's Persons of Significant Control (PSC) details or the required statements associated with them.

**registered office**
An academy's official address at which legal and other documents can be validly served and at which certain company records must be kept if not kept at a SAIL. For a single academy this is likely to be the school itself.

The majority of information filed with Companies House can be inspected by a member of the public. As well as administrative correspondence which is not put on the public record, there are a few exceptions (s. 1087 CA 2006) to what may be inspected including:

◆ directors'/trustees' residential addresses; and
◆ documents supporting a proposal to use certain words or expressions in the company name.

Anyone can gain access to basic information free of charge:

◆ company name
◆ registered number
◆ registered office address
◆ names and service addresses of directors/trustees
◆ **accounting reference date** (always 31 August)
◆ date last accounts were made up to and when the next accounts are due

**accounting reference date**
The date that marks the end of a company's accounting year end for the purposes of preparation and filing of statutory accounts.

◆ date last confirmation statement was made up to and when the next confirmation statement is due.

There is a Follow service which allows registered users of Companies House to receive an e-mail alert of any transaction as soon as it has been accepted. The e-mail contains a link to the filing history where it is possible to download a copy of the document free. The service can be particularly useful for trusts that use an external agent to provide company secretarial services as the trust will receive an automatic confirmation when documents or accounts have been filed.

Companies House has a mobile app which provides easy access to basic company information, filing history and appointment of **officers**. It does not include any chargeable information and there is no need to register to use the app. Information includes company address, trustee and company secretary appointments, filing history, when the confirmation statement is due to be filed or if it is overdue. It is possible to store a list of 'favourites' so that they can easily be watched and the app will flag if the confirmation statement is due or overdue.

**officer**
A director, manager or secretary of an academy (under CA 2006, s. 1173 of the Companies Act 2006). In the case of an 'officer in default' this is broadened to include any person who is to be treated as an officer of the company for the purposes of the provision of the Companies Act in question.

Copies of documents and forms filed can be obtained by visiting Companies House in person or by ordering by phone for postal delivery. Some charges will apply.

# 11. Ofsted

The Office for Standards in Education, Children's Services and Skills (Ofsted) is responsible for the inspection and regulation of all state-funded schools including academies.

The common inspection framework (effective from September 2015) sets out how Ofsted inspects academies as well as maintained schools, non-association independent schools, further education and skills provisions and registered early years settings in England. It is intended to bring a consistency of inspection irrespective of the legal status or phase of education across those organisations to which it applies.

Inspection of schools in England falls under the provisions of section 5 of the Education Act 2005; hence, full inspections are known as 'section 5 inspections'. Regulations require that section 5 inspections for those schools to which it applies take place 'within five school years from the end of the school year in which the last inspection took place'.

Certain schools are exempt from section 5 inspection including academies and free schools that were judged to be outstanding in their overall effectiveness at the most recent section 5 inspection. This includes academies, where the overall effectiveness of the school prior to conversion, was outstanding.

A section 8 'short inspection' can take place at any time if there are concerns about performance, concerns are raised as a result of risk assessment or structural changes, such as adding a new key stage or amalgamating with another school. Alternative provision academies, special schools and pupil referral units will not be exempt from routine inspection even if they were previously judged outstanding but will be subject to section 8 inspection.

Section 8 inspections are made where:

◆ short inspections of schools judged to be good at their most recent section 5 inspection and those outstanding schools that are not exempt from section 5;

◆ monitoring inspections of schools judged as requires improvement;

◆ monitoring inspections of schools judged as having serious weaknesses;

◆ monitoring inspections of schools judged as requiring special measures;

◆ any inspection that is undertaken in other circumstances where the inspection has no specific designation, known as 'section 8 no formal designation inspection'; and

◆ unannounced behaviour inspections.

Section 8 inspections can convert to a full section 5 inspection in certain situations:

◆ usually within 48 hours, if there are serious concerns about safeguarding or behaviour, or if the quality of education provided by a school is thought to have declined to be inadequate;

◆ when there are no significant issues with safeguarding or behaviour, but potential concerns about either the quality of education or leadership and management are identified, the inspection will not convert. Instead, Ofsted will publish a letter setting out the school's strengths and areas for improvement. A section 5 inspection will then take place later, typically within 1 to 2 years. This will give the school time to address any weaknesses and seek support from appropriate bodies. In the meantime, the letter will be clear that the school's current overall effectiveness judgement has not changed;

◆ when there is reason to believe that a school may be improving towards an outstanding judgement, Ofsted will publish a letter confirming that the school is still good and setting out its strengths and priorities for further improvement. A section 5 inspection will then take place within one to two years, giving the school time to consolidate its strong practice. However, requests from schools for early inspections will be considered. The majority of short inspections will confirm that the school remains good and, as now, Ofsted will return to carry out another short inspection after approximately three years.

Generally, an inspection of new schools will not take place 'until they are in their third year of operation'. As a school becomes an academy, the predecessor school is closed and a new academy technically opens. This means that inspection will also be deferred until the third year of operation unless there are specific concerns.

The Common Inspection Handbook (December 2017) states:

> 'The contribution of governors to the school's performance is evaluated as part of the judgement on the effectiveness of leadership and management.'

> It is clear that Ofsted recognises the importance of those involved in governing schools in ensuring overall school performance. The framework also offers some flex around different governance arrangements that may be in place stating that inspectors will 'seek to meet those responsible for governance' which could be academy trustees and sponsor representatives, but could also be a local governor where governance functions have been delegated by the board. In some cases, the local governing body will only be advisory so that inspectors should 'ensure that meetings are with those who are directly responsible for exercising governance of the school and for overseeing its performance.'

According to the Handbook:

Inspectors will consider whether governors:

◆ work effectively with leaders to communicate the vision, ethos and strategic direction of the school and develop a culture of ambition;

◆ provide a balance of challenge and support to leaders, understanding the strengths and areas needing improvement at the school;

◆ provide support for an effective headteacher or are hindering school improvement because of a lack of understanding of the issues facing the school;

◆ performance manage the headteacher rigorously;

◆ understand the impact of teaching, learning and assessment on the progress of pupils currently in the school;

◆ ensure that assessment information from leaders provides governors with sufficient and accurate information to ask probing questions about outcomes for pupils;

◆ ensure that the school's finances are properly managed and can evaluate how the school is using the pupil premium, Year 7 literacy and numeracy catch-up premium, primary PE and sport premium, and special educational needs funding; and

◆ are transparent and accountable, including in recruitment of staff, governance structures, attendance at meetings and contact with parents.

### Making it work 2.1

**An academy graded 'Good' receives a section 8 short inspection and the inspectors identify weaknesses in pupil progress and attainment. Results from the previous year were below floor level and data is poor. Ofsted subsequently publishes a letter stating the shortcomings and the academy is advised that a section 5 will take place in the next year or two. The academy's grading remains 'Good' during this period.**

**A neighbouring academy graded 'Good' also receives a section 8 short inspection during which a serious safeguarding issue is identified. The inspection converts to a full section 5 inspection the following day when the academy is judged to be 'inadequate' due to major operational issues and lack of oversight. The grading is immediately impacted.**

# 12. Schools Causing Concern

The DfE expects local authorities and Regional Schools Commissioners (RSC) to work with school leaders to drive improvements. It sets out guidance for local authorities and Regional Schools Commissioners on how to work with schools to support improvements to educational performance, and on using their intervention powers in guidance on Schools Causing Concern.

This publication was updated in February 2018 and significantly broadened the expectations beyond the existing provision for coasting schools and schools with concerns about performance standards or safety. The performance standards definition includes provision for a warning notice where there has been a serious breakdown in the way a school is managed or governed.

The guidance sets out examples of evidence which may indicate that governors could be failing to deliver on one or more of these core roles, but it is important to recognise that the examples are not formal criteria like the Ofsted framework nor is the list exhaustive. The evidence mentioned in the guidance is:

- High governor turnover.
- A significant, unexplained change to their constitution.
- The governing body having an excessive involvement in the day-to-day running of the school.
- Lack of appropriate engagement with data. This might include, but is not limited to, data on pupil learning and progress or staff recruitment.
- Not sufficiently managing risks associated with strategic priorities and school improvement plans.
- Evidence of poor financial management and oversight, such as through consistent overspending the school's budget beyond agreed thresholds.

The guidance explains that these situations could all indicate a serious breakdown of management or governance that may prejudice standards. In such circumstances, the local authority (or RSC where, for example, a local authority has failed to act swiftly or robustly or lacks the capacity) may want to investigate and, where appropriate take action early by issuing a warning notice. In the case of a school with a religious designation, the local authority or RSC should raise concerns about governance with the appropriate religious body at the earliest opportunity.

The guidance also expects that local authorities (or RSCs where, for example, a local authority has failed to act or lacks the capacity to do so) should also consider issuing warning notices to their maintained schools that have not responded robustly or rapidly enough to a recommendation by Ofsted to commission an objective external review of their governance arrangements. Such recommendations are normally made in the Ofsted report of an inspection if a school is judged as requiring improvement where governance is judged to be weak.

Governors are reminded that they do not need to wait for an Ofsted inspection recommendation to seek an external review of their governance arrangements. Local authorities (or RSCs where, for example, a local authority has failed to act swiftly or robustly or lacks the capacity to do so) may consider issuing such a recommendation where they have concerns about the quality of a maintained school's governance, before considering more formal intervention. Guidance is available on commissioning and conducting such external reviews

# 13. Local authority

Trusts are state-funded schools that are independent of local authority control. Local authorities do not have direct responsibility for the school. However, local authorities do have ongoing responsibilities relating to schools and pupils and there will be an ongoing relationship of some kind with all trusts.

The local authority retains responsibility for school place planning ensuring that there are sufficient spaces for pupils. This will require liaison with trusts to agree expansion or putting out to tender for new academies in the area. The local authority can provide funding for certain educational capital projects such as expansion projects to meet basic need for demand.

The local authority is responsible for the provision of home to school transport and must make arrangements for all eligible students. It must look to establish a sustainable transport infrastructure.

The local authority also continues to have a number of statutory duties relating to vulnerable learners. These include maintaining Education, Health and Care Plans (EHCPs), educating pupils who are excluded from school and monitoring and tracking children who are missing education.

Local authorities have significant responsibilities with regards to safeguarding. Every local authority must establish a Local Safeguarding Children Board (LSCB) for their area (s. 13 Children Act 2004). The LSCB has a range of roles and statutory functions including developing local safeguarding policy and procedures and scrutinising local arrangements.

# 14. National Leaders of Education

Headteachers, executive headteachers and CEOs can apply to be appointed as a National Leader of Education (NLE). The individual must be able to show that they are a strong school leader with experience of effectively supporting schools in challenging circumstances; they must:

◆ have a track record of strong school leadership with at least three years' headship experience;

◆ have a track record of providing effective school-to-school support which has led to improved outcomes for pupils over a sustained period;

◆ have the full support from the school's governing body and a reference from a commissioner of school-to-school support; and

◆ be located in a target area or be prepared to work in one (application rounds are targeted to focus on areas of greatest need to ensure that all schools can access effective support).

If they are selected, the NLE's school will become a national support school (NSS). For a school to qualify as an NSS, it must:

◆ be judged to be at least good by Ofsted;

◆ demonstrate sustained high pupil performance and progress over the last three years; and

◆ have the capacity to support schools in challenging circumstances to improve.

# 15. National Leaders of Governance

Experienced chairs of governors can apply to become an NLG. They must be able to show that they:

◆ have a strong track record
  - for leading school improvement, evidenced by pupil performance data
  - in relationship management within and beyond your school
  - of effective governance

◆ be chair of a school with sustained high pupil performance and progress over the last three years and be above current floor standards;

◆ have at least two years' experience as a chair of governors in the last five years;

◆ have the ability to support other chairs to strengthen their governing body, using their coaching and mentoring skills;

◆ be committed to quality of education for all students, including those in schools they are not accountable for;

◆ be able to meet the time commitment;

◆ have the full support of their governing body; and

◆ have written support from a commissioner of school-to-school support, such as local authority, teaching school alliance, dioceses or regional schools commissioner's office who would be willing to deploy them as a NLG if they were designated.

NLGs provide support to a school/academy that meets specific criteria:

◆ identified as being in need of significant improvement by DfE, Ofsted, a teaching school, local authority or diocese;

◆ where attainment is below the current minimum standards set;

◆ in transition to academy status or MAT;

◆ where the chair of governors is new; and

◆ where working practices for a chair, headteacher or leadership group need developing.

The NLG is expected to support at least one school per year. The first five days of support in each financial year is expected to be provided free of charge. However, additional days over the course of the financial year may be charged to the recipient or commissioner of support and charges/payment arrangements should be negotiated in advance.

# Chapter summary

◆ As charitable companies limited by guarantee, trusts are regulated and controlled by charity and company law as well as specific guidance and regulation produced in relation to trusts including the Academies Act 2010, the Companies Act 2006, the *Academies Financial Handbook*, letters to accounting officers and the Academies Accounts Direction.

◆ The Department for Education (DfE) is the ministerial department responsible for children's services and education. The Education and Skills Funding Agency (ESFA) is the executive agency, sponsored by the DfE, accountable for funding education and skills for children, young people and adults.

◆ Trusts must be aware of and comply with the requirements of DfE documentation including the *Governance Handbook, Competency Framework for Governance* and Clerking Competency Framework.

◆ The Schools Commissioners Group works with school leaders to take action in underperforming schools. Each Regional School Commissioner is supported by a headteacher board (HTB).

◆ Trusts must be registered at Companies House and details updated to reflect changes. The confirmation statement and annual accounts must also be filed in accordance with the time limits.

◆ Ofsted (Office for Standards in Education, Children's Services and Skills) is responsible for inspection and regulation of all state-funded schools including academies.

◆ The RSC and LAs have duties and powers to intervene where schools are causing concern.

◆ Local authorities have ongoing responsibilities particularly with regard to school place planning, home to school transport and a number of statutory duties relating to vulnerable learners. Local authorities have significant responsibilities with regards to safeguarding.

◆ Headteachers, executive headteachers and CEOs can apply to be appointed as a National Leader of Education (NLE) if they can show that they are a strong school leader with experience of effectively supporting schools in challenging circumstances.

# Part two

## Governance

### Overview

This part explains the different types of governance structures that are available for academies. It outlines the nature of an academy's constitution as set out in its articles, how the roles and responsibilities of the officers are delineated and how responsibility is delegated through an academy. The roles of clerk and company secretary are explored in detail.

Students will gain a broad understanding of the different governance structures and a more detailed understanding of the roles and responsibilities of officers and delegation of authority.

## Learning outcomes

In this module you will:

◆ Understand how the legal structures of academies impact on governance.

- ◆ Understand the roles and responsibilities of the board of trustees, board committees and members.
- ◆ Understand the roles and responsibilities of the clerk and the company secretary.

# Chapter three
## Governance structures

**CONTENTS**

## 1. Introduction

This chapter outlines the legal and governance structures that shape trusts and their constituent academies. All trusts are set up as charitable companies limited by guarantee. Trusts in this context includes single academy trusts (SATs), multi-academy trusts (MATs), umbrella trusts, free schools, university technical colleges (UTCs) and studio schools.

This incorporated legal form means that every trust has its own legal personality. It is a legal entity distinct from those involved in running it and it can enter into contracts, own land and assets and can sue and be sued in its own right. The company does not have any shareholders but has members who act as guarantors and promise to contribute a nominal amount if the trust is would up. The members are not necessarily involved in the running of the trust unless they have also been appointed to the board. Those who constitute the board are directors for the purposes of company law, trustees for the purposes of charity law and governors for school improvement purposes. The DfE now generally refers to them as trustees but previous versions of the model articles called them 'directors' or 'governors'.

As registered companies established under the Companies Act 2006, trusts are required to comply with the constitution or rules set out in the **articles of association** as well as complying with the statutory requirements set out in the legislation particularly with regard to reporting and transparency arrangements. Certain information including details of trustees must be registered with Companies House and an annual confirmation statement and annual report and accounts must be submitted. Academies must also maintain registers setting out information about the company and the individuals involved in running it.

**articles of association**
The academy's main constitutional document which sets out the rules regarding internal management, decision making and the running of the trust as well as its liabilities.

Academies cannot be run on a profit basis or directly operated by a for-profit company. However, some for-profit companies operate MATs through not-for-profit subsidiary companies.

# 2. Single academy trusts (SATs)

The first academies were large secondary schools which had the benefit of an external sponsor providing significant financial backing. They were established as single academies and had their own separate legal identity. Later, the programme was expanded to allow successful schools to convert to academy status; secondary, primary and special schools were able to choose to become a single academy.

A SAT is responsible for one school and is indistinguishable as an entity from the school. It has its own funding agreement with the Secretary of State for Education and, consequently, its own articles of association.

The DfE has stated that every application to convert to a SAT structure will be judged on its own merits but consideration will include:

◆ Exam results from the last three years
◆ Pupil progress over the last three years
◆ Most recent Ofsted inspections
◆ The school's capacity to be successful and sustainable as a SAT
◆ The school's finances.

The DfE's preference is currently for maintained schools converting to academy status to form a MAT with other converters or to join an existing MAT. In any event, the Governance Handbook makes clear that it expects a SAT 'to support one or more other schools, whether maintained schools or academies. Such academies can choose what they do to support another school or schools and how they do it, but it must be intended to raise standards'.

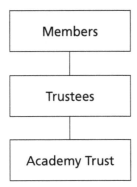

**Figure 3.1:** SAT structure

## Stop and think 3.1

**Trusts have utilised an existing corporate structure, that of the charitable company limited by guarantee. Over time, the DfE's preferred structure and arrangements have modified so, for example, many early academy converters adopted a flat governance structure where all trustees were also members whereas now a structure with no overlap is preferred.**

**How does the structure afforded as a charitable company limited by guarantee affect the governance arrangements of a trust? What are the benefits and drawbacks?**

**What issues are likely to arise for a trust where the DfE's preferred approach has changed?**

# 3. Multi-academy trusts (MATs)

The expectation is now that schools will convert into a MAT structure, either to join an existing MAT or as part of a new MAT. The *Governance Handbook 2017* states: 'Governance structures that span more than one school create an opportunity for more effective governance.'

Maintained schools looking to convert to academy status can establish a so-called 'empty MAT' if it can show capacity. In this case, the converting school is the sole academy school within a MAT structure with the intention that other schools will join.

Many schools, particularly smaller schools, will be aware that they lack the resources to convert alone and will want to join with others in a MAT. Schools that are already in a hard federation will be required to convert to academy status and join a MAT with all the other member schools. Many schools will also wish to strengthen long-established partnership or cluster arrangements which have already developed close working relationships between the schools.

The company structure applies to the MAT itself so that there is one board of trustees and one group of members. The MAT is a single legal entity which is responsible for running each of the individual academies or schools within the trust.

The terminology is confusing as the individual 'schools' are known as academies although they are not trusts in a legal sense.

The MAT is a single legal entity which will have its own vision and strategy which overarches all the academies within it. The trust can establish separate 'local governing bodies' (LGBs) or 'academy committees' for each academy or across clusters. However, there is huge variation between MATs regarding the amount of flexibility and delegation of responsibility to individual academies. LGBs do not need to be constituted by a majority of trustees nor do they need a majority of trustees present at meetings to form a **quorum**.

The MAT board must agree a scheme of delegation which makes clear whether there is delegation to a LGB. However, it must be remembered that any LGB has no legal status and is a form of committee of the board; any delegation of powers can later be retracted or varied by the board.

All teaching and support staff are employed by the MAT whether they work in central services or within one of the academies.

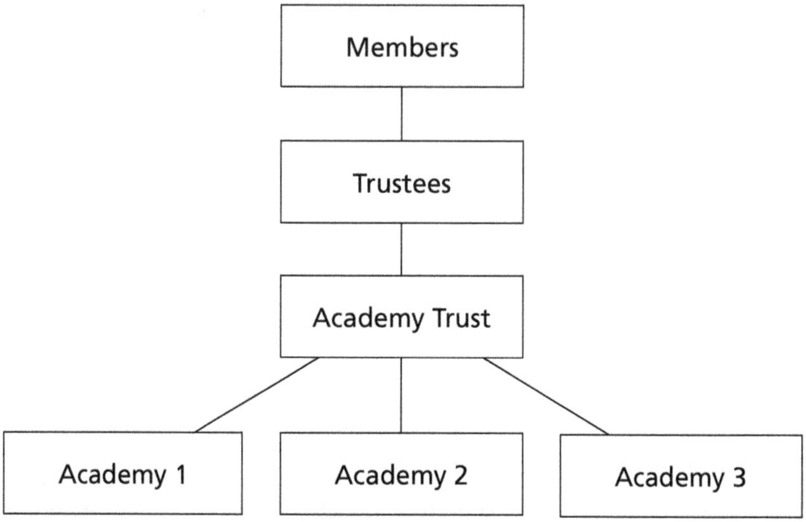

**quorum**
In relation to a board meeting or a members' meeting, the minimum number of directors or members respectively who must be present in order for the meeting to be validly constituted.

**Figure 3.2:** MAT structure

# 4. Church schools

There are memoranda of understanding in place between the DfE and the Church of England, and the DfE and the Catholic Church. These were jointly developed by the DfE and the National Society, and the DfE and the Catholic Education Service, respectively. These formal agreements set out the key principles to apply where schools become academies or action is taken to support, challenge or intervene in any underperforming Catholic or Church of England school.

In principle, schools with different governance structures such as community, foundation and faith schools, can join in a single MAT. However, the Catholic Bishops' Conference of England and Wales have dictated that Catholic schools can only convert in MATs solely comprised of Catholic schools.

Church of England schools can join with community schools in a MAT as long as the governance structure fits their governance arrangements (i.e. **voluntary controlled** schools will need 25% foundation trustee positions on the board whereas **voluntary aided** schools need 75%).

Catholic schools must seek the permission of their Diocesan Bishop and, in Church of England schools, the permission of the Diocesan Director of Education to convert to academy status.

**voluntary controlled**
A maintained school with a quarter of the board of directors appointed by a foundation or trust, usually a religious body. The foundation may own the land, but will have less direct influence than in a VA school.

**voluntary aided**
A maintained school with a majority of the board of governors appointed by a foundation or trust, usually a religious body, which may also own the land and contribute financially.

## Making it work 3.1

**The Salisbury Diocesan Board of Education (SDBE) has adopted a pragmatic approach to academisation. It supports Church of England schools to explore MAT status in a structure that protects the Christian character of the school and meets the needs of pupils. It will agree to schools joining MATs alongside voluntary aided, voluntary controlled and community schools but requires that the representation of any VA or VC school is maintained at member, director and local governor level. The SDBE itself is a corporate member in any such arrangement.**

**The SDBE has also established its own MAT, the Diocese of Salisbury Academy Trust (DSAT) which is open to church and non-church schools.**

# 5. Other academy arrangements

There are a number of other arrangements that either are, or involve, academy structures. For example, a free school is an academy and differs only in the way that it is created.

## 5.1  Umbrella trusts

The **umbrella trust** model is no longer favoured by the DfE. The *Governance Handbook* states that the DfE will not approve the conversion to academy status of schools planning to join an umbrella trust or allow existing trusts to join such an umbrella trust. Nevertheless, a number of umbrella trusts are still in existence.

The umbrella is a collaborative arrangement whereby each of the individual schools is established as a SAT in its own right, with a charitable company which over-arches them (i.e. the umbrella). The form was particularly favoured by schools who wished to gain the benefits of joining together in a group with others but still protect their own ethos; it allowed schools with different

**umbrella trust**
An academy chain whereby the over-arching academy, or umbrella, is a charitable trust in its own right and each of the individual schools is a single academy.

governance structures such as community, voluntary controlled and voluntary aided to join in a formal structure without any changes to representation by a faith or foundation body on the individual academy's governing board.

Academies within an umbrella trust can decide on the level of collaboration and joint working. It is possible to establish central services, employ staff and develop a shared vision and strategy. However, in practice, many umbrella trusts develop a much looser arrangement in which the single academies are independent. Unfortunately, umbrella trusts have not produced the level of governance and collaboration required in a self-supporting system and the more formalised approach of the MAT model is now preferred.

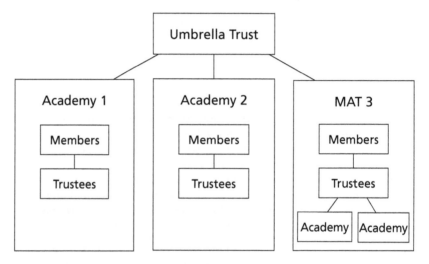

**Figure 3.3:** Umbrella trust structure

### 5.2 Free schools

Free schools were introduced in 2010 influenced by similar models in Sweden and New Zealand and the Charter movement in the US and Canada.

Free schools are a type of trust and, therefore, structured as a charitable company limited by guarantee in the same way as any other trust. Free schools can be mainstream, special, alternative provision or 16- to 19-year old schools. They are set up by a group of parents, teachers, charities, existing schools or other organisations, the majority being set up by existing schools or trusts.

To be successful, a free school application must prove that there is local demand and the school is wanted by both parents and students. This may be demonstrated by reference to a shortage of school places in the area, by offering to raise standards or offer a different choice, or to provide unique support for deprived children or those with particular needs.

Since February 2016, all new schools are established as free schools. If a local authority thinks there is a need for a new school in its area it must seek proposals to establish an academy (free school).

Independent schools can convert to academy status, but they do so by using the free school mechanism.

Once established a free school is simply a new academy.

## 5.3 Studio schools

Studio schools were introduced in 2010 and are also a form of academy. They are schools for 14 to 19-year olds which offer mainstream academic qualifications alongside vocational project-based practical learning. They are set up with the backing of local businesses and employers and follow workplace opening hours with a 9am to 5pm working day and year-round timetable. Study is combined with paid work placements. Studio schools aim to provide students with a strong grounding in English, maths and science whilst developing skills required by employers such as team working, reliability, punctuality and good communication. Studio schools are intended to be small with around 300 students.

## 5.4 University Technical Colleges (UTCs)

UTCs are also a form of academy which offer technically orientated and practical courses taught alongside core GCSE subjects. They are co-educational and all-ability and are sponsored by universities and employers. There is a focus on disciplines such as engineering, manufacturing and construction which require modern, highly specialised equipment. These are taught alongside general business and ICT skills.

Generally, UTCs have around 500–800 pupils drawn from a wide catchment area that can stretch across a number of local authorities.

UTCs are for pupils aged between 14–19 years of age since this is considered by universities and employer sponsors as an appropriate age for young people to be following a more specialised technical route. However, it has proved challenging to recruit pupils at this age in a number of areas. Consequently, some UTCs have now either closed or converted to secondary schools and expanded their age range.

UTCs are also a form of academy. The model articles of association provide that the majority of the board of trustees is made up of nominees of the employer and university sponsors.

## Test yourself 3.1

1.  **What would a school need to show to be approved to convert as a SAT?**

2.  **Why might a school consider setting up as a MAT?**

3.  **What is a MAT and what is the legal status of its academies?**

4.  **What should church schools consider if looking to join with non-church schools in a MAT?**

# 6. Sponsors

The first academies were failing schools that were supported by an external organisation. Primarily this involved a significant injection of capital to build new school buildings and to turn around the fortunes of the failing school.

Sponsorship no longer requires the provision of large sums of money although many sponsors will dedicate time and resources in their role. Sponsorship now generally involves provision of school improvement services. It will not always relate to failing school but may involve those that are too small or otherwise vulnerable to survive alone or where specialist expertise or knowledge is required. It arises in UTCs and studio schools where local employers and universities bring valuable input and opportunity.

Any of the following can apply to become an academy sponsor:

- ◆ Successful school
- ◆ Further education college
- ◆ Sixth form colleges
- ◆ Higher education institution/universities
- ◆ Businesses and entrepreneurs
- ◆ Educational foundations
- ◆ Charities and philanthropists
- ◆ Faith communities.

The most common sponsors are now successful converter academies. However, this is slightly confusing as, when a failing school is 'sponsored' and joins a MAT, it is subsumed into the overall governance structure and effectively ceases to exist as a separate legal entity (though the individual academies continue as separate schools with their own Ofsted judgment).

The lead sponsor will have majority control of a sponsored SAT or MAT and will be able to appoint the majority of members and, thereby, trustees.

# 7. Memorandum and articles of association

The memorandum and articles of association are appended to the funding agreement and must be uploaded to the trust's website.

## 7.1 Memorandum

**Memorandum of Association**
Document confirming the three 'subscribers' who wish to form the academy and become its members. The memorandum has no ongoing significance once an academy has been incorporated.

The **memorandum** is a simple document which sets out the name of the company (i.e. the trust) and provides the name of at least three 'subscribers'. The subscribers can be real or corporate persons, so they could be individuals or companies or organisations such as the sponsor of the academy. The subscribers provide a declaration that they wish to form the trust and they become the first members. Once the company is incorporated the memorandum has no real practical purpose.

## 7.2 Articles of association

The articles of association are the constitution of the company and set out the rules regarding internal management, decision making and the running of the trust as well as its liabilities.

Schools are expected to adopt the DfE model documentation on incorporation or conversion and are not expected to make significant changes. The model articles have changed significantly over time with new versions being developed. Given this, it is essential to refer to the specific articles for a MAT or SAT to understand the requirements and governance provisions that apply: many trusts' articles do not reflect the latest model articles published by the DfE.

The main current model can be used by mainstream, special, 16–19, alternative provision academies and free schools, as well as by studio schools. The same version has alternative sections for use by MATs incorporating such academies.

Although schools are generally not expected to make changes to the model articles, the DfE has indicated its willingness to approve any application by academies that wish to adopt the latest model.

The standard clauses in the model articles comprise:

◆ *Objects*. The purpose and range of activities that the trust is set up to carry out; as a charitable company, the objects are appropriately limited. The current objects clause in the model articles is to 'advance for the public benefit education in the United Kingdom' in particular 'by establishing, maintaining, carrying on, managing and developing school/s'. The model version is adapted according to whether it is a MAT or SAT and the type of provision offered whether mainstream, alternative provision, 16–19 or special academy.

◆ *Powers*. The powers that may be exercised by the academy in furtherance of its objects are set out and include: 'to raise funds', 'to acquire, alter, improve and … to charge or otherwise dispose of property', 'to employ such staff, as are necessary' and 'to pay out of funds of the trust the costs, charges and expenses of and incidental to the formation and registration of the academy trust', as well as numerous other powers that enable a trust to operate.

   The clause states: 'The income and property of the Academy Trust shall be applied solely towards the promotion of the Objects.'

◆ *General meetings*. There are detailed provisions relating to meetings held by members (general meetings). The calling of general meetings and notice requirements, proceedings at meetings, voting and the appointment of proxies is set out.

◆ *Trustees*. The constitution of the board including the various types, number and appointment of trustees is set out (see Chapter 4).

◆ *Clerk to the trustees*. The trustees appoint a clerk 'at such remuneration and upon such conditions as they may think fit'. The clerk cannot be either a trustee or the CEO/principal, although a trustee may act as clerk for the purposes of any meeting where the clerk fails to attend. The clerk may also be the company secretary, but there is no requirement for the duality of roles nor is there any formal requirement to appoint a company secretary.

◆ *Chair and vice-chair of the trustees*. The board must elect a chair and vice-chair of the board each academic year. Employees of the trust are not entitled to be elected. Generally, they will hold office until a successor has been elected, but they will cease to hold office if they:

   – cease to be a trustee

   – is employed by the trust

   – is removed from office.

The board may agree to remove the chairman or vice-chairman subject to:

   – the removal being confirmed by a resolution passed at a second meeting of the trustees held not less than fourteen days after the first meeting; and

   – the matter being specified as an item of business on the agenda for both meetings.

◆ *Powers of trustees*. The board can 'manage' the 'business of the Academy Trust' and may 'exercise all the powers' of the trust. In particular, they can 'expend the funds' of the trust and 'enter into contracts on behalf' of it. The articles cannot be amended so as to retrospectively invalidate the actions of the trustees.

◆ *Conflicts of interest*. Any trustee with a 'direct or indirect duty or personal interest' which conflicts or could conflict with his/her role as a trustee should disclose it as soon as s/he becomes aware of it. This will include any employment or remuneration received from the trust.

**minutes**
A formal record of the proceedings of a meeting and the decisions made.

◆ *The minutes*. **Minutes** of **board meetings** must be drawn up and kept in a book kept for the purpose by the clerk. Once approved by the board, the minutes are signed by the person acting as chair at the same or next subsequent meeting.

**board meeting**
A formal meeting of the board of directors.

◆ *Committees*. The board can establish any committee and determine the constitution, membership and proceedings that will apply which must be reviewed annually. Separate committees known as Local Governing Bodies (LGBs) may be established in a MAT for each academy or for a group of academies. Persons who are not trustees may be appointed to a committee and given voting rights. Generally the majority of members of a committee must be trustees except in the case of an LGB where this is not a requirement.

◆ *Delegation*. The board can delegate any power or function to an individual trustee, committee, the CEO/principal or any other holder of an executive office. Such delegation must be made in writing and can be made subject to any conditions that the board wish to impose and may be revoked or altered. The individual or committee must report to the board when the delegated authority has been exercised and any action taken or decision made, or if it is sub-delegated to another person.

◆ *CEO/Principal.* The board appoint the CEO (sometimes known as executive principal or executive headteacher) in a MAT or the principal in a SAT. The board delegate the powers and functions they consider are required for 'the internal organisation, management and control' of the MAT/SAT.

◆ *Meetings of trustees.* The articles do not set out detailed requirements for board meetings which are largely governed by the Companies Act 2006. The board must hold at least three meetings in every school year. The quorum for the meeting and any vote is 'three Trustees, or where greater, any one-third (rounded up to a whole number) of the total number of Trustees holding office at the date of the meeting'.

◆ *Patrons and honorary officers.* The trustees can appoint a 'patron' who is not a member or trustee but who holds an honorary office. They will decide the period of office that will apply.

◆ *The seal.* The seal may only be used on the authority of the board or a committee of trustees. In practice, seals are rarely used by private companies today.

◆ *Annual report and accounts.* The annual report and accounts (also known as the Annual Report and Financial Statements) should be prepared in accordance with SORP and filed with DfE by 31 December.

◆ *Annual return/Confirmation Statement.* The trustees are responsible for ensuring that the Confirmation Statement (which replaced the **annual return**) is filed at Companies House.

◆ *Notices.* Apart from notices calling a meeting of the trustees, any notice should be in writing or given 'using electronic communications to an address for the time being notified for that purpose to the person giving the notice'.

◆ *Indemnity.* Any trustee, officer or auditor of the trust is entitled to be indemnified against any liability incurred whilst in that role in connection with any court action. This means that as long as the individual is acting within their capacity and has acted honestly and reasonably in all the circumstances, they will be recompensed for any loss.

◆ *Rules.* The board can make 'such rules or bye laws as they may deem necessary or expedient or convenient for the proper conduct and management of the Academy'.

**annual return**
A return of information that all companies must make to the registrar of companies within every 12-month period providing a snapshot of the company including its directors, principal business activities and registered office.

## 7.3  Changes to the articles

To make changes to the articles, the trust must make an application for approval to the Secretary of State via ESFA. The application should usually be supported by a business case setting out the proposal, although some fast-track significant changes do not require a business case; these relate to expansions, age-range changes (by up to three years), adding boarding provision and amending admissions arrangements in old-style funding

**special resolution**
A members' resolution requiring a majority in favour of 75% or over.

agreements. Formal approval of the Secretary of State is still required in these cases. Changes will generally be possible to bring articles into line with up-to-date model versions.

The change is effected by a **special resolution** of the members (75% majority).

### Stop and think 3.2

**Take a detailed look at the model articles of association on the DfE's website to understand current preferred structures. Then compare with the articles of various SATs and MATs – academies are required to publish their funding agreement, to which the articles are appended, on their websites.**

# 8. Becoming an academy

There are various different routes by which academies come into being. The original precursors of academies were newly founded state-funded schools independent of local authority control. All newly created schools are now set up as academies or free schools.

Later, existing maintained schools became academies either by being sponsored in an effort to improve or as a strong, good or outstanding school, as a converter academy. Over time, MAT structures have evolved and are now encouraged by the DfE; existing academies are increasingly moving to join with other MATs. In some instances, MATs have not proved to be achieving the school improvement required and the RSC has got involved to re-broker existing academies.

### 8.1 Conversion

The first converter academies were 'outstanding' schools which were able to become single academy trusts (SATs) and retain their independence. These were larger schools with sufficient staff and resources to stand alone as individual education establishments, the majority were secondary schools. The programme was opened up to any schools graded 'good' or 'outstanding'. In addition, a school will need to demonstrate that it is successful and sustainable:

◆ Above national average pupil attainment and progress
◆ Healthy finances.

The academy programme has been further expanded to allow for all schools, irrespective of Ofsted grading, to opt to convert. However, any school with a grading less than 'Good' will need to demonstrate how the MAT they wish to join will aid their school improvement journey; they would not be permitted to convert to become a SAT.

The DfE has set out a process for conversion:

**1.** Pre-application
◆ Register interest with the DfE which will appoint a project lead.

◆ Read the *Academies Financial Handbook* to understand the financial responsibilities of a trust.

◆ Read *Multi-academy trusts: Good practice guidance* which explains what RSCs look for when approving new academies. This is becoming an increasingly important point with the developing role of head teacher boards and the RSC in considering applications.

◆ Undertake research on different academy structures.

◆ Obtain consent of:

- Governing board

- MAT (for schools wishing to join an established MAT)

- The trust or foundation (for foundation schools and voluntary schools with a foundation)

- The religious body (for church and faith schools)

◆ Prepare the application

◆ Start informal discussions with staff about the Transfer of Undertakings (Protection of Employment) Regulations 2006 (TUPE) process.

◆ Get an actuarial assessment on pension contributions.

◆ Gather all land registration documents.

◆ Compile a list of:

- Contracts

- Assets

- Service-level agreements

- Licences

- Sport England or Football Association grants.

**2.** Apply to convert

◆ Complete the application form

◆ Notify the local authority.

**3.** Set up or join a trust

◆ The academy order will be granted (usually between two to six weeks after receipt)

◆ Arrangements will be made for the £25,000 support grant to be made available

◆ Receive the funding allocation pack which includes an indicative funding allocation letter

◆ Prepare to set up your trust – appoint a solicitor, statutory consultation, complete the land questionnaire, submit draft memorandum and articles of association, submit draft funding agreement

◆ Set up the trust (if establishing a new trust) – register with Companies House, appoint trustees

◆ Appoint local governing body (if establishing or joining a MAT).

4. Transfer responsibilities to the trust
◆ Transfer land to the trust
◆ Commercial transfer agreement
◆ Undertake TUPE process for staff
◆ Establish arrangements for staff pension registrations
◆ Agree use of shared facilities
◆ Agree changes to contracts for unfinished building works
◆ Seek DfE approval for transfer of any loan responsibilities.

5. Prepare to open as an academy
◆ Finish statutory consultation
◆ Finalise funding agreement
◆ Open a trust bank account and send details to ESFA
◆ Appoint accounting officer, trust officers and auditors
◆ Register with the Information Commissioner's Office (ICO) and appoint a Data Protection Officer
◆ Arrange insurance
◆ Undertake Disclosure and Barring Service (DBS) checks as appropriate
◆ Establish a complaints procedure
◆ Notify Get Information About Schools
◆ Receive new unique reference number (URN)
◆ Notify exam boards.

6. Open as an academy
◆ Receive welcome letter and information pack from ESFA
◆ Receive first payment from ESFA
◆ Submit support grant expenditure certificate
◆ Publish funding agreement on academy website
◆ Submit financial returns to ESFA
◆ Complete land and buildings valuation within six weeks of converting.

## 8.2  Joining a multi academy trust (MAT)

However, the DfE have made clear that it expects schools to form or join MATs when they become academies.

It is a relatively simple process to join an existing MAT that has the governance structures already in place to allow it. Any school looking to convert must be happy that the MAT they select fits with their vision and ethos and robust due diligence must take place. Once a school joins a MAT, it is very difficult to get out again and then it will not be by its own volition.

Issues may arise where a school wishes to join an existing MAT which does not have an appropriate governance structure. It is a particular issue for church schools and consideration must be given to the Diocesan proportion of the board/members.

## Making it work 3.2

**There are a number of mixed MATs in which schools in a particular partnership or cluster have joined together. They have experience of working together and have aligned visions so there is every reason to think that the formal arrangement proposed by the MAT structure will work well. The mixed MAT model articles allow for diocesan representation at board and member level of 25% of the total. This means that some church schools can join i.e. any voluntary controlled schools (which have a 25% diocesan representation on the governing board).**

**Unfortunately, voluntary aided schools, which have a 75% diocesan representation on the governing board, are unable to join unless the DDE agrees to 'give away' its majority.**

Separate applications must be made by each of the schools involved if a new MAT is going to be established. Each governing board must pass a resolution to convert to become an academy. The proposal must set out how the proposed school will support school improvement and ensure that weaker schools improve.

Schools in an existing federation must comply with the School Governance (Federations) (England) Regulations 2012, as amended in 2015. Federations are where two or more maintained schools work together under one over-arching governing board. Any federated school must have the approval of at least 50% of its 'prescribed governors' before it can apply to convert to academy status:

- the headteacher
- parent governors
- staff governors
- foundation governors.

Theoretically, individual schools in a federation could decide to convert to academy status at different times. If the federation consists of only two schools, this would necessitate the federation being dissolved. One school leaving a larger federation would not necessarily impact unless it was a forced academisation which may get attention from the RSC as clearly the federation is failing to ensure school improvement.

### 8.3   Forced academisation

Any school that is deemed to be failing will be required to become an academy and join a MAT that can support it. One of the RSC's responsibilities is 'improving underperforming maintained schools by providing them with support from a strong sponsor' which means that a MAT will be identified to take over responsibility for any school which is underperforming, which will usually be prompted by an Ofsted inspection giving a grading of Inadequate. The school may have little control over the course that academisation takes and the MAT that they join.

Schools deemed to be 'coasting' will also be required to join a MAT. A coasting school is one which has failed to ensure that pupils reach their potential for a period of three years. A 'floor standard' is set, below which results should not fall. The definition is intended to avoid temporary 'blips' where a particular cohort has dropped below floor standard. The requirement also considers performance for attainment as well as progress so that a particularly challenging cohort may fail to achieve expected standards of attainment but have strong progress data.

The government has now announced that the coasting measure will be removed in moves to replace the confusing system of failing and coasting measures with one coherent approach.

In addition to these provisions for schools which have been judged by Ofsted to be inadequate or meet the coasting definition, the DfE Guidance on Schools Causing Concern explains that warning notices may be given to schools which otherwise give cause for concern – for example, where the school's performance data is below floor standards or where leadership and governance has broken down or safety is threatened. Performance standards and safety warning notices may be given where:

1.   The standards of performance of pupils at the school are unacceptably low and are likely to remain so.
2.   There has been a serious breakdown in the way the school is managed or governed which is prejudicing, or likely to prejudice, such standards of performance.
3.   The safety of pupils or staff at the school is threatened (whether by a breakdown of discipline or otherwise).

Schools that fail to comply with a warning notice may be eligible for formal intervention which can include making an academy order.

# 9. Mergers and acquisitions

There is an increasing trend for SATs and MATs to merge into larger MATs. It rapidly became obvious that SATs and small MATs often simply do not have the resources to be sustainable. Various figures for the optimal number of pupils or schools necessary to make a MAT financially viable have been suggested but there is no definitive number as many other factors will be relevant such as geographical proximity, the scope and remit of central services, governance structure, etc.

Joining a MAT is often regarded as a one-way ticket. Once a school joins, it ceases to exist as a separate legal entity and any local governing body will not have the authority to decide to split away. An application could be made to the RSC for consideration if the relationship breaks down, but it is difficult to know in what circumstances this would be successful.

More commonly academies are removed from MATs by the RSC and 're-brokered' where performance has not been acceptable. There are no formal guidelines around re-brokerage and the conditions leading to it, but it is likely to be where there has been poor performance but the MAT is not deemed to have the capacity to support school improvement in the timescales required. It is now fairly standard practice for academies to be removed from one MAT by the RSC and accepted into another MAT.

The Memorandum of Understanding between the DfE and the National Society contains provisions whereby the RSC will engage with the Diocesan Board of Education (DBE) 'at the earliest opportunity' if a church academy is underperforming and 'in the view of the RSC requires urgent remedial action' or is 'failing to maintain and develop its religious character and ethos to the satisfaction of the DBE'. In such a case, one of the consequent actions may be re-brokering the academy into a different MAT with an appropriate governance structure.

# 10. Land issues

The legal adviser will arrange for the school's land to be transferred to the trust. To do so, the land questionnaire must be completed and land and title searches conducted. The land transfer advice document is used to complete the model documentation. The documents and transfer arrangements will depend on the existing ownership of the land.

Community schools are sited on local authority land. The trust will usually enter a long-term lease for a term of 125 years with the local authority.

If the land is owned by a trust or foundation or by the school's governing body, the transfer of the freehold is effected by use of the relevant model directions.

If land is held by a trust or foundation that is not the diocese, transfer of the use of the land will be effected by use of the relevant model trust modification orders.

Land on which church schools operate often has a mixture of ownership where, commonly, the diocese owns the land and buildings and the local authority owns the playing field. In this case, the local authority land will be transferred on a long-term lease and a land supplemental agreement will transfer the use of school buildings.

Occasionally, land may be temporarily leased to the trust under a tenancy at will if there is insufficient time to negotiate the lease. However, this is strongly discouraged by the DfE.

Following conversion, a land and buildings valuation must be completed within six weeks. A land and buildings information form should be completed with basic background data and provided to the DfE which instructs valuers to carry out a desktop valuation exercise. The resultant valuations are consolidated into the financial statements within the Sector Annual Report and Accounts (SARA).

## Chapter summary

◆ All trusts are charitable companies limited by guarantee with their own legal personality. A single academy trust (SAT) has only one school/academy whereas a multi-academy trust (MAT) has the potential for many schools/academies.

◆ Church of England and Catholic schools have restricted options regarding joining MATs with schools with different governance structures. They must obtain the approval of the diocese prior to conversion.

◆ Umbrella trusts are a collaborative arrangement of SATs joined by an over-arching company; they are no longer favoured by the DfE. Free schools are newly created academies. Studio schools and University Technical Colleges offer a particular educational experience but are forms of academies.

◆ Sponsors must show that they can support school improvement but rarely offer additional financial input. The most common sponsors are now successful converter academies. The lead sponsor will have majority control of a sponsored SAT or MAT and will be able to appoint the majority of members and trustees.

◆ The memorandum and articles of association are appended to the funding agreement and set out the constitution and rules of the company. Changes may be made to the articles subject to the Secretary of State's approval and a members' resolution.

◆ All new schools are academies or free schools. Existing schools can choose to convert to academy status and the DfE's presumption is that they will join or start a MAT. Failing or coasting schools may be forced to join a MAT.

◆ There has been an increase in mergers of SATs and MATs to create bigger, financially viable organisations. It may be difficult for academies to leave a MAT once they have joined unless they are re-brokered by the RSC.

◆ Arrangements must be made to transfer use of the school buildings and land to the trust. The method will differ according to the land ownership.

# Chapter four
# Roles and responsibilities

**CONTENTS**

## 1. Introduction

This chapter outlines the roles of those involved in governance of trusts.

Trusts are charitable companies limited by guarantee with a two-tier governance structure consisting of members and trustees. Their structure is dictated by company law as enshrined in the Companies Act 2006 and set out in the individual trust's articles of association.

All trusts, both SATs and MATs, are a single legal entity and have one body of members and trustees.

It is possible to be both a member and a trustee and many of the early single academy converters had a flat governance structure where all trustees were also appointed as members. This is no longer considered an acceptable governance model as it lacks robustness and the Department for Education (DfE) thinks there will be reduced objectivity and an increased risk of unchecked 'group think'. The Governance Handbook 2017 states:

> 'The department's view is that the most robust governance structures will have a significant degree of distinction between the individuals who are Members and those who are Trustees. … The department's strong preference is therefore for at least a majority of Members to be independent of the board of Trustees.'

# 2. Members

**member**
A person or corporate body whose name is entered in the academy's register of members.

The **members** have a similar legal standing to the shareholders in a company limited by shares, but instead of a shareholding, members in a trust offer a guarantee. The amount of the guarantee is set at a maximum limit of £10 which is written into the articles of association. This £10 will only be payable as a contribution towards the 'debts and liabilities' of the trust and 'costs, charges and expenses' if it is wound up while they are a member or within a year of them ceasing to be a member.

As the trust is a charitable company, members, including any company or for-profit organisation appointed as a member, are not allowed to participate in any profit (e.g. by receiving dividends).

The DfE recommends that trusts have at least five members and that there is a separation of powers between the members and the board (i.e. that they are not all the same people). The members in the current model articles do not take office by virtue of their role on the board – previous versions had the chair of the board as a member, *ex officio*. There is an increasing recognition of the need for a 'significant degree of separation' between the individuals who are members and those that are trustees; consequently, an increasing number of trusts are opting to amend their articles to reflect this. The Academies Financial Handbook 2018 makes clear that 'If members sit on the board of trustees this may reduce the objectivity with which the members can exercise their powers.'

## Making it work 4.1

**An infant and junior school converted and formed a two-school MAT. The MAT was approached by other primary and nursery schools in the area who felt their ethos aligned with that of the MAT. After due diligence was carried out by all concerned parties these schools also became part of the MAT at which point the trustees decided to review the governance structure. All the original members were the original trustees (i.e. it was a flat governance structure). The final structure was the recommended five members, all of whom were independent and not trustees. The presence of independent members and the separation between the trust board and members makes the new structure more robust from a governance point of view.**

### 2.1 Appointment of members

The subscribers to the memorandum, whose names were added during the company formation process, are the first members of the trust. Members can be natural persons (i.e. people) or corporate bodies (e.g. a Diocese or sponsor organisation). A foundation or sponsor organisation will often be a signatory.

The articles set out the details regarding the appointment of members as well as their removal and termination of membership.

Members are formally appointed when their name is entered into the company's register of members. There must be at least three members, though the DfE recommends that trusts should ideally have at least five. The *Academies Financial Handbook 2018* states that having at least five members:

◆ provides for a more diverse range of perspectives; and

◆ ensures members can take decisions via special resolution without requiring unanimity.

Difficulties can be encountered where there are only three members. If one member wished to leave immediately and would not cooperate in appointing a replacement, the resignation would not be effective since the articles state that a member cannot resign unless 'after such resignation the number of Members is not less than three'. Also, decisions requiring a special resolution, such as the appointment of a new member, require a voting majority of 75% which is impossible without unanimity if there are only three members.

There are generally four members in MATs of Church of England voluntary controlled (VC) schools or mixed MATs of VC and non-church schools. This means that diocesan representation is 25%. The same proportion 25%/75% would need to be applied if the trust wished to have more than four members.

External sponsors (i.e. that are not the MAT itself) or the foundation will be a member in its own right and will generally appoint the majority of members. The members themselves may appoint additional members.

For non-sponsored 'community MATs' the members appoint any additional or replacement members. Suitable candidates are often identified and recommended for appointment by the trustees. Occasionally, older articles allow for appointment of members by the board of trustees.

Earlier versions of the articles automatically appointed the chair of the board as a member but this is no longer included in the model articles.

The current model articles do not permit employees of the trust to be appointed as members. The *Academies Financial Handbook 2018* is clear that employees 'must not be members' unless permitted by the trust's articles.

Every person nominated to be a member must sign a written consent and sign the register of members.

## Test yourself 4.1

**Why is it practical to have more than three members even though the model articles provide for only three as a minimum?**

## 2.2  Responsibilities and rights

The *Academies Financial Handbook 2018* explains that members should be 'eyes on and hands off' and 'avoid compromising the board's discretion'.

However, the members have 'a strong interest' in ensuring that the board has plans to address issues where governance has become 'dysfunctional', it can remove and replace the board or individual trustees with the 'skills necessary for effective governance'.

Members may appoint new members and the current model articles provide that they make the majority of appointments to the board. They also have powers to remove the majority of members and trustees.

The members delegate the general power to the board to oversee the management of the trust; the board, in turn, delegates the day-to-day operational control to the CEO/principal. How much of the strategic direction and vision is set by the members will depend on the organisational and governance structure; trusts with a sponsor or external body such as a diocese involved, may have a great deal more direction from members. The *Governance Handbook* is clear that members should remember that they should be 'eyes on and hands off' and must 'avoid over stepping their powers or undermining the board's discretion in exercising its responsibilities'.

The members have control of changing the trust's constitution (subject to approval by the Secretary of State). They make any changes to the articles by passing a special resolution.

The members have the power to change the name of the trust and, ultimately, to wind up the trust.

Company law gives members the rights to:

- Receive a copy of the Memorandum and Articles of Association.
- Receive notices of general meetings, proposed written resolutions and audited accounts and annual report.
- Attend, speak and vote at general meetings.
- Require the trustees to call a **general meeting**.
- Remove a trustee from office.
- Appoint and remove an auditor.
- Appoint proxies to vote at general meetings.
- Inspect the register of members on reasonable notice during normal office hours.

**general meeting**
A formal meeting of an academy's members.

It is the members who have the powers to amend the articles, change the name of the trust company and, ultimately, to wind up the trust.

## Stop and think 4.1

**What considerations might there around who to appoint as members and how could that be reflected and defined in the articles?**

## 2.3 Restrictions and remedies

The members are prevented from benefiting from the trust except in limited circumstances by the provisions of the articles. A member who is not also a trustee may:

◆ benefit as a beneficiary of the trust

◆ be paid reasonable and proper remuneration for any goods and services supplied

◆ be paid rent for premises let if the amount of rent and other terms of the letting are reasonable and proper

◆ be paid interest on money lent to the trust at a reasonable and proper rate (subject to maximum 2% below base lending rate of a UK clearing bank or 0.5%, whichever is the higher)

Any payments made must be 'reasonable in all the circumstances' and 'in the interests of the trust to contract with that member rather than with someone who is not a member'. Any such decision must be considered by the board and specifically minuted.

Members must declare any business or pecuniary interests which will be published on the trust website.

Members have protection against 'unfair prejudice': if a member/s believes that the trust's affairs are being, have been or are likely to be 'conducted in a manner that is unfairly prejudicial to the interests of members generally or of some part of its members (including at least him/herself), they can petition the court for a remedy (Companies Act 2006, s. 994). In such a case, which would be extremely rare, the member would have to demonstrate that the prejudice was unfair and that their rights/interests had been prejudiced. If the petition is successful, the court can make any order it sees fit which will often require the trust to do, or refrain from doing, the act complained of (Companies Act 2006, s. 996).

**shadow director**
A person who has not been appointed as a director but who directs or gives instructions to an academy's true directors.

Members can bring a derivative action on behalf of the trust against a trustee, former trustee or **shadow director** under s. 260 of the Companies Act 2006 (i.e. it allows members to sue an individual trustee on behalf of the trust). A cause of action could arise from an actual or proposed act or omission by a trustee involving:

**directors' general duties**
Seven general duties of directors which are set out in the Companies Act 2006.

◆ negligence

◆ default (the failure to perform a legally obligated act)

◆ breach of duty (including '**general duties**' or any other duty)

◆ breach of trust.

**derivative claim**
A claim brought by a member of a company against a director on the academy's behalf in accordance with the procedure set out in the Companies Act 2006.

Negligence may be ratified by the board, disbarring any **derivative claim**.

Derivative claims are time-consuming and expensive and are likely to arise extremely rarely.

## 2.4  Ceasing to be a member

Membership automatically terminates if a member:

- in the case of a corporate entity, ceases to exist and is not replaced by a successor institution;
- in the case of an individual, dies or becomes incapable by reason of illness or injury of managing and administering their own affairs; or
- becomes insolvent or makes any arrangement or composition with their creditors generally.

Members may be removed by the person that appointed them. In addition, the members can agree by special resolution (75% majority) to remove any additional member (other than a foundation/sponsor appointment). The subscribers to the memorandum can be removed where remaining members 'agree unanimously in writing'.

The first members are those listed as subscribers to the memorandum. They can be removed when the other members 'agree unanimously in writing'. The DBE cannot be removed in this way from a church trust or mixed-MAT.

All removals must be 'in the interests of the academy trust'.

A member can resign at any stage by lodging notice in writing signed by the person/s entitled to remove them. Their resignation will take effect immediately provided that three members remain in office.

# 3. Trustees

Since the trust is its own legal person, the liability of members and trustees is limited except in certain circumstances, such as where they have acted fraudulently or improperly. This 'corporate veil' separates the legal entity of the trust from the real people involved giving them some level of protection.

## 3.1  Tripartite role

The trustees have a tri-partite role as:

- Trustees for the purposes of charity law.
- Directors of the charitable company for the purposes of company law.
- Governors for the purposes of school improvement.

The DfE's favoured term is currently 'trustee' but usage differs from trust to trust. Some trusts, particularly those with church academies, use the term 'directors' to distinguish them from the trustees who own the land.

Trustees remain accountable for the responsibility even if they delegate to others to carry out. Although the trustees are responsible for the control and administration of the trust, they are not the trust.

## 3.2  Appointment of trustees

The articles will determine the number and category of trustee which dictates how they are appointed. No more than one-third of trustees, including the CEO/ Principal, can be trust staff. With the exception of any *ex officio* roles, trustees are generally appointed for a term of four years. It is possible for a trustee to be re-elected or re-appointed, although the National Governance Association (NGA) recommends that 'governors should serve no more than two terms of office (eight years) in any one school' which is in line with good practice in the charity sector.

Subject to limitations set out in the articles, there is no maximum number of trustees. However, care should be taken to ensure that the board has the necessary skills and expertise to fulfil its role without it becoming too big and unwieldy. The *Governance Handbook 2017* states:

> 'All boards should be tightly focused and no larger than they need to be to have all the necessary skills to carry out their functions effectively, with everyone actively contributing relevant skills and experience.'

Trustees are appointed or elected via a number of routes:

◆  *Member appointments*. The current model articles provide that the majority of trustee appointments are made by the members. They can use such process as they may determine. Often the trustees will identify the need of the board and notify members, sometimes recommending suitable candidates for appointment.

◆  *Foundation/sponsor appointments*. Where there is a foundation or sponsor arrangement, a number of trustee positions will be retained for appointment by them. Selection may be made on any basis that the Foundation/sponsor chooses.

◆  *Parent trustees*. A SAT should have a minimum of two parent trustees on the board who are elected by parents and other individuals exercising parental responsibility for registered pupils at the academy. The articles may allow for parent trustees to be appointed by the board.

There is no obligation for a MAT to have parent trustees on the board if there are at least two parent governors on each LGB. Of course, there may still be trustees who are parents of pupils at MAT academies but they will not be elected or appointed AS parents.

Although parent trustees must be a parent of a pupil at the academy at the time when they are elected/appointed, they will not be required to terminate their position if that pupil leaves. That board is responsible for making all necessary arrangements for a parent trustee election and ensure that it is conducted via a secret ballot if it is contested. If there are insufficient nominees to fill the vacancies, the board can appoint a person who is the parent of a registered pupil at the academy or if this is not possible a person who is the parent of a child of compulsory school age.

◆   *Co-opted trustees*. The board may also appoint co-opted trustees subject to any limitation on number set out in the articles.

◆   *CEO/principal*. The members can appoint the CEO/principal as a trustee if that individual 'agrees so to act'. The CEO/principal will benefit from an *ex officio* role in older versions of the model articles, but this has now been removed from references in the *Academies Financial Handbook 2018* to bring it into alignment with the current model where the senior executive leader does not automatically become a trustee.

◆   *Staff trustees*. Earlier versions of the model articles for SATs had some trustee positions allocated to elected or appointed staff trustees. This is no longer the case and there is no longer any requirement to appoint staff. The DfE's *Governance Handbook* states the strong preference is for no employees other than the CEO to serve as trustees to retain clear lines of accountability through the trust's single senior executive leader. This is a distinct shift from earlier model versions of the articles which often allowed the headteachers of MAT academies to hold a position on the board by virtue of their role.

◆   *UTCs*. Nominees of the employer and university sponsors must together form the majority on the board in a UTC.

### 3.3   Chief executive officer/principal and executive officers

The articles recognise that the day-to-day running of the trust will be delegated to the CEO in a MAT or the principal in a SAT. Various titles are given to these individuals in specific trusts (e.g. executive headteacher, executive principal, headteacher, etc).

In the current model articles, the CEO/principal will not automatically hold an *ex officio* place on the board by virtue of their position (unlike previous versions). Instead, the members can appoint the CEO as a trustee subject to the CEO's agreement to do so.

The NGA does not think that the CEO/principal should be a trustee, although they recognise that they should be required to attend board meetings. They state that the dual role of the CEO/principal in 'presenting plans, giving advice and providing information' to the board creates an inherent conflict of interest if they are at the same time a member of that board.

### 3.4   Selection of trustees

There has been a gradual move away from the stakeholder model of representation on the board. The focus is now on ensuring that individuals are selected for appointment on the basis of the skills and experience they offer which are matched against the board's current requirements or perceived weaknesses. Efforts should also be made to appoint a diverse board made up of highly qualified skilled/experienced individuals from varied backgrounds which will promote better corporate governance. Diversity criteria should include gender, age, ethnicity, educational and social diversity.

The *Governance Handbook 2017* states:

> 'The membership of the board should therefore focus on skills, and the primary consideration in appointment decisions should be acquiring the skills and experience the board needs to be effective. Boards should therefore develop a skills-based set of recruitment criteria which they should share with any third parties, such as trust Members or a foundation or sponsor, that has a role in appointing people to the board.'

It is good practice to undertake regular skills audits which can identify gaps in skills and drive the board training programme. The recognition of any gaps can also help to ensure a focused search and appointment process for new trustees.

## Test yourself 4.2

1. **What routes are there for trustees to be appointed/elected to the board?**

2. **What issues are there with appointing the CEO/principal to the board?**

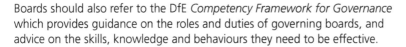

Boards should also refer to the DfE *Competency Framework for Governance* which provides guidance on the roles and duties of governing boards, and advice on the skills, knowledge and behaviours they need to be effective.

## 3.5  Eligibility

Company law contains restrictions on who is suitable to be appointed as a director. In addition, the articles provide that an individual:

◆ Must be aged 18 or over at the date of election or appointment.

◆ Not a current pupil of the academy (or any academy in a trust).

In addition, they must not be appointed:

◆ During a period of disqualification, whether in the UK or in an overseas jurisdiction.

◆ During any period of undischarged bankruptcy (without the permission of the court).

The trust's auditor is not eligible for appointment as a trustee.

## 3.6  Directors' duties

The *Academies Financial Handbook 2018* states that trustees '**must** apply the highest standards of governance and take full ownership of their duties'. It makes specific reference to sections 170–181 of the Companies Act 2006 which sets out 'general duties' that apply to directors. They have a duty to:

- act within powers – acting in accordance with the trust's constitution and only exercising powers for the purposes for which they were conferred;
- promote the success of the trust;
- exercise independent judgement;
- exercise reasonable care, skill and diligence;
- avoid conflicts of interest;
- not accept benefits from third parties; and
- declare interest in any proposed transaction or arrangement.

Directors have a fiduciary duty to act with the 'utmost good faith'.

The *Academies Financial Handbook 2018* also states that trustees 'must ensure regularity and propriety in use of the trust's funds, and achieve economy, efficiency and effectiveness'.

## 3.7   Liability

Trustees' liability will usually be covered by any officers' and directors' insurance arrangements made by the trust. The model articles specifically provide that trustees can 'benefit from any indemnity arrangement purchased at the trust's expense or any agreement so agreed with the Secretary of State to cover the liability of trustees' such as a risk protection arrangement. The articles provide that such arrangements should cover 'any negligence, default or breach of trust or breach of duty of which they may be guilty' as long as it does not arise as a result of:

- any claim arising from any act or omission which the trustees (or any of them) knew to be a breach of trust or breach of duty or which was committed in reckless disregard to whether it was a breach of trust or breach of duty or not; and
- the costs of any unsuccessful defence to a criminal prosecution brought against the trustees (or any of them) in their capacity as directors of the trust.

Although trustees have a responsibility to act with the utmost good faith, they are unlikely to acquire liabilities unless they recklessly or knowingly did something wrong. A trustee found to have acted fraudulently could receive a prison sentence of up to ten years under criminal law. There are also various instances where a trustee could be disqualified from acting as a director of a UK company for up to 15 years as well as receive a fine.

Members could potentially bring a derivative claim against a trustee for an actual or proposed act or omission by a trustee involving:

- negligence
- default (the failure to perform a legally obligated act)
- breach of duty (including 'general duties' or any other duty)
- breach of trust,

as long as the action complained of has not been ratified by the board.

Trustees could also find themselves at risk of legal action or a fine if they have not fulfilled their duties. Trustees are responsible for fulfilling the company secretarial function and may be personally liable for filing failures with Companies House. There is an automatic late filing penalty on an increasing scale if the annual accounts are delivered late and trustees could find themselves criminally liable.

## 3.8 Termination of office

The model articles provide for trustees to be appointed/elected for a fixed term of office of four years. This excludes any post which is held *ex officio* (i.e. by virtue of their position or status). At the end of that period the term of office will lapse. Any trustee can be re-appointed or re-elected. The articles do not contain any restrictions on the length of time that a trustee can serve, but the *Governance Handbook* explains that care should be taken when looking to re-elect the chair as, in some circumstances, 'a change of chair may be necessary for the board to remain invigorated and forward looking'. The NGA recommends that trustees should not remain on the board for more than eight years with a maximum of six years as chair. This is echoed in the *Governance Handbook* which suggests that strong chairs should move on to another school or trust after a 'reasonable time (e.g. two terms of office)'.

Trustees can resign from office by notice to the trust at any time. However, the articles provide that it will only take effect if at least three trustees remain in office after the resignation.

The model articles provide that a trustee can be removed during their term of office by the 'person or persons who appointed or elected him' or by **ordinary resolution** of the members. In this case, those removing the trustee must give written notice of it to the clerk. As the trustee is also a company director there are formal processes to be followed for the removal of a company director to maintain compliance with company law and trusts should seek advice from their legal advisors or company secretary if they are contemplating removal of a trustee.

**ordinary resolution**
A decision/resolution requiring approval by a majority of an academy's members.

The model articles also provide that the trustees can resolve that a trustee's office be vacated if they have been absent from all trustees' meetings without consent for a period of six months.

## 3.9 Disqualification

The court has power to make an order disqualifying an individual from promoting, forming or taking part in the management of a company without the leave of the court (Company Directors' Disqualification Act 1986). The model articles provide specific instances which will be regarded as disqualification, if a trustee or a member of a trust committee including any local governing body:

◆ has been declared bankrupt and/or his estate has been seized from his possession for the benefit of his creditors and the declaration or seizure has not been discharged, annulled or reduced;

**disqualification order**
A court order preventing
a person from, among
others, acting as a director
of a company without the
consent of the court for
the period of time specified
in the order. Breach of a
disqualification order is a
criminal offence.

◆   is the subject of a bankruptcy restrictions order or an interim order;

◆   is subject to a **disqualification order** or a disqualification undertaking
    under the Company Directors' Disqualification Act 1986 or to an order
    made under s. 429(2)(b) of the Insolvency Act 1986;

◆   has been removed from the office of charity trustee or trustee for a charity
    by an order made by the Charity Commission or the High Court on the
    grounds of any misconduct or mismanagement in the administration of the
    charity for which he was responsible or to which he was privy, or which he
    by his conduct contributed to or facilitated;

◆   has, at any time, been convicted of any criminal offence, excluding any
    that have been spent under the Rehabilitation of Offenders Act 1974 as
    amended, and excluding any offence for which the maximum sentence is a
    fine or a lesser sentence except where a person has been convicted of any
    offence which falls under s. 178 of the Charities Act 2011; and

◆   has not provided to the board chair a disclosure and barring service check
    at an enhanced disclosure level under s. 113B of the Police Act 1997. In
    the event that the certificate discloses any information which would in the
    opinion of either the chair or the CEO/principal, confirm their unsuitability
    to work with children that person shall be disqualified.

A trustee will also automatically cease to hold office:

◆   on becoming incapable by reasons of illness or injury of managing or
    administering their own affairs; and

◆   if he ceases to be a trustee by virtue of any provision in the Companies Act
    2006 or is disqualified from acting as a trustee by virtue of section 178 of
    the Charities Act 2011.

### 3.10 Shadow and *de facto* directors

The Companies Act 2006 provides that a director will be 'any person occupying
the position of director, by whatever name called'. In a trust, directors are
commonly referred to as governors or trustees but are still legally the directors.

**de facto director**
A person acting as a
director who has not
been formally or validly
appointed.

A **de facto director** (which literally means director 'in fact') may arise where
a person acts as a director even though they have not been validly appointed.
This may be due to an error, omission or oversight in the appointment process.
Typically it will arise where a trust attempts to appoint an 'associate trustee'
in the same way as the governing board of a maintained school; this is not
permissible in a trust. Anyone who does become a *de facto* director is subject
to the same general duties and legal responsibilities as a legitimately appointed
director.

There is no determinative test as to whether someone is a *de facto* director, but
the Court of Appeal set out a number of relevant considerations in the leading
case of *HMRC v Holland* (2010):

◆   the concepts of a shadow director and a *de facto* director are separate but
    overlap;

- the key consideration in determining whether someone is a *de facto* director is to ask whether they have assumed a responsibility to act as a director;
- it must be determined objectively: the individual's own thoughts on the matter are irrelevant;
- it is relevant whether the company considered the individual to be a director and held them out as such and whether third parties considered that person to be a director;
- the court must look at the acts in context and consider their cumulative effect; and
- the fact that a person is consulted about directorial decisions, or asked for approval, does not, without more, make them a director.

The Companies Act defines a 'shadow director' as 'a person in accordance with whose directions or instructions the directors of the company are accustomed to act'. This will relate to anyone who has a significant influence over the workings of the board that goes beyond advice given in a professional capacity. Again, it is a broad definition. Case law has considered the factors to take into account:

- communications were either a 'direction' or 'instruction';
- it is not necessary for a shadow director to give directions or instructions over all areas of the company's activities;
- advice of a non-professional nature can constitute a direction or instruction;
- it is not necessary to show that the board acted in a subservient manner;
- the majority of the board were accustomed to following the directions and instructions and not only a number of individuals;
- it must be shown that the directors act on instructions, the mere giving of them is insufficient; and
- a person can be a shadow director if s/he is involved in the internal management of the company.

Shadow directors can be either natural persons or a legal person such as a company, charity or other organisation.

Like *de facto* directors, shadow directors will acquire responsibilities and liabilities. This puts them into a vulnerable position personally as they may not be covered by any insurance provision in place as they were never formally appointed. The general duties set out in the Companies Act will apply to both *de facto* and shadow directors and they may find themselves subject to a disqualification order.

The *Academies Financial Handbook 2018* explicitly states that trusts must not have *de facto* or shadow directors.

### Making it work 4.2

**A large secondary school graded 'Outstanding' converted to become a SAT. It wished to recreate the existing structure and representation on the governing board. However, it had historically had an 'Associate Governor' position for the chair of the PTA who came along to all governing board meetings and voted alongside other governors. They were advised to formally co-opt the PTA chair as a trustee under the provisions of their articles; attempting to appoint them as an 'associate' would mean that they were a *de facto* director and leave that individual exposed on a personal level.**

### 3.11 Time off work

Unlike maintained school governing boards, there is no legal requirement for employers to give reasonable time off work to carry out their duties. However, many employers encourage their employees to become trustees or governors and gain board-level experience.

The *Governance Handbook* recognises that the 'learning and development benefits' that employees gain 'more than compensate for the flexibility and time off that staff may need to fulfil their governance duties'. The Confederation of British Industry (CBI) identifies clear parallels between the ways in which 'governing bodies set strategic direction and hold school leaders to account for delivery of educational outcomes, and the activities of corporate boards in developing a business vision and evaluating senior executives on its achievement'.

## 4. Role of the board

According to the funding agreement, the trustees are 'responsible for the general control and management of the administration of the Academy Trust'. In so doing, the board must 'have regard to any Guidance on the governance of Academy Trusts' that is issued by or on behalf of the Secretary of State such as the *Academies Financial Handbook* or *Governance Handbook*.

According to the *Governance Handbook*, all boards have three core functions:

◆ ensuring clarity of vision, ethos and strategic direction;

◆ holding executive leaders to account for the educational performance of the organisation and its pupils, and the performance management of staff; and

◆ overseeing the financial performance of the organisation and making sure its money is well spent.

There are, however, responsibilities beyond these including, but not limited to, those related to the board's role as:

- employer and therefore compliance with employment law;
- controller of premises (e.g. health & safety, environmental health);
- having wider financial responsibilities (e.g. HMRC Revenue & Customs, Charity Commission);
- admissions authority;
- appellant body for complaints, appeals, panels etc;
- being responsible for operating within company law; and
- data controller.

The board is a corporate body. Therefore, any decision making is a collective process; if a resolution is passed, it is binding on all trustees who must stand by that decision even if they do not agree with it or voted against it. In keeping with this, the minutes will not record the actual number of votes for and against a particular resolution. The model articles provide that 'a declaration by the chairman that a resolution has been carried or carried unanimously, or by a particular majority, or lost, or not carried by a particular majority and an entry to that effect in the minutes of the meeting shall be conclusive evidence of the fact without proof of the number or proportion of the votes recorded in favour of or against such resolution'.

## 4.1 The chair

The articles provide that trustees must elect a chair and vice-chair of the board each year. They must not be trust employees. The *Governance Handbook 2017* states that the focus should be on 'appointing someone with the skills for the role, not just the willingness to serve'.

It is possible to appoint more than one person to share the role of chair or vice-chair. However, the board would need to ensure that this was in the best interests of the trust and did not result in a loss of clarity of leadership.

The *Academies Financial Handbook 2018* states that the chair is 'responsible for ensuring the effective functioning of the board and setting professional standards of governance'.

The *Governance Handbook 2017* is clear that it is essential to have an effective chair and vice-chair with the ability to 'provide visionary strategic non-executive leadership'. The chair must give the board clear leadership and direction and they are ultimately responsible for ensuring that the board operates effectively. They play a 'vital role in setting the highest of expectations for professional standards of governance' and should make sure that 'everyone understands what is expected of them' including trustees and any members of committees. It is an onerous role which requires significant people skills encouraging the board to work together as a team, 'building their skills, knowledge and experience', making sure that everyone is contributing and actively involved and not afraid to have 'honest conversations'.

The DfE *Competency Framework* for Governance also provides further guidance in the role of the chair.

The chair does not automatically have any rights or responsibilities except as delegated by the board. However, the board may delegate a general power for the chair to act in cases of urgency where a delay in exercising the function would be likely to be 'seriously detrimental to the interests of the school, a pupil, parent or member of staff'. As with any delegation of power, its exercise must be reported to the next board meeting.

Generally, the chair and vice-chair will remain in office for one year unless they:

◆ cease to be a trustee;
◆ are employed by the trust; and
◆ are removed from office.

The vice-chair will cease to hold their office automatically if they are elected as chair.

The board may remove the chair or vice-chair from office by passing a resolution as long as:

◆ the removal is confirmed at a second board meeting held not less than 14 days after the first meeting; and
◆ the removal is specified as an item of business on the agenda for both meetings.

The reasons for proposing the removal of the chair or vice-chair must be stated at the second meeting with an opportunity given to the chair and/or vice-chair, as appropriate, to make a statement in response.

The board should have due regard to succession planning so that any change in the chair does not impact negatively on the board's effectiveness.

The *Governance Handbook 2017* notes that there are no formal restrictions on the number of times a chair can be re-elected, but states that sometimes 'a change of chair may be necessary for the board to remain invigorated and forward looking'. The NGA recommends that chairs should consider standing down after six years in one school/academy.

If a board decides that they do not have a candidate with the appropriate skills, it can advertise and recruit a chair who is appointed to a vacant position on the board to take up the role.

# 5. Local Authority Associated Persons (LAAPs)

The model articles set strict limits on the number of LAAPs that can be appointed as members and trustees in order to avoid 'influenced company status'. Academies were intended to be free of local authority (LA) control and the provisions were included to ensure that this did not happen by means of appointing individuals to take control of the board. Individuals wishing to be appointed as a trustee must get approval of the LA with which they are associated.

A person is regarded as a LAAP if:

◆ they are a member of a LA (elected councillor);

◆ they are an officer of the LA (direct employee);

◆ they are both an employee and either a director/trustee, manager, secretary or other similar officer of a company which is under the control of the LA; or

◆ at any time within the preceding four years they have been a member of the LA.

This is a broad definition which could encompass employees of LAs such as police officers, fire officers, teachers at maintained schools, etc. The restriction should be kept under review as it could mean that potential new trustees cannot be appointed.

An individual will be regarded as a LAAP even if the LA with which they are associated has no connection with the trust. The relevant percentage limit can be reached even if all the LAAPs are connected with different LAs.

A LA is:

◆ a county council;

◆ a district council (including metropolitan boroughs, non-metropolitan districts/boroughs and unitary authorities);

◆ a London borough council;

◆ a parish council; and

◆ a community council.

## Stop and think 4.2

**Taking into account the definition of a Local Authority Associated Persons, think what information should the Board seek from prospective candidates before appointing them to the Trust Board.**

The number of votes exercisable by LAAPs must not exceed 19.9% of the total number of votes exercisable by members. In practice, this means that no LAAP can be appointed as a member unless there are at least six members (the current DfE preferred model allows for five). To avoid this situation, the articles allow for the votes of the other members 'having a right to vote at the meeting' to be increased on a pro-rata basis.

Similarly, LAAPs must make up less than 20% of the total number of trustees with the number of votes exercisable by LAAPs on any resolution not exceeding 19.9% of the total number of votes exercisable by trustees. Again, the votes of the other trustees may be increased on a pro-rata basis.

The trustee/member is deemed to have resigned immediately if their appointment/election would exceed the limit set. They will also be deemed to have resigned immediately if they are a trustee/member and subsequently become a LAAP. There are no such restrictions on those serving on local governing bodies or advisory boards in a MAT.

### Test yourself 4.3

**What limitations are there on appointing Local Authority Associated Persons?**

## 6. Local governors

Many MATs operate a local governing body (LGB) structure where various responsibilities and powers of the board are delegated. It is one method of achieving local accountability and engaging with local stakeholders.

The model articles allow for the trustees to appoint LGBs responsible for one or more academies. LGBs can be established in accordance with the wishes of the board with regards to the 'constitution, membership and proceedings'. Unlike other trust committees, LGBs do not need to have a majority of members who are trustees or vote where the majority of members of the committee present are trustees.

There is now a clear direction from the DfE that it is looking for a separation of powers between the different layers in trust governance structures. The *Governance Handbook* specifically highlights the need for 'complementary and non-duplicative roles for the board, any committees or local governing bodies (LGBs), and MAT executives'.

Any local governors will not be trustees unless they are also appointed to sit on the MAT board. This means that the charity and company law requirements do not apply directly to them. They will, of course, need to recognise the Nolan principles in all their activities. The board will often require LGBs and their governors to adopt a code of practice. Local governors must also undergo DBS checking and declare any conflict of interest which must be managed in the normal way.

Interestingly, the charity law restrictions on payment to trustees do not apply to local governors which means that, in theory, they could be paid for discharging their role. However, the *Governance Handbook* makes clear that trusts considering payment of people to sit on LGBs or other committees 'should review very carefully, whether this is in the best interest of the trust and whether this would be an appropriate use of public funds'. Generally, payment would only be acceptable for a time limited period (e.g. 'bringing in highly skilled individuals to oversee the turnaround of an underperforming academy').

# Chapter summary

◆ All trusts, both SATs and MATs, are a single legal entity and have one body of members and trustees. The DfE preference is for there to be a majority of members who are independent of the board of trustees.

◆ Members offer a guarantee set at a maximum limit of £10 payable towards costs if the trust is wound up. Members are not allowed to participate in any profit of the trust by receiving dividends.

◆ The subscribers to the memorandum are the first members; subsequent members can be appointed by the sponsor or foundation and the other members. The current model articles do not permit employees to become members. Their main responsibilities are: the power to change the articles and appointment and removal of trustees and auditors. Members can resign, be removed or membership will terminate if they die/cease to exist or becomes insolvent.

◆ Trustees are trustees for the purposes of charity law, directors for the purposes of company law and governors for the purposes of school improvement. The articles determine who can appoint, elect or remove trustees, no more than one third of whom can be employees. In the current articles, the members can appoint the CEO/principal as a trustee subject to their consent. The term of office is usually four years though they may resign, be removed or will cease to hold office in certain circumstances. Shadow and *de facto* directors are not permitted. There are strict limits on LAAPs.

◆ Trustees are 'responsible for the general control and management of the administration of the Academy Trust'. The board makes decisions and operates as a corporate body. A chair and vice-chair must be elected each year.

# Chapter five
# The clerk and the company secretary

## CONTENTS

## 1. Introduction

This chapter outlines the role of the governance professional within a trust, the appointment of a clerk and/or company secretary and the remit of these roles.

This chapter also outlines the statutory registers that must be maintained by the trust as a company and the ongoing requirements to Companies House.

## 2. The governance professional

There is an increasing recognition of the need to appoint a professionally trained and experienced individual to provide robust governance advice and support. Legal advisers may be kept on retainer but this is costly and there are limitations on the support available. The growing importance of the role has been acknowledged in the DfE Clerking Competency Framework and the government's support for the clerking development programme. The framework recognises that boards governing different types and sizes of trusts will have different clerking needs: the board of a large MAT may have greater need for expert advice and support in structuring and operating multifaceted governance arrangements. It is for the chair and the executive leader, together with the board, to consider which knowledge and skill areas outlined in the framework are most important for their clerk in their particular context and in relation to the scale and complexity of their organisation. Whatever their clerking needs, all boards should have high expectations for the professionalism of the service they receive.

This is particularly applicable with the growth and development of MATs where the requirements differ between trusts as a result of having different articles and internal schemes of delegation. Consequently, many MATs now employ a dedicated head of governance/company secretary who is the guardian of the governance process and the constitutional conscience of the board. Some trusts also separate the company secretary role and duties from the secretary to the board.

However, a governance professional attracting a higher salary is not necessary for every academy within a MAT. Many MATs have now adopted a two-tier governance support structure where clerks or minute-takers are engaged for the individual academies and line managed by the governance professional.

The board appoint the 'clerk' or other governance professional 'at such remuneration and upon such conditions as they may think fit'. It must, therefore, ensure that remuneration is appropriate for the role with the scope and remit of that role set out in a written job description.

If the clerk/company secretary is an employee of the trust they should be subject to the normal performance management system used by the trust. This means that the clerk/company secretary will benefit from a process that reviews the past year to identify mistakes and build on successes by using objective setting. Where the role is contracted through an external provider or the clerk is self-employed there should be a similar process for a review of the performance of the contract or service level agreement.

A good performance management process will also provide for appropriate training and support, identifying gaps and allowing for continuous development. The educational landscape has experienced significant change over the last few years and this is likely to continue until academisation and the development of the MAT has matured. In the meantime, all clerks/company secretaries/governance professionals will need to undertake continuing professional development to keep abreast of the latest requirements.

The DfE Clerking Competency Framework is likely to be of use in identifying areas for development. It is structured around four competencies:

◆ *Understanding governance*. Enables the clerk to make an important contribution to the effectiveness of the board, resulting in better quality advice on legal and procedural matters, more accurate recording of discussions and decisions and enable more efficient use of the board's time.

◆ *Administration*. Taking care of the basics enables the chair and the board to make more effective use of their time and focus on strategic matters; high-quality paperwork leads to better informed decision making, and clear record-keeping enables compliance and accurate reporting to others both within and outside the organisation.

◆ *Advice and guidance*. Contributes to better and more efficient decision making and helps the board to manage the risk of non-compliance with legal and regulatory frameworks, helps the board stay focused on its strategic functions.

◆   *People and relationships.* Essential to establishing open communication and ensuring smooth information flow between the board, the executive leaders and, where required, staff, parents and the local community.

## 2.1  Clerk

The model articles provide that the board should appoint a clerk or secretary to the board. However, it does not specify exactly what that role should entail or what it should look like. The *Academies Financial Handbook 2018* states that the board should appoint a person as clerk to the board who is 'someone other than a trustee, principal or chief executive of the trust'.

In a MAT, the board can choose to appoint one person as clerk to the board of trustees but different clerk/s to any committees or LGBs since it may be impractical for the same person to do it all. It may even be possible that a simple minute-taker is used to service the meetings with a governance professional taking an advisory role.

Every board needs a clerk to provide administrative support and guidance on procedural matters. One important duty is the preparation of minutes of meetings which will be amongst the first documentation viewed by Ofsted inspectors and other external bodies when assessing the quality of provision. It is, therefore, essential that the clerk can produce accurate minutes that conform to the latest best practice.

The DfE now widely advocates the use of 'professional-quality clerking' which, in the Clerking Competency Framework, is regarded as is 'critical to the effectiveness of a governing board in fulfilling its core strategic functions'. The clerk provides:

◆   administrative and organisational support;

◆   guidance to ensure that the board works in compliance with the appropriate legal and regulatory framework, and understands the potential consequences for non-compliance; and

◆   advice on procedural matters relating to the operation of the board.

Particularly in larger and more complex organisations, professional clerking may involve 'designing structures and procedures for the sound governance of the organisation'. The scope of the role and the range of responsibilities will differ according to the academy setting and requirements of the board. The clerk may advise the board on governance and constitutional matters and the management of information to comply with legal requirements.

Clerks need adequate training and qualifications to give them a working understanding of the law and procedures relevant to academies and have a thorough knowledge of the funding agreement and articles of association that apply to their trust and their particular requirements.

The clerk should be mindful of the Nolan principles and carry out their duties in line with them. The Competency Framework explains that they should take account of equality legislation 'recognising and encouraging diversity and inclusion. Effective governance will impact on the quality of education and on outcomes for pupils and this should be understood by the clerk.

Often in the past the role of clerk was undertaken by the school secretary or bursar. However, these relationships had significant difficulties arising from the conflicting reporting lines. Technically, at least, the clerk is appointed by the board of trustees and reports to the chair of the board. This can present an impossible situation for an individual who reports to the headteacher in their day job but to the chair of the board in their role as clerk. There is a growing recognition that these internal arrangements are no longer appropriate; efforts must be made to ensure a clear separation of functions and lines of reporting.

Increasingly, professional, independent clerks are engaged. A professional clerk can provide appropriate legal and regulatory guidance where applicable as well as having an unbiased view: they can focus on making sure that governance is done well.

The clerk must not be a trustee or the principal/headteacher/CEO. They are not entitled to vote at board meetings. If the clerk fails to attend a meeting, the board may appoint a trustee to act as clerk and they will still be able to take part in discussions and vote.

Whilst the clerk is appointed by the board, they report to the board chair. The clerk will be key to ensuring the effective running of meetings by providing practical support and legal and procedural guidance where necessary. The clerk is responsible for preparing the legal record of proceedings at meetings.

## 2.2  Company secretary

Prior to the Companies Act 2006, all private companies were required to appoint a designated company secretary. This requirement was removed unless there is a provision in the articles of association. Whilst the model articles do not contain this requirement a trust may choose to do so and MATs are increasingly appointing senior governance professionals to fulfil this role.

The company secretary is a high-ranking professional and the chief administrative officer of the trust who is registered as such at Companies House. Their role and responsibilities will differ enormously from trust to trust. However, as well as holding a key governance role, they may advise on legal and regulatory matters, finance and accounting, risk management and the development of strategic planning.

There is no legal or regulatory definition of the company secretarial role and there is no typical arrangement. The remit must be clearly defined by the terms of the contract of employment. Trustees should carefully consider the most appropriate arrangements to meet the needs of their trust.

There is potential overlap here with the clearly defined role of the chief finance officer (CFO) in the *Academies Financial Handbook* which stipulates that 'the CFO should play both a technical and leadership role, including ensuring sound and appropriate financial governance and risk management arrangements are in place, preparing and monitoring of budgets, and ensuring the delivery of annual accounts'.

As a result, the role of company secretary is often subsumed in the role of business manager/finance director. Many trusts call their clerk the company secretary, but this is purely for the maintenance of Company House and associated registers. A company secretary assists the board in the decision-making process by providing information and guidance; they are adviser to the board and to the chair. They will generally be responsible for leading on the administrative aspects of running a company including the maintenance of Companies House records. Commonly, a company secretary will deal with some of the following:

**statutory registers**
Books/registers containing information relating to an academy's directors, members etc, which academies must maintain in accordance with the Companies Act.

- organising meetings of trustees and meetings of members, attending the meeting to provide support and advice and preparation of the minutes;
- maintenance of the **statutory registers**;
- assisting with the preparation of the annual report and accounts;
- ensuring compliance with the Companies Act, the articles and other DfE/ESFA guidance;
- updating the information held by the Registrar of Companies when appropriate;
- preparing and filing the annual confirmation statement;
- ensuring that decision making is in line with the articles and scheme of delegation; and
- acting as adviser to trustees on governance best practice and changes to legislation and guidance.

Professional firms of solicitors or accountants often offer company secretarial services which will manage Companies House requirements and provide basic legal support relating to company law. However, this is an expensive solution and can lead to time delays. As MATs grow, both in size and diversity, trustees look to appoint dedicated in-house specialist governance support.

There appears to be an emerging practice in MATs to employ a qualified company secretary or governance professional at MAT level and then appoint clerks to service the individual academy councils. In this situation, the clerks will often be line-managed by the company secretary and will be guided by the Scheme of Delegation and requirements of their own trust.

However, for many trusts, there is a lack of understanding of the role of the company secretary and how this differs from a clerking role. As a result, many clerks take on some or all of the functions normally identified as being those of the company secretary. Sometimes, filing or other registration functions are outsourced to a professional company secretarial service. Unfortunately, this leaves the clerk without the status or protection as an officer inferred in the articles and usually without the proper recognition or remuneration for the role.

Whatever approach, the trustees are ultimately responsible for ensuring that requirements are met and that anyone appointed to the company secretarial role is adequately trained. Where no company secretary has been appointed, any potential liability will fall on the trustees.

The company secretary is regarded as an 'officer' of the trust company. This means that they can sign the majority of forms for filing at Companies House (though in practice this is largely now done online). They can also be a signatory to any documents that need the signatures of two officers of the trust company. This does also mean that the company secretary can find themselves potentially liable as an 'officer in default' with respect to breaches of the Companies Act provisions.

## Stop and think 5.1

**Consider how the needs of a variety of MATs and SATS can be best met through the appointment of clerks, company secretaries and governance professionals. What might their respective roles be and how can they operate to support the board, local governing bodies (if any) and the executive?**

# 3. Statutory registers

All companies including trusts are required by provisions within the Companies Act 2006 to maintain specific records known as statutory registers or statutory books. The registers should generally be kept at the registered office. They must be kept up-to-date with any changes that take place and maintained for the life of the trust.

The registers may be written, printed or in machine-readable form (i.e. an electronic register). Certain information can be kept only on the public register held by Companies House rather than by holding statutory registers at the company. This is only possible in respect of:

◆ register of members;
◆ register of directors/trustees;
◆ register of secretaries;
◆ register of directors'/trustees' residential addresses; and
◆ register of people with significant control (PSC).

It is an offence to fail to maintain the statutory registers which may be punishable by a fine imposed on the company itself and every officer of the company in default.

Although the contents of the registers are largely held at Companies House, the registers are the official records of the trust.

## 3.1 Register of members

The register must maintain:

**(a)** the names and addresses of the members;

**(b)** the date on which each person was registered as a member; and

**(c)**   the date at which any person ceased to be a member.

Members are not registered at Companies House (although they are registered on Get information about schools) and the register provides evidence of member appointments. The model articles provide that:

> 'Every person nominated to be a Member of the Academy Trust shall sign a written consent to become a Member and sign the register of Members on becoming a Member.'

Older versions of the articles allow the members to either provide a written consent or sign the register.

## 3.2  Register of directors/trustees

The register must contain details of each trustee's:

**(a)**   name and any former name;

**(b)**   a service address;

**(c)**   the country or state (or part of the United Kingdom) in which s/he is usually resident;

**(d)**   nationality;

**(e)**   business occupation (if any); and

**(f)**   date of birth.

If the trustee is a corporate body, the register must contain details of:

**(a)**   corporate or firm name;

**(b)**   registered or principal office; and

**(c)**   information on legal form and registration details.

Trustees may opt to use the registered office of the trust as their service address so that their private, residential address is kept separately and is not disclosed to members of the public. The register of directors/trustees must be open to inspection:

**(a)**   by any member of the company without charge; and

**(b)**   of any other person on payment of such fee as may be prescribed (subject to the provisions of the Freedom of Information Act 2000).

The register should record the date of termination or resignation of every trustee.

## 3.3  Register of secretaries

The register must maintain details of formal appointments of secretaries to the trust. In the case of an individual, this should be:

**(a)**   name and any former name; and

**(b)**   address.

For a company or firm, the register should contain:

**(a)** corporate or firm name;

**(b)** registered or principal office; and

**(c)** information on legal form and registration details.

Although not legally required, it is useful to include the date of appointment and date of termination of each secretary which will be required to complete the relevant annual report.

## 3.4 Register of directors'/trustees' residential addresses

Trustees must disclose their residential address to the trust and this should be recorded in the register. This information will remain confidential and will not be open to public inspection.

## 3.5 Register of people with significant control

All companies must maintain a register of people who have 'significant control' over them (PSCs). PSCs can be an individual or a legal entity who:

- holds more than 25% of voting rights at general meetings;
- holds the right to appoint a majority of the board of trustees;
- actually exercises or has the right to exercise significant influence or control;

or

- actually exercises or has the right to exercise significant influence or control over the trust or firm, which is not a legal entity, which has significant control over the company.

The register must contain:

- name
- date of birth
- nationality
- county, state or part of the UK where the PSC usually lives
- service address
- usual residential address
- Date the individual became a PSC
- which of the conditions for being a PSC the individual meets – the official wording must be used
- any restrictions on disclosing the PSC's information that are in place – the official wording must be used

If the trust is unable to confirm the information about any PSCs, it must note this on the register with the wording:

'The company has identified a registrable person in relation to the company but all the required particulars of that person have not been confirmed.'

If there is no registrable person, a register must be kept which states:

'The company knows or has reasonable cause to believe that there is no registrable relevant legal entity in relation to the company.'

If the trust has attempted to get the information from a PSC but they have not responded, a statement should be included:

'The company has given a notice under section 709D of the Act which has not been complied with.'

Details of the PSC must be included in the trust's register and notified to Companies House within 14 days. The annual confirmation statement filed with Companies House also confirms that the information on PSCs held on the public register is accurate irrespective of any changes in the previous 12 months.

All PSC information apart from home address and the day of birth is available to the public. An individual may apply, in exceptional circumstances, to protect the PSC information so that it is not disclosed.

### 3.6 Register of interests

Although there is no statutory requirement for a register of interests, the *Academies Financial Handbook 2018* states:

'The academy trust's register of interests must capture relevant business and pecuniary interests of members, trustees, local governors of academies within a multi-academy trust and senior employees.'

The register should extend to cover not only trustees and members, but anyone with delegated authority either as an individual or by membership of a local governing body or other trust committee. Each person or corporate body should be required to complete a declaration on appointment which is updated annually. As a minimum, the declaration should require details of:

◆ directorships, partnerships and employments with businesses;

◆ trusteeships and governorships at other educational institutions and charities; and

◆ for each interest: the name of the business; the nature of the business; the nature of the interest; and the date the interest began.

The *Academies Financial Handbook 2018* has detailed guidance around related party transactions: all transactions must be reported to ESFA and those which, either individually or cumulatively, exceed £20,000 must have prior approval from ESFA. As a result, great care must always be taken with any actual or perceived conflict of interest where it relates to a related party. The register must include 'any relevant material interests arising from close family relationships between the academy trust's members, trustees or local governors. It must also identify relevant material interests arising from close family relationships between those individuals and employees'.

The register of interests should be routinely updated each year and any time that there is any change. It is normal practice to include a standing item on meeting agenda to remind attendees of their duty to declare any conflict of interest or loyalty with any agenda item. The register of interests is also presented to board meetings so that trustees can refer to the details and update as necessary.

## 3.7 Register of gifts, hospitality and entertainments

The *Academies Financial Handbook 2018* requires academies to have 'a policy and register on the acceptance of gifts, hospitality, awards, prizes or any other benefit which might be seen to compromise their judgment or integrity'.

All members, trustees, governors and staff should be made aware of the policy and be required to make declarations. The policy will generally set *de minimis* levels below which declarations need not be made; this will mean that teaching staff will not need to declare every end of term gift from a pupil below a set value. Declarations need to be made and recorded even if the gift, hospitality or entertainment is refused with a note to this effect.

The Bribery Act 2010 provides that any individual who is involved in bribery, either by offering or accepting a bribe, will be guilty of an offence. A trust could also be found to have committed an offence if it, or someone acting on its behalf, is found to be involved in bribery. It is a defence for a 'commercial organisations' including a trust to have 'adequate procedures designed to prevent persons' from involvement in bribery.

## 3.8 Inspection of registers

Trust members can inspect some of the registers maintained by the trust free of charge:

◆ register of members
◆ register of directors
◆ register of secretaries

Anyone else can inspect these records as well, subject to payment of the necessary fee. Subject to receiving a request on the correct period of notice, the trust must make the records available on a day chosen by the trust which is a normal working day. The notice period required will be:

◆ at least two working days if the trust has given notice of a forthcoming general meeting or circulated a written resolution; otherwise
◆ 10 working days.

**Test yourself 5.1**

1.   **What are the 'statutory registers' that trusts are required to keep under the Companies Act 2006?**

2.   **What registers must be kept under provisions contained in the Academies Financial Handbook 2018?**

3.   **What registers are open to inspection and who by?**

# 4. Companies House

Companies House is an executive agency of the Department for Business, Energy and Industrial Strategy. The main functions of this government body are to:

◆   incorporate and dissolve limited companies;

◆   examine and store company information; and

◆   make information available to the public.

All limited companies including trusts must be registered at Companies House which will allocate their 'registered number'. Under provisions of the Companies Act 2006 and other legislation, all companies must provide information to Companies House to maintain the 'register' which is available for public inspection. There is a duty to notify Companies House of any relevant event such as a change in the registered office or change in trustees; the majority of changes should be notified within 14 days. It is a key responsibility for trustees to be aware of and observe the filing requirements at the appropriate times. Failure to comply with filing obligations is an offence and could result in prosecution and fines for the trust and its officers. Ultimately, Companies House has the power to remove a company from the register.

The Companies Act 2006 requires all companies including trusts to file a copy of the report and accounts for each financial year. Under the requirements of the Companies Act, the accounts must be submitted within nine months from the end of the accounting period (i.e. by 31 May).

The first filing deadline is calculated on the basis of the incorporation date of the company which may not correspond to the conversion date or date when operations started. In this case, accounts can be prepared for a period of more than 12 months and delivered to Companies House within 21 months of the **date of incorporation** or three months from the accounting reference date, whichever is longer.

**date of incorporation**
The date on which a company was formed.

The registry for companies registered in England and Wales is in Cardiff with a satellite office in London. Search, inspection and copying facilities are available at both offices.

## 4.1 Public record

The majority of the information filed at Companies House is open to inspection by the public. Along with certain administrative correspondence which is not put on the public record, there are some exceptions to the information available for inspection including:

◆ directors'/trustees' residential addresses; and

◆ documents supporting a proposal to use certain words or expressions in the company name.

Basic information is available free of charge:

◆ company name;

◆ registered number;

◆ nature of business (sic);

◆ registered office address;

◆ names and service addresses of directors/trustees;

◆ accounting reference date;

◆ date last accounts were made up to and when next accounts are due; and

◆ date last confirmation statement was made up to and when the next one is due.

It is possible to obtain copies of specific forms and documents that have been filed subject to payment of a small fee.

Company searches using company name or registration number can be carried out online using the WebCheck facility on the Companies House website. A list of the company's filing record can be viewed.

## 4.2 Filing changes by hard copy

Trusts must update the Companies House records by making a filing whenever a relevant event take place:

◆ change of registered office;

◆ notification of single alternative inspection location;

◆ appointment of trustees;

◆ resignation of trustees (their term will not automatically expire) ;

◆ any change in trustees' details;

◆ change of secretary; and

◆ change of articles.

In addition, a copy of any members' written resolution must be delivered to Companies House within 15 days of it being passed.

Trusts must also submit a confirmation statement and the annual report and accounts each year.

To file in hard copy, the correct form relevant to the particular change or notification must be used. These can be downloaded free from the Companies House website or can be purchased from a legal stationer.

Documents can be delivered to Companies House by post or delivered by hand. It is possible to obtain a receipt by enclosing a copy of the covering letter together with a pre-paid addressed return envelope. Companies House will barcode the date of receipt on the copy letter and return it.

Documents must be printed on plain white, A4 size paper with a matt finish with black text that is clear, legible and of uniform density.

Companies House states that failure to follow guidance on completion of forms can result in documents being rejected:

◆ use black ink or black type;
◆ use bold lettering (some elegant thin typefaces and pens give poor quality copies);
◆ do not send a carbon copy;
◆ do not use a dot matrix printer;
◆ photocopies can result in a grey shade that will not scan well;
◆ use A4 size paper with good margin;
◆ supply in portrait format (i.e. with the shorter edge across the top); and
◆ include the company name and number.

Forms contain a checklist of information that needs to be included.

The original form, signed by an authorised person (i.e. a trustee or the company secretary) should be submitted.

Amendments to the articles and the audited annual report and accounts must always be filed in hard copy.

## 4.3  WebFiling

**electronic filing**
A form or document filed with Companies House in electronic format using either approved software or the Companies House WebFiling service.

There is an increasing move by Companies House towards **electronic filing** by means of the WebFiling service. However, it is not yet possible to submit all returns of information electronically and some returns continue to be required in hard copy, printed and sent to Companies House.

WebFiling is faster and more secure than traditional hard copy filing. WebFiling can be used for:

◆ changes of trustees, secretary, company name or address; and
◆ the confirmation statement.

Companies must register with Companies House to use the service. However, filing may only be done by a user with a registered email address, password and authentication code. The security code is sent by email whereas the company authentication code is posted to the registered address.

Filing online is quick and an email confirmation is automatically sent when a change has been made with a further email when it has been accepted or rejected. The charge for filing the confirmation statement via WebFiling is lower than that for submission in hard copy.

An 'eReminders' service is available for WebFiling which sends out email reminders to up to four addresses that the accounts and the confirmation statement are due.

Companies can opt into the **PROOF (PROtected Online Filing)** service by committing to submit all documents electronically. Companies House will reject attempts to lodge paper filings unless accompanied by form PR03 completed with the authentication code for the following:

**Protected Online Filing**
An agreement between an academy and Companies House that the academy will always file certain information electronically.

◆   change of registered office address;

◆   appointment or termination of trustee and company secretary;

◆   changes in trustee's or secretary's details; and

◆   the confirmation statement.

Companies House also offers the Monitor service which is part of their strategy to support organisations in protecting against corporate identity theft. Once signed up to the service, Companies House will send an e-mail notification every time a form or document is filed to the individual monitoring it – it helps to ensure that fraudulent filings are quickly identified. There is no limit to the number of companies that can be monitored so an individual can sign up to be notified about any others it may wish to follow!

## Test yourself 5.2

1.   **What filings must a trust make to Companies House?**

2.   **What are the advantages and disadvantages of WebFiling?**

### 4.4  Confirmation statement

Every company must file a confirmation statement annually at Companies House within 14 days of the 'end of each review period' which is either:

**(a)**   the period of 12 months beginning with the day of the company's incorporation; or

**(b)**   each period of 12 months beginning with the day after the end of the previous review period.

## Making it work 5.1

**The trust company was incorporated on 1 May 2017. The first confirmation statement must be made up to 1 May 2018. All subsequent confirmation statements must be filed within 28 days of the made-up date of 1 May. An offence will be committed by the trust, every trustee, the secretary and any other officer in default.**

The confirmation statement reviews and confirms that the information held on the public record at Companies House is correct in respect of:

◆ the name of the trust;

◆ the registered number;

◆ the date to which the confirmation statement is made up;

◆ the standard industrial classification (SIC) code;

◆ the principal business activities of the company;

◆ the type of company (i.e. private);

◆ the registered office address;

**single alternative inspection location**
A location at which certain company

◆ the address (**single alternate inspection location** – SAIL) where the company keeps certain company records if not at the registered office, and the records held there;

◆ company secretary (corporate or individual), where applicable;

◆ the company's trustees (corporate or individual); and

◆ people with significant control (PSCs).

The details supplied on the confirmation statement are a snapshot of the information accurate at a particular date known as the 'made-up date'. A trust may submit confirmation statements as often as it wishes provided it files at least one every 12 months.

The confirmation statement includes a 'standard industrial classification' (SIC) code of five digits which identifies the company's business. In the case of academies, the relevant codes will usually be:

◆ 85100 Pre-primary education

◆ 85200 Primary education

◆ 85310 General secondary education

◆ 85320 Technical and vocational secondary education.

A trust could have more than one SIC code where it operates across phases.

The trustees and secretary (where applicable) are responsible for filing the confirmation statement on time. Failure to do so is a criminal offence and may result in legal action against the company and its officers.

The confirmation statement must be signed by a trustee or the secretary or submitted via the WebFiling service by a registered user.

## 4.5 Notification of single alternative inspection location (SAIL)

The statutory registers need not necessarily be kept at the registered office, for example when a professional firm is engaged to maintain the records. In this case, the trust must notify Companies House of the location where the company records and registers are kept – the SAIL. There can only be one SAIL, so a trust cannot keep different records in different locations.

The trust must notify Companies House of the:

◆ company number

◆ company name

◆ address of the SAIL.

WebFiling can be used or Form AD02 submitted to notify the SAIL address. Companies House must also be notified when documents have relocated to the SAIL address (Form AD03) or moved back to the registered office (Form AD04).

The SAIL and the records held there must be included in the confirmation statement.

# Chapter summary

◆ The model articles require the board to appoint a clerk or secretary to the board. The clerk must not be a trustee or the principal/headteacher/chief executive and is not entitled to vote at board meetings.

◆ A trust may choose to appoint a company secretary, the chief administrative officer who is registered as such at Companies House. They will be potentially liable as an 'officer in default' for any breaches of Companies Act provisions.

◆ Governance professionals are increasingly appointed especially in MATs where there is often a two-tier governance support structure with clerks or minute-takers engaged for individual academies and line managed by the governance professional.

◆ The board appoint the 'clerk' or other governance professional 'at such remuneration and upon such conditions as they may think fit'.

◆ Statutory registers must be maintained in respect of members, directors/ trustees, secretaries, directors'/trustees' residential addresses and people with significant control. A register of interests and register of gifts, hospitality and entertainments must also be kept. Certain registers may be inspected, subject to the payment of a fee and sufficient notice; members can inspect them free of charge.

◆   Trusts must be registered at Companies House and provide information
to update the register. The majority of the information filed is open to
inspection by the public. Documents can be filed either in hard copy form
or online via the WebFiling service, though the latter benefits from PROOF
and Monitor. Every company must file a confirmation statement annually
confirming information held. Notification must be given if the company
records and registers are kept at a place other than the registered office
(i.e. a single alternative inspection location).

# Chapter six
# Meetings and decision making

**CONTENTS**

## 1. Introduction

This chapter outlines the way that business decisions are made in trusts. It considers how meetings are held and the requirements imposed on them both for members' meetings and trustees' board meetings. It also considers how decision making can be formally conducted outside of meetings. There is guidance and recommendations around minute taking.

The chapter also outlines committee structures in trusts and how the decision-making authority is delegated to ensure an effective and efficient organisation.

## 2. General meetings and decision making

Members' meetings are known as 'general meetings' and are closely regulated by the Companies Act 2006, which contains a chapter on the requirements (Part 13, Chapter 3).

There is no requirement for private companies to hold an annual general meeting (AGM) unless it is set out in a company's articles. However, the current model articles require that an AGM is held for trusts. Whilst the AGM is often used as an opportunity to present the annual report and financial statements to the members, they do not need approval as they will have been formally approved by the board.

Where a trust's articles require it to hold an AGM, no more than 15 months may elapse between AGMs. The first following incorporation must take place within 18 months.

Trustees usually call general meetings. If they do not do so, members holding at least 5% of the total voting rights of all the members able to vote at the meeting can request a meeting; within 21 days of the request, trustees must call a meeting for a date not more than 28 days after the date of the notice. If the trustees do not call a meeting, members representing over half of the members' total voting rights may call a general meeting within three months.

The model articles require 14 clear days' notice of general meetings to be given. The model articles require that notice shall be given to all the members, to the trustees and auditors. This period cannot be shortened although a longer period could be set in the articles. A meeting can be held on short notice if a majority of the members holding at least 90% of the voting rights agree. A formal notice containing details of the business to be conducted, the date, time, place and details about appointing a proxy must be sent to every member, trustee and the auditor. It can be given in hard copy, electronic form, by means of a website or a combination – notice will not be invalidated if an individual entitled to receive notice did not do so 'due to accidental omission or non-receipt'.

The model articles provide that the quorum is two members, which can include a representative of a corporate member or validly appointed proxies. If the quorum is not reached within half an hour of the schedule start time, the meeting will be adjourned to the same day, time and place the following week or whenever the trustees decide. Members can also agree to adjourn the meeting to a later date although no additional meeting can be conducted at the later meeting.

The current model articles provide for members to elect one of themselves to be the chair for the meeting although some earlier versions stipulate that the chair of trustees will chair the meeting. Trustees are entitled to attend and speak at general meetings even if they are not also a member, but they will not have a vote.

Most resolutions will be regarded as ordinary resolutions and require a simple majority (i.e. at least 50% plus one of the votes cast) to be passed. Decisions relating to the constitution or the future of the trust will be made on a special resolution, which requires 75% majority of the votes cast in person or by proxy:

◆    changes to the articles;
◆    change of name of the trust;
◆    any resolution required by the articles to be a special resolution; and
◆    the appointment of members.

A copy of any members' special resolution must be filed at Companies House within 15 days.

Each member has one vote, but they will not be able to use it if they owe any money to the trust or if there is a perceived or actual conflict. Voting will be on a show of hands and the chair will declare whether the resolution is passed. A poll can be demanded before a vote or on the declaration of the result of the show of hands by:

◆ the chair;

◆ at least two members having the right to vote at the meeting; and

◆ a member or members representing not less than one-tenth of the total voting rights of all members having the right to vote at the meeting.

A poll must be taken not more than 30 days after it was requested. A poll on the election of chair or adjournment of the meeting must be taken immediately.

Members are entitled to appoint a proxy to attend the general meeting on their behalf and who can speak or vote for them. The member must appoint a proxy by submitting a signed formal document prepared and submitted in accordance with the articles.

## Test yourself 6.1

1.  **How many members are required for a general meeting to be quorate?**

2.  **What majority is required to pass a special resolution and when might it be used?**

3.  **What could prevent someone who is present at a general meeting from voting?**

# 3. Trustees' meetings

Unlike members' general meetings, which have detailed provisions contained within the Companies Act 2006, trustees have a degree of flexibility around the conduct of their board meetings. The model articles also provide that trustees 'may regulate their proceedings as they think fit' subject to the limitations contained within the articles.

## 3.1 Calling meetings

The model articles provide that there must be 'at least three meetings in every school year'. The *Academies Financial Handbook 2018* requires that the board and its committees must meet 'regularly enough to discharge their responsibilities and ensure robust governance and effective financial management arrangements'. Whilst the board must meet at least three times a year, if it meets less than six times in a year it must provide a description of how effective oversight of funds was maintained with fewer meetings for inclusion in the governance statement accompanying the annual accounts.

The board should consider the requirements of their trust carefully when setting a meeting schedule to ensure the ability to achieve a quorum whilst enabling effective financial oversight. The *Academies Financial Handbook* suggests that larger trusts should consider meeting more frequently. The trustees must be confident that whatever schedule they adopt allows them sufficient time to enable them to comply with their duties to the trust and ensure that they exercise their duty of care. Dates will generally be set in advance considering important milestones in the academic year that will need to be addressed, such as approval of the budget, annual accounts or to consider pupil performance data. Ideally a schedule is created that allows meetings of advisory councils and committees to take place and the preparation of minutes that can be presented to the board if necessary.

Irrespective of whether dates have been set in advance, the meeting must be formally called or 'convened' by the clerk. Normally the clerk will follow the directions of the board or instructions given by the chair (as long as the latter is not inconsistent with any direction given by the board). Three trustees may requisition a meeting by 'notice in writing given to the clerk' who is then under a duty to convene a meeting 'as soon as is reasonably practicable'.

A valid notice and agenda must be circulated to trustees prior to the meeting. The notice must specify the date and time of the meeting and where it will take place; the articles specify that it must be in writing and 'signed by the clerk'. Without a formal notice sent in sufficient time, the meeting would theoretically be unconstitutional and decisions could be challenged as invalid. The notice must be sent to each trustee at the address given by them; in practice, this is now generally effected via email. However, the articles provide that the process will not be invalidated if any individual does not receive the notice or agenda.

The model articles require at least seven clear days' notice of meetings to be given, although some earlier versions require 14 clear days' notice. This means that notice must usually be given on Wednesday of week one for a meeting for a meeting on Thursday of week two.

Meetings may be called on 'short notice' if the chair, or vice-chair if there is no chair or if they are absent, determines that there are 'matters demanding urgent consideration'.

A copy of the agenda should be circulated with the notice. The agenda sets out the items of business to be discussed at the meeting and should be carefully constructed to direct the business and enable a smooth flow to the meeting allowing a proper focus on the important items. It can be useful to allocate time periods to individual items according to their importance to keep the meeting on track. However, care should be taken that it does not restrict important discussions or lead to guillotining of appropriate debate in the interests of timekeeping.

A decision to rescind or vary a decision of a previous board meeting can only be made where it has been included as a specific item of business on the agenda.

Any reports or other documentation to be considered at the meeting should be circulated with the agenda. This is necessary on a practical level to give trustees the time to read and understand the contents so that the meeting can operate efficiently.

## 3.2 Managing meetings

Only trustees have the right to attend board meetings. Other members of senior staff, particularly the CEO/principal (if not a trustee) and the CFO may be invited as advisors to the board. Care should be taken to avoid any individual being regarded as a shadow or *de facto* director.

The chair is responsible for ensuring the smooth running of the board meeting. They must allow sufficient time to each agenda item so that each is addressed and decisions are made in an orderly fashion. They should facilitate open discussions, which allow all trustees to state their opinions.

When documents or reports have been provided, it is accepted that they have been read and considered by trustees prior to the meeting. The person responsible for a report should 'speak to the report' so that they outline the issues and comment on the contents rather than giving a summary. Meeting time should be spent on questions or discussions about the contents of the report and any decisions to be made.

Where it has not been possible to provide a written report to trustees ahead of the meeting and the chair permits discussion of the item, a short synopsis should be given.

It should be clear when any decisions are made: the chair should formally propose the resolution or summarise the decision, take a vote and declare whether it is carried or defeated.

## 3.3 Quorum

The quorum or minimum number of trustees that must be present to validly conduct business at a meeting is set out in the model articles as the greater of:

◆ three trustees; or
◆ one-third (rounded up to a whole number) of the total number of trustees holding office at the date of the meeting.

If the quorum is not present, any decisions taken will not be valid and could be challenged. The current model articles enable trustees to attend either in person or via telephone/video conferencing. This has introduced a level of flexibility around attendance at meetings and may be welcomed by trustees with a corporate background who are used to regular teleconferencing.

If the number drops below the quorum, the meeting must be 'terminated forthwith' or immediately closed. Care must be taken to note that the quorum remains if any trustee leaves the meeting or if a trustee has a conflict of interest with an issue under discussion and they will not participate in the consideration of the issue and not be counted in the quorum. If the meeting has been adjourned and there is further business that has not been covered, the clerk must call another meeting 'as soon as is reasonably practicable' but within seven days of the original date of the meeting.

In the unlikely event that the total number of trustees appointed is less than the quorum (i.e. two or less) the articles provide that the remaining trustees may act 'only for the purpose of filling vacancies or of calling a general meeting' of the members.

The articles also provide that the quorum is raised to two-thirds (rounded up to a whole number) of 'the persons who are at the time Trustees' where a vote is being taken on the removal of a trustee or the removal of the chair.

### 3.4  Voting

Decisions or 'resolutions' are passed by a majority of the votes cast by the trustees' present. Each trustee has one vote except where there is an equal division of votes cast for and against a resolution in which case the chair will have an additional 'casting vote'.

Voting is normally conducted on a show of hands although trustees can use any mechanism they choose. Typically, a secret ballot is used where a resolution is contentious or if trustees do not wish to publicly declare their vote. The chair declares that a resolution is carried or not. Once a vote is passed it is binding on all trustees irrespective of whether they voted in favour of it.

The articles contain restrictions on the number of LAAPs that can be trustees. There is also provision that if the number of LAAPs present and voting at any meeting exceeds this threshold then the votes are weighted; the articles provide that the 'votes of the other Trustees having a right to vote at the meeting will be increased on a pro-rata basis'.

Other people such as the finance director/school business manager often attend board meetings. They are invited to attend in an advisory capacity and do not have a vote. Care must be taken that any such individuals are not regarded as shadow/*de facto* directors.

## Test yourself 6.2

1.  **What is the quorum for a board meeting and what happens if it is not met?**

2.  **How are decisions made in a board meeting?**

### 3.5  Conflicts of interest and loyalty

Trustees must declare if they have any other interests which could potentially influence or corrupt their decision making or be seen to do so. Any conflict arising from a 'direct' personal interest or an 'indirect' interest through a relative must be declared. Interests could be pecuniary or non-pecuniary. Pecuniary interests are any that can be measured in monetary terms or relate to money, though interests could relate to a huge range of other circumstances, not relating to money, which give rise to a conflict situation.

Any trustee with an interest will be excluded from any discussion and decision-making process concerned. They will not be eligible to vote on any resolution where they have an interest or could be seen to have a potential interest.

Trustees must complete a declaration of interests upon appointment to the board and updated annually or any time there is any change. Each meeting should start with an item for trustees to declare any conflict of interest or loyalty with any item on the agenda. The Register of Interests should be presented to each board meeting for confirmation that the details contained are accurate and up-to-date.

The Charity Commission guidance paper CC29 'Conflicts of Interest – a guide for charity trustees' also provides guidance on conflicts of loyalty. In these cases, the trustee does not stand to gain any benefit but their decision making at the trust could be influenced (or be seen to have the potential to influence) by their other interests (e.g. where their loyalty could conflict with their loyalty to the sponsor/foundation that appointed them to the board) another organisation such as their employer or another charity of which they are a trustee or to a member of their family or other **connected person** or organisation. If there is a conflict of loyalty, or potential to be a conflict or perceived conflict, the trustee should declare the interest, the other trustees must decide what level of participation, if any, is acceptable. The trustee could:

◆ fully participate in the decision;

◆ stay in the meetings where the decision is discussed and made but not participate; or

◆ withdraw from the decision-making process.

**connected person**
Person who is considered to be connected with a director such as a spouse or civil partner, any other person with whom the director lives with in an enduring family relationship, the director's children and stepchildren, the director's parents and a body corporate in which the director has an interest in at least 20% of the share capital.

### 3.6 Telephone/video attendance

The current model articles provide that trustees can participate in board meetings 'by telephone or video conference' providing that the trustee gives at least 48 hours' notice. The trustee must also provide either the telephone number on which s/he can be reached and/or details of the video conference suite. If 'reasonable efforts' to 'appropriate equipment' to allow the trustee to attend via telephone/video are unsuccessful, the meeting may still proceed subject to usual rules around quorum.

### 3.7 Adjournments

The trustees can resolve to terminate a meeting 'forthwith' despite there being further items on the agenda that have not been considered. In this case, the clerk must convene another meeting 'as soon as is reasonably practicable, but in any event within seven days'. The date and time of that further meeting should be agreed by trustees before the adjournment takes place.

# 4. Written resolutions

The model articles contain provisions enabling members and trustees to make decisions by means of written resolutions. Trust committees including local governing bodies may also use the written resolution provisions as long as it is permitted by the trust scheme of delegation. The requirements for written resolutions are set out in the Companies Act 2006, Part 13, Chapter 2.

A 'resolution in writing' of members requires the same proportion of votes as would be required at a general meeting (i.e. 50% plus one for an ordinary resolution or 75% for a special resolution). It is a requirement that the proposed resolution is sent to all members. The trustees are obliged to circulate a members' written resolution and any accompanying statement if a request is received from members representing not less than 5% of the total voting rights of all members entitled to vote on the proposed resolution.

A written resolution by trustees requires the unanimous consent of all trustees who were entitled to 'receive notice' of the meeting and may be more difficult to achieve.

Consent may be achieved through 'several documents in the same form'. So, every member or trustee (as appropriate) could sign a separate copy of the resolution.

The resolution will only be passed when the required number of members or all trustees have signed and returned the written resolution. A cut-off date should be set for return of resolutions and if no date is set, the proposed written resolution fails 28 days after the date of circulation.

Copies of the signed written resolutions should be retained in the minute book.

The written resolution procedure is not permitted where the resolution proposed is to remove a trustee or the auditor.

A copy of the written resolution must be delivered to Companies House within 15 days of it being passed.

**Test yourself 6.3**

**What is a written resolution?**

# 5. Minute taking

The Companies Act 2006 requires 'minutes of all proceedings at meetings of [a company's] directors to be recorded' (s. 248). The model articles state that minutes must be 'drawn up and entered into a book kept for the purpose by the person acting as Clerk for the purposes of the meeting'.

Section 355 of the Companies Act 2006 also requires 'minutes of all proceedings of general meetings' to be kept.

The minutes are 'draft' until the next such meeting and will then be signed by the person acting as chairman. Once approved and signed, the Companies Act 2006 states that the minutes are 'evidence' of the proceedings in the meeting, in particular that:

◆ the meeting was duly held and convened;

◆ all proceedings at the meeting were deemed to have duly taken place; and

◆ all appointments at the meeting were deemed valid.

Minutes can be set aside by the court if inaccuracies can be demonstrated.

Minutes of board meetings will also be inspected by Ofsted and ESFA and will be used to demonstrate whether trustees are fulfilling their duties and are central to the leadership and management of the trust. Minutes are also a practical tool for trustees and the executive involved to evidence decisions and delineate any next actions required. It is essential to have a trained clerk or minute-taker. The DfE Clerking Competency Framework advises that 'professional clerking also informs the board's accountability to others through minutes that provide evidence of challenge and scrutiny of the executive, and the board's overall ability and capacity to govern the organisation well'. The effective skills and behaviours in the framework also includes that the clerk 'makes good judgements about which discussion points to capture in the minutes and is aware of the importance of recording dissenting voices or challenges from the board and records all decisions to produce accurate minutes and actions from the meeting'.

There are certain accepted protocols for minute-taking:

◆ Minutes are written in the past tense.

◆ Minutes are written in the third person (i.e. 'he', 'she', 'it' and 'they').

◆ Items should be numbered.

◆ Plain English should be used and acronyms avoided (if it is necessary, define them at the first usage).

◆ Short sentences and paragraphs should be used to make them easy to read.

◆ Use an accessible layout – consider how minutes will appear on laptops, tablets and smartphones.

◆ Make action points and resolutions easily identifiable.

◆ Reference supporting documentation without replicating their contents.

◆ Record any legal or procedural advice from the clerk.

◆ The record is subject-based and does not reflect who said what – though it must reflect any challenge presented. Ofsted like trustees' support, challenge and specific questions asked to 'pop' out of the page and many boards have adopted an approach where questions are literally highlighted or put into a different colour. Questions asked or challenges presented should not identify the individuals concerned – the board is a corporate body. The responses to challenge and questions should also be recorded.

The board is a corporate body, so takes collective responsibility for all decision making; once passed, a resolution is binding on all trustees, whether or not they voted for it. The number of votes for, against and abstentions is not recorded in the minutes.

The draft minutes should be prepared as soon after the meeting as practicable and forwarded to the chair. The chair may check for accuracy but should not add any information or make any changes that will affect the meaning; stylistic, typographical or other such errors should be corrected. The approved minutes will be circulated to all board members and others who the board agree are entitled to see them, such as the CEO/principal (if not otherwise a trustee), finance director, etc. The minutes remain technically in draft until they are approved at the next meeting.

The Companies Act requires minutes to be kept for at least 10 years from the date of the meeting. However, it is the Charity Commission's view that they should be kept for the lifetime of the charity and it is recommended practice to do so. Any papers presented to the meeting should be retained where these are necessary to understand the contents of the minutes.

It is possible to keep the minute books in electronic form. However, the law is rather unclear about the evidential value as there could be doubt about whether the chair signed the minutes or whether amendments were made by hand. It would be necessary to demonstrate the integrity of such electronic versions should they ever need to be produced during legal proceedings.

Trustees and members have the right to inspect minutes of general meetings.

The current model articles provide that copies must be made available at every academy for inspection by anyone of certain documents:

- the agenda for every board meeting;
- the draft minutes of every board meeting if they have been approved by the person acting as chairman of that meeting;
- the signed minutes of every board meeting; and
- any report, document or other paper considered at any board meeting.

There is no requirement to upload copies to the trust website.

## 5.1  Content of the minutes

- Heading – name and registered number of trust.
- Date, time and location of meeting.
- Names of those present (i.e. trustees for board meeting – note if they are present by telephone conferencing if appropriate).
- Names of those 'in attendance' (i.e. other persons present who are not trustees such as the finance director).
- Apologies – those who have informed the meeting that they would be absent and whose apologies have been accepted.

- ◆ Absent – trustees who are not present but who have not given apologies nor have their apologies been accepted.
- ◆ Chair – identify who is the chair.
- ◆ Confirmation that the meeting was quorate.
- ◆ Declaration of interests.
- ◆ Minutes of the last meeting must be formally approved.
- ◆ Matters arising from the minutes – any action points or follow up.
- ◆ Items of business and resolutions.
- ◆ Any other business.
- ◆ Closing time of the meeting.

The minutes do not provide a verbatim report of what was said at a meeting: they are formally structured to enable a reader to see that business has been properly conducted and that trustees have provided appropriate support and challenge to the CEO/principal.

## Stop and think 6.1

**Find examples of minutes from board and general meetings. What elements of good practice are evident? What is missing? How might the minutes be improved?**

### 5.2  Confidential items

Any confidential items should be treated with great care. They should be included in the agenda for the meeting in very general terms. Commonly they will be dealt with at the end of the meeting so that any persons who cannot be present can leave early. Confidential items can relate to matters such as items involving individuals or pay settlements. It could also relate to items that are 'commercially sensitive' or not yet in the public domain (e.g. discussions around whether to academise or internal restructuring).

The minutes of the meeting will contain a single high-level reference to the confidential item. A separate 'part two', confidential minute of the discussion is prepared, although this is usually much less detailed than the main minutes. The minutes are headed up in exactly the same way as the main minutes and will be signed and approved in the same way, although it will make clear that they are confidential through use of the header and sometimes a watermark.

Consideration should be given to the way in which confidential minutes are circulated to trustees; it may be possible to table very short minutes, but anything shared by e-mail should be encrypted or otherwise secured. Traditionally confidential minutes are printed on pink paper to distinguish them from the normal minutes. They should be stored separately in a locked filing cabinet, accessed only by authorised persons. This practice may be relaxed where the matters discussed subsequently come into the public domain and are no longer confidential in nature.

# 6. Committee structures

The trust has the freedom to set up as many committees as are appropriate and enable effective governance, except where audit and financial oversight are concerned. According to the *Academies Financial Handbook 2018*, the board must establish a committee to provide 'assurance to the board over the suitability of, and compliance with, its financial systems and operational controls, and to ensure that risks are being adequately identified and managed' (i.e. a finance committee).

If a trust has annual income over £50 million it must establish a dedicated audit committee. Other trusts can decide whether to establish a dedicated audit committee or whether the functions should be subsumed into another committee such as the finance committee. All other committees are entirely optional. MATs often have committees known as local governing bodies (LGB) or academy councils which are linked to individual academies. There is also an increasing use of MAT hubs or cluster advisory councils in larger MATs where oversight of academies is conducted on a more regional or cluster basis, allowing them to feed into the board in a more constructive fashion.

The constitution and terms of reference for all committees should be drafted and reviewed each year; this must include details about membership and proceedings of the committee so there is clarity about its role and remit and how work should be conducted. It is essential that trustees understand the purpose for setting up any committee and its functions so that it assists the board to work effectively.

The articles provide that, apart from LGBs which do not require any trustee involvement, any committee must have a majority of members who are trustees. The quorum must be based on a majority present being trustees and 'no vote on any matter shall be taken at a meeting of a committee' unless the majority of committee members present are trustees.

## 6.1 MAT local governing bodies/advisory councils

The model articles permit the board to establish committees known as LGBs for one or more academy within a MAT to provide local oversight. However, there is no obligation on the trustees to do so in the current model articles; some earlier versions of the articles require either an LGB or advisory council at an academy level.

The LGBs are board committees and do not have a separate legal identity. The constitution, membership and proceedings of all committees, including LGBs, is agreed by the board. The delegation must be reviewed at least annually and can be increased, reduced or taken away! An LGB may be established with a purely advisory function and without any delegated authority.

## Making it work 6.1

**In January 2016, the large MAT E-ACT removed LGBs, replacing them with 'academy Ambassadorial Advisory Bodies' chaired by a board appointee. There is a centralised process for monitoring standards which is overseen by the trust board.**

The MAT board can decide on the level of responsibility that it will delegate to any LGB and whether this will relate to oversight of teaching and learning or will involve financial oversight as well. Whilst accountability is not delegated, remaining with the board, functions and powers can be delegated to LGBs such as authority to approve certain policies or elect the LGB chair. It can decide not to retain LGBs or to have committees that are responsible for a group or cluster of academies.

The 'earned autonomy' model is often popular in community MATs. In these cases, the stronger, more effective academies and LGBs are given more responsibility for oversight than those academies that are struggling, have an adverse Ofsted grading or do not have the level of expertise necessary on their LGB.

MATs can choose not to have any parent trustees on the board. However, in this case the LGB must have at least two parent local governors. Having parent governors on LGBs also helps strengthen links with local stakeholders and enables the 'local voice' to be heard.

Where individual academies retain local governing boards or academy councils, 'local governors' are effectively committee members. It is possible to appoint individuals to act as governors on an LGB if they are not a trustee and there is no requirement to have a majority of trustees on any LGB.

## Making it work 6.2

**An infant school and a junior school shared a site but were separate schools. The governing bodies of both schools decided to convert and form a MAT. Both schools had their own local governing bodies which had delegated responsibilities and were accountable to the trust board. After the MAT had been established for a few years the board felt that the two LGBs would function better as one body. This would allow the local governors to have an oversight of both schools and would also help in transition of pupils from the infant to the junior school. The trust presented this proposal to the two LGBs who were also in favour of this and subsequently amalgamated. They elected one chair and two vice chairs to facilitate communication with the two heads. The new LGB was smaller and it was decided that 'natural wastage' would be the mechanism to reduce the number of local governors.**

### 6.2  Audit committee

Only trusts with an annual income over £50 million are required to have a dedicated audit committee. Other trusts may choose to do so or may incorporate the functions of an audit committee within another committee, typically the finance committee. The *Academies Financial Handbook* states that the committee must provide assurance to the board 'over the suitability of, and compliance with, its financial systems and operational controls, and to ensure that risks are being adequately identified and managed'.

Trust staff must not be appointed to the audit committee although they must attend to provide information and participate in discussions as required. This means that where the audit committee function is carried out by a finance committee, staff must not participate as members when audit matters are discussed even though they may be a member of the finance committee. The accounting officer and chief financial officer and other relevant senior staff will routinely attend the committee.

The audit committee must to agree a programme of work to 'provide its assurance on financial controls and risks', which in a MAT must extend to the financial controls and risks at constituent academies.

The audit committee's work will inform the governance statement within the annual report and accounts and provide assurance to the external auditors.

# 7. Delegation of authority

The board is ultimately accountable for the operation of the trust. However, it can delegate the responsibility for tasks and grant authority to carry them out to:

◆ board committees including local governing bodies;
◆ individual trustees (e.g. the chair); and
◆ members of the executive (e.g. the CEO or CFO).

The board must decide on the remit of any delegation and any conditions to be imposed.

In a MAT, it is essential to ensure an effective working relationship between the board and academies. What that will look like will differ enormously from MAT to MAT. There may be a high degree of delegation to individual academies or a much-more restricted, centre-out approach: either way, proper communication channels must be set up to ensure that individual academies understand and follow the trust policies and procedures to the level required.

Some MATs take a much more authoritative approach and are led from the centre. Here, individual academies may have little input to trust policy. The trust will, however, need to ensure that there is appropriate communication and feedback from the academy is taken into account.

The model articles provide:

> 'Any such delegation shall be made in writing and subject to any conditions the Trustees may impose and may be revoked or altered.'

It is good practice to have a single document scheme of delegation, which summarises all delegations. Any general delegation that is made during a meeting should be clearly minuted. Legally, unless any decisions are delegated, they must be made by the board, which would be impossible on a practical level.

It is necessary that anyone to whom a power or function has been delegated, reports to the board when it has been exercised at the 'meeting of the trustees immediately following the taking of the action or the making of the decision'. In practice, this is often done by sharing the minutes of meetings held where it has been evidenced. Although decisions or action taken must be reported to the board, there is no requirement for the board to ratify any decisions.

## 7.1  Schemes of delegation

It is essential that there is clarity around the delegation of any powers. Any delegation must be clear and documented, specifying:

- ◆ who is given authority;
- ◆ what the authority is and any limits; and
- ◆ how the exercise of delegated powers will be monitored by the board.

The *Academies Financial Handbook 2018* requires that the trust board approves a written scheme of delegation of financial powers to maintain 'robust internal control arrangements'. Levels of financial expenditure should be established so that there is clarity about the size of contract or purchase agreement that can be entered into at every level in the trust's hierarchy.

The *Academies Financial Handbook* also references the scheme of delegation to explain governance arrangements required by the *Governance Handbook*; this must be published on the trust website. It states: 'MATs may delegate responsibilities in proportion to the strength of individual academies and the skills and expertise of the people on their LGBs.' However, trusts are 'free to decide which functions they delegate' and there is a range of options about 'governance structures and levels of delegation'. Trusts must decide what works best for the particular circumstances and academies involved.

Those matters 'reserved for the board' should be established and made explicit. These will be high-level strategic matters such as approval of the vision and strategy, approval of business plans, approval of the annual budget and the annual report and accounts.

The model articles require any committee or individual to whom authority has been delegated, to report to the board 'immediately following' the exercise of that power, whether that be the taking of an action or making a decision.

# Chapter Summary

◆ The current articles require an AGM of the members to be held each year. General meetings are usually called by the board but can be requested by members. Fourteen clear days' notice must be given and the quorum is two members. Trustees can attend and speak at general meetings but do not have a vote. Decisions involving significant change to the trust require a special resolution and 75% majority.

◆ There must be at least three trustees' meetings in every school year with the notice and agenda circulated at least seven clear days beforehand. Only trustees have the right to attend board meetings and the quorum is at least three trustees or one-third of the trustees, whichever is higher, though they may attend by telephone/video. Trustees usually vote on a show of hands.

◆ Members and trustees may use the written resolution procedure. To succeed, a member resolution requires the same proportion of votes as would be required at a general meeting whereas it requires the unanimous consent of all trustees.

◆ Minutes of member and board meetings must be taken and retained. They remain draft until approved at the next meeting and signed by the chair and, then, are evidence of the proceedings at the meeting. Once passed a resolution is binding on all irrespective of whether an individual voted for it. Copies of the minutes must be made available. Confidential matters should be recorded as a separate 'part two' minute.

◆ A trust may set up as many committees as it wishes but it must have a finance committee. MATs often have committees known as local governing bodies (LGB) or academy councils which are linked to individual academies. The constitution and terms of reference for all committees should be drafted and reviewed each year. Trusts with an annual income over £50 million must have a dedicated audit committee.

◆ The board can delegate authority, though it remains accountable. The board must decide on the remit of any delegation and any conditions to be imposed and must set them out in writing with a Scheme of Delegation. Any committee or individual to whom authority has been delegated must to report to the board following exercise of that power.

# Part three

## Risk, compliance and policies

### Overview

This part examines the process of risk management. It looks at how different types of risk are identified, managed and tolerated and the factors that influence the treatment of risk. It considers statutory and regulatory compliance and how information, especially electronic data, should be managed. It also explains the types of reviews that can be used to ensure robust governance practices.

Students will gain a broad understanding of the legal and regulatory requirements for academies as well as best practice around risk management and reviews that can be put in place.

## Learning outcomes

In this module you will:

◆   Understand the importance of assessing and managing risk in academies.

- ◆ Understand how to comply with legal and regulatory requirements for academies.
- ◆ Know how legal requirements for information management are met.
- ◆ Know the procedures around performance management and internal and external reviews.

# Chapter seven
# Risk management

**CONTENTS**

## 1. Introduction

This chapter outlines how risk should be identified and managed in a trust. It also considers particular ways of sharing risk via insurance or the risk protection arrangement and looks at the way that some specific risks should be considered.

Whilst every organisation is subject to risks daily, effective governance will identify and monitor those risks to ensure that they are managed and controlled as far as possible. As a trust is the recipient of public funding and is incorporated as a charitable company, resources must be safeguarded against harm

Risk management is defined by the International Organization for Standardization (ISO) as 'coordinated activities to direct and control an organisation with regard to risk'. ISO has developed International Standards which set out principles and guidelines on the selection and application of systematic techniques for risk assessment and managing risk effectively.

The *Academies Financial Handbook 2018* states: 'The trust **must** manage risks to ensure its effective operation.'

The risk management process should involve:

◆ adoption of a risk policy;
◆ identifying risk;

◆ analysis of specific risks;

◆ evaluation and modification of risk; and

◆ ongoing monitoring.

The trust board has an overarching responsibility for ensuring that there are effective risk management arrangements in place. It is integral to corporate governance and should inform all board decision making. It may be necessary for trusts to take risks in order to seize opportunity but risks taken should be proportionate and not reckless. The vision and objectives should be attained but the trust's resources protected. Risk management has both strategic and operational aspects which must be dealt with accordingly.

# 2. Types of risk

According to the ISO: 'Risks affecting organizations may have consequences in terms of societal, environmental, technological, safety and security outcomes; commercial, financial and economic results, as well as social, cultural and political reputation impacts.'

Every trust must develop a framework for effective risk management whether by adopting ISO Standards or otherwise.

Each trust will need to identify the risks that potentially affect it which will differ according to activities, structure and environment. However, possible risk categories to consider are:

◆ governance

◆ operational risk such as health and safety

◆ accidental loss or damage

◆ finance risk

◆ environmental and external risk

◆ reputational risk

◆ safeguarding risk

◆ law and regulation compliance risk

◆ staffing risks such as inability to recruit

◆ terrorist activities or hoaxes

Some risks will arise because of the trust's primary role as a service provider. 'Knowledge' risk will arise if there is insufficient knowledge or understanding amongst trust staff or trustees. As MATs grow increasingly more complex and diverse, there will also be a need to consider the internal 'relationship' risk whereby there is ineffective collaboration across academies or across departments.

## Stop and think 7.1

**Thinking of the trusts or academies that you are aware of, what risks do they face? Which would be significant risks?**

Effective financial oversight is a key aspect of risk management and this is guided by the requirements of the *Academies Financial Handbook*. Trusts are the recipients of public funding and are subject to stringent controls and reporting obligations. Nevertheless, trustees must give proper consideration to funding and financial processing as a risk area.

The trust must recognise and manage present and future risks to ensure its effective and continued operation. The trust should maintain a risk register.

# 3. Risk appetite and risk tolerance

Risk can never be entirely eliminated. However, different trusts may decide to accept a different level of risk depending on their particular circumstances. Every trust should carefully consider its desired risk profile, taking account of its legal obligations, business objectives and public expectations. There will be no one-size-fits-all risk management process and this will vary from time to time. Therefore, risk management must be continually updated in response to identified risk and periodically re-assessed and enhanced.

According to the Institute of Risk Management, risk appetite can be defined as 'the amount and type of risk that an organisation is willing to take in order to meet their strategic objectives'. Different trusts will have different risk appetites depending on their culture, development and objectives and these may change over time. Risk tolerance is the acceptable level of risk that the trust can actually cope with – this may be influenced not only by the risk appetite of the board but also by external obligations imposed by ESFA.

Trust boards must have a clearly articulated risk appetite and set the risk tolerance in relation to the various risks that affect the organisation. The purpose of a risk management strategy is to reduce the likelihood and impact of serious harm occurring and the major risks facing the trust must be identified and managed to keep in line with the policy that is adopted. The model wording included in the *Academies Accounts Direction 2017–2018* regarding risk recognises the limitations of the risk management process:

> 'such a system is designed to manage rather than eliminate the risk of failure to achieve business objectives, and can provide only reasonable and not absolute assurance against material misstatement or loss'.

# 4. Risk management

Risk management is a process whereby the risks are methodically examined and 'managed'. Every trust must develop its own risk strategy framework which involves:

- risk identification
- risk estimation (assessing likelihood and impact)
- risk prioritisation
- risk mitigation
- risk monitoring
- risk reporting

Although risk can never be eliminated entirely, every effort must be taken to make sure that the potential risks are identified and managed in the most appropriate way. Risk management ensures that students, staff and resources are protected. It is not a static reporting system but a framework which constantly reviews the risks, anticipating and responding to changes in social, environmental and legislative requirements and ensuring that risk management becomes part of the culture and organisational structure of the trust.

The risk management strategy is the responsibility of the trust board although, in practice, much of the risk management activity is delegated to relevant staff to oversee. Nevertheless, the board should be aware of the major risks facing the trust at any time and be aware of the approach to risk management that is being taken.

## 4.1 Risk identification

This involves recognising what can happen (the risks) as well as considering when, where, how and why they might arise.

Financial risk is specifically identified by ESFA and clear guidance set out in DfE guidance including the *Academies Financial Handbook* and the *Academies Accounts Direction*. Trusts are the recipients of public funding and, therefore, particular care must be taken in its management.

Identification of risk involves not only looking at what can go wrong but also when an event occurs that is beneficial (e.g. a sudden increase in pupil numbers).

The *Academies Accounts Direction 2017–2018* explains that a recently established trust 'will have a heightened risk profile' since controls and procedures will not have been in place for the full financial period, the accounting officer may be still developing an understanding of their role and there may be immature or developing governance structures. Certain matters may heighten the risk profile in an established trust:

- culture (attitude and values) within the trust;
- a change in accounting officer, chief finance officer or significant changes in the board of trustees;

◆   an expansion of the number of academies within the academy trust; and

◆   changes to the scheme of delegation or major accounting systems.

## 4.2  Risk estimation

Risk assessment will primarily look at the result of an event that will impact negatively. However, consideration must also be given to the potential positive impact of a risk: any change can destabilise an organisation and even something good can pose a risk!

Risks are analysed according to the expected potential loss as well as the likelihood of the risk occurring. They can then be prioritised with those judged to present the greatest probability of occurring as well as the greatest potential loss being highest and these should be managed first. This could be scored on a scale of 1–5:

**1.**   Likelihood

–   extremely unlikely; rare occurrence

–   unlikely

–   moderately unlikely

–   very likely

–   extremely likely; frequent occurrence

**2.**   Impact

–   minor impact in limited areas

–   minor impact in many areas

–   significant impact; would not affect continued operations in short-term but might in long-term

–   significant impact; in medium term; relates to substantial operational areas

–   fundamental to continuing operations.

The scores for likelihood and impact are multiplied to produce a total score.

## 4.3  Risk prioritisation

Risks can then be ranked by numerical value so that they can be prioritised to focus on significant risks.

A risk register should be used to record all risk information. The board should establish what level of risk is tolerable and the register colour-coded accordingly – it is standard practice to 'RAG-rate' risk registers. Items coloured green are kept under review; consideration should be given to action on those coloured amber; any items coloured red should be subject to immediate action.

## 4.4  Risk mitigation

The board is under a particular obligation to manage any significant risk – any risk that may threaten the survival of the trust or seriously weaken it.

A common risk management approach is to follow the mnemonic SARA:

◆ **S**hare risk – outsource the activity or transfer the risk through insurance.

◆ **A**void risk – change the plan or the activity so that the problem is not encountered.

◆ **R**educe risk – make changes that mitigate or control the risk.

◆ **A**ccept risk – note the risk and take the chance that it, or part of it, might arise.

Each risk should be considered in turn and then SARA applied; the most appropriate risk management approach should be selected. If the risk can be 'avoided' or 'reduced', an action plan must be developed. If it is not possible to mitigate the risk, it should be either 'shared' by taking out insurance or setting up outsourcing arrangements or should be 'accepted' and the risk to the trust formally noted.

It is essential that a lead individual is identified and noted in the risk register. They will be responsible for making sure that the action plan is carried out or that insurance or outsourcing arrangements are effected.

The board is responsible for the strategic approach to risk management and should specifically approve any risks that are accepted without treatment.

Trusts should be conscious of 'gross and net risk' in the register. The gross risk value will initially be recorded; however, mitigating action may be taken which will reduce the overall risk score to the net risk value. The impact of the mitigating actions can be quantified and an assessment made as to their cost effectiveness.

The risk management process is a continuous, cyclical process of review and management.

The *Academies Financial Handbook 2018* makes clear that trusts **must** act on any advice given to them and 'must cooperate with risk management auditors and risk managers, and implement reasonable risk management audit recommendations made to them'.

### Stop and think 7.2

**From what you know or have read about academies, consider some typical risks and how these should be managed (ie shared, avoided, reduced or accepted):**

◆ **the school building was destroyed by fire, flood, etc**

◆ **key employees were no longer available (resigned, ill, injured, etc)**

◆ **the school was graded Inadequate by Ofsted**

◆ **there was a significant and sudden decrease/increase in pupil numbers**

◆ **cash flow is inappropriately managed**

◆ **a significant safeguarding incident takes place**

◆ **pupil performance is poor**

◆ **data protection breach**

## 4.5 Risk monitoring

Risks should be constantly monitored to ascertain whether the likelihood or impact has changed, for example:

◆ the nature of the risk is changing or has changing;

◆ existing controls are inadequate or not functioning; and

◆ new mitigating measures are put in place.

Whilst the risk register will be used by the senior leadership team as a live document for monitoring purposes, regular monitoring reports or an updated register must be put before trustees. Typically, the audit committee will review the risk register as well as any risk reduction plan and guidance contained in the internal audit monitoring report.

The *Academies Financial Handbook 2018* highlights that ESFA publishes guidance on reducing fraud and advises that trusts should refer to this information and to the findings from ESFA's investigation reports, as part of its risk management approach.

## 4.6 Risk reporting

Risk management needs to be a holistic and responsive system. The process is informed from many different levels within the trust and warning indicators can be used to put in place remedial action. Risk management should be reported to stakeholders as part of the annual report (Companies Act 2006 and SORP 2015). The trustees' report must include a section setting out the principal risks and uncertainties facing the trust that have been identified by the trustees. The focus should be on those risks that could seriously affect the performance, future prospects or reputation of the trust, including its viability. Any factors that are likely to affect performance or risk going forward should be identified. The risk management process should be outlined together with a summary of the plans and strategies for managing those risks identified as priorities.

The trust's financial risk management objectives and its exposure to financial risks including credit, cash flow and liquidity risks must be disclosed, unless 'not material for an assessment of its position and performance'. However, the *Academies Accounts Direction 2017–2018* explains that as the financial instruments dealt with by trusts are 'largely bank balances, cash and trade creditors, with limited trade (and other) debtors, it is likely that only minimal disclosure will be required' as this information will not be material to the assessment of the 'trust's assets, liabilities, financial position and its results' (Large and Medium-sized Companies and Groups (Accounts and Reports) Regulations (SI 2008/410) Schedule 7, s. 6(1)). It may be necessary to make reference to any defined benefit pension schemes, such as the Teachers' Pension Scheme, particularly where there is a deficit as this may be material.

The risk management framework must be embedded into the culture and values of the trust so that it is reflected in the policies and procedures and informs overall management and strategy.

Although it is essential to minimise or eliminate risk as far as possible, the risk management process must be proportionate and balanced. The time and cost of increasingly complex risk management processes could quickly outweigh the benefits to be achieved.

## Test yourself 7.1

1. What are the main steps in a risk management process?

2. What risk treatment or strategies should be considered?

### 4.7 Business continuity and disaster recovery plans

There are some events and threats which, although likely to be extremely unlikely, would threaten the operation and reputation of the trust as well as the safety of the organisation and anyone connected with it. Abnormal situations which may fall under this may include extreme weather, natural disasters or terrorism.

The *Academies Financial Handbook* specifically states that: 'The trust's management of risks must include contingency and business continuity planning.' This plan will set out a strategy in the event of a major disaster and it should be developed and maintained in line with latest guidance and information available. The likelihood of a disaster happening is small, but the impact would be very great. Having an agreed strategic recovery plan ensures that disruption is minimised and normal operations can be restored as quickly as possible. Business continuity planning should be incorporated within the normal risk management processes.

## Making it work 7.1

**In December 2015, schools in Carlisle were affected by serious flooding after storm Desmond hit the North West coast. Some of these schools had previously been flooded in 2005. The governing boards of these schools should have put in place continuity plans which would have set out the steps that would be taken if the scenario arose again.**

In business continuity planning, the trust plans for a crisis occurring. It cannot know what exactly will occur but it can consider different scenarios and outcomes and decide what will happen to minimise the impact. For example, what alternative premises could be used if the school building is destroyed or not available for use – how can the 'business' (i.e. teaching and learning) continue, as far as possible, to ensure the trust's 'continued and effective operation'.

# 5. Risk register

The *Academies Financial Handbook 2018* requires that trusts 'should maintain a risk register' but it does not set out any specific requirements around what this should cover or the format in which it is held.

The risk register should be retained in a format that is easy to use and to update. It needs to be easily accessible by trustees and the senior leadership team so that risk can be identified, tracked and monitored and risk controls put in place as appropriate. The risk register should encompass all areas identified and include a mechanism to highlight the biggest risks. It should also be kept under regular review and amended to reflect any changes.

A common approach uses a spreadsheet format which puts the identified risks down the left-hand side. Each is then scored according to the likeliness of it occurring and the potential impact if it does occur. A score between one and five is typically used: the two scores are then multiplied together to give a final figure. The scores for each risk can then be prioritised. Risk registers can be extended to include consideration of the trust's attitude to a risk (i.e. a trust might have a higher risk tolerance level in relation to certain types of risk).

| No. | Category | Risk description | Consequence | Comment | Likelihood | Impact | Likelihood × Impact score | Priority ranking | Risk owner |
|---|---|---|---|---|---|---|---|---|---|
| P1. | People | Quality of provision drops and pupil numbers fall | | | 2 | 5 | 10 | | DS |
| P2. | | Inability to attract quality staff | Pupils fail to make good progress. Poor Ofsted grading. Not school of choice. | Recruitment very challenging. | 3 | 5 | 15 | | DS |
| P3. | | Lack of capacity – understaffed/ stretched/ overloaded | Work incomplete. Missed deadlines. Increased errors. Unreasonable pressure on staff. | | 4 | 5 | 20 | | DS |
| P4. | | Staff negligence – lack of compliance with policy and procedures | Potential for compensation claims. | External training and support engaged through SLA | 1 | 4 | 4 | | DS |

**Table 7.1: A small excerpt from a risk register looking at risks relating to people**

# 6. Insurance and risk protection arrangements

Adequate arrangements must be set up for those risks identified to be 'shared' via insurance. Some risks are easily insurable (e.g. material damage or third-party liability). The *Academies Financial Handbook* is clear: 'The academy trust must have adequate insurance cover in compliance with its legal obligations or be a member of the academies risk protection arrangement (RPA).'

According to the *Academies Financial Handbook*, if the trust is not a member of the RPA, it 'should determine its own level of commercial insurance cover to include buildings and contents, business continuity, employers' and public liability insurance and any cover required'. Purchase of insurance should always be in accordance with normal purchasing decisions and best value for money.

There is a statutory requirement for all trusts to have employers' liability insurance under the provisions of the Employers' Liability (Compulsory Insurance) Act 1969. Trusts can be fined for failure to hold current insurance. Employers' liability insurance will cover the cost of compensation payments and legal fees granted where an employee successfully claims for any injuries or illness sustained as a result of their employment.

Other insurances which should be considered are:

◆ Trustees' and officers' liability.
◆ Absence management, rehabilitation and supply cover.
◆ Buildings, contents and property damage including accidental or malicious damage.
◆ Business interruption.
◆ Equipment breakdown for engineering and computer equipment, including statutory inspections of pressure, lifting or other plant.
◆ Public liability.
◆ Motor/minibus and occasional business use for teachers' vehicles.
◆ Out-of-school clubs and holiday clubs.
◆ Pupils' personal accident.
◆ Pupils' personal effects including educational trips.

The level of cover provided in respect of any identified risk should be carefully calculated and kept under regular review.

ESFA runs a risk protection arrangement (RPA) which is a voluntary risk pooling scheme. It provides a mechanism by which losses that materialise are reimbursed from a pooling arrangement that is underwritten by government funds.

The *Academies Financial Handbook* suggests that trusts 'should consider the RPA unless commercial insurance provides better value for money'. All SATs and MATs, including free schools, special academies, alternative provision academies, UTCs, studio and PFI schools, can opt in to the RPA.

The scope of the RPA covers: material damage, business interruption, employers' liability, third-person liability, governors' liability, professional indemnity, employee and third person dishonesty, money, personal accident, United Kingdom travel and legal expenses. The RPA does not cover all risks including motor vehicles, overseas travel, statutory engineering inspections and works of art, and alternative arrangements will need to be made.

Trusts 'opt in' to the RPA scheme and a per pupil (per place for special and AP trusts) deduction with be made at source from GAG. It is set at £20 per pupil/place until 31 August 2018.

A trust may join or leave the RPA at any time, though it must give at least three months' notice to the RPA Administrator of its intention to leave.

## Test yourself 7.2

**What is the RPA and how does it work?**

# 7. Specific risks

## 7.1  Health and safety

The Health and Safety at Work Act 1974 requires that any employer must ensure, as far as possible, the 'health, safety and welfare at work' of all employees as well as protecting other people who might be affected by their activities such as pupils or visitors. The trust must also ensure that premises are 'safe and without risks to health'.

It is obviously not possible to eliminate all risks but the trust must take all steps necessary 'so far as is reasonably practicable' so anything that would be technically impossible or the cost of which would be so disproportionate to the risk would not be essential.

However, it is important to carry out risk assessments and manage those risks that are identified so far as possible.

There is a significant amount of regulation around health and safety and specialist guidance should be sought. The main requirements on the employer are set out in the Management of Health and Safety at Work Regulations 1999 (SI 1999/3242). The Health and Safety Executive (HSE) has produced a leaflet *Five Steps to Risk Assessment* which gives information on the requirements on employers beyond carrying out a risk assessment:

- Make arrangements for implementing the health and safety measures identified as necessary by the risk assessment.
- Appoint competent people (often themselves or company colleagues) to help them to implement the arrangements.
- Set up emergency procedures.

◆ Provide clear information and training to employees.

◆ Work together with other employers sharing the same workplace.

The HSE and Institute of Directors suggest three essential principles of effective leadership in health and safety in their *Guidance to Directors* (INDG 417):

◆ Strong and active leadership from the top:

 − visible, active commitment from the board;

 − establishing effective 'downward' communication systems and management structures; and

 − integration of good health and safety management with business decisions.

◆ Worker involvement:

 − engaging the workforce in the promotion and achievement of safe and healthy conditions;

 − effective 'upward' communication; and

 − providing high-quality training.

◆ Assessment and review:

 − identifying and managing health and safety risks;

 − accessing (and following) competent advice; and

 − monitoring, reporting and reviewing performance.

There is a lot of useful guidance on the HSE website including a health and safety checklist for classrooms.

Part of risk management will be to ensure that all staff receive appropriate health and safety training and guidance.

As an employer, trusts must either display the HSE-approved law poster or must provide a copy of the equivalent leaflet to every worker. They set out in simple terms what the employer and workers must do.

Adequate and appropriate equipment, facilities and qualified first-aid personnel should be provided (Health and Safety (First Aid) Regulations 1981 (SI 1981/917)). There must be emergency procedures in place in the event of an incident and workers should be made aware of the process to be followed (Management of Health and Safety at Work Regulations 1999 (SI 1999/3242)).

Certain serious workplace accidents, occupational diseases and specified dangerous occurrences that qualify as 'near misses', must be reported to HSE under the provisions of RIDDOR (Reporting of Injuries, Diseases and Dangerous Occurrences Regulations 2013 (SI 2013/1471)). Examples of injuries that occur in schools are given on the HSE website and indicates that the following will not normally be reportable:

◆ Accidents to pupils sustained in PE lessons (unless the pupil is killed or taken to hospital for treatment or was work-related).

◆ Sporting injuries (unless they arise out of or in connection with a work activity).

◆ Injuries sustained in a road traffic accident on the way to school in the school bus.

◆ Injuries sustained on a school trip abroad.

## Test yourself 7.3

**1. What do the HSE and Institute of Directors suggest are the three essential principles of effective leadership in health and safety?**

**2. Give an example of a typical injury that will not be reportable under RIDDOR.**

## 7.2  Off-site activities

Many trusts obtain a generic parental consent that will cover local trips and visits carried out during the normal school day. A specific consent will be required if such trips take place outside normal school hours or if off-site activities involve a higher level of risk.

## 7.3  Safeguarding

Academies including free schools and AP academies must have regard to any guidance given by the Secretary of State with regard to arrangements to safeguard or promote the welfare of pupils – Schedule to the Education (Independent School Standards) Regulations 2014, paragraph 7(b). Statutory guidance is provided in Keeping Children Safe in Education: Statutory Guidance for Schools and Colleges (September 2016). It defines 'safeguarding and promoting the welfare of children' as:

◆ protecting children from maltreatment;

◆ preventing impairment of children's health or development;

◆ ensuring that children grow up in circumstances consistent with the provision of safe and effective care; and

◆ taking action to enable all children to have the best outcomes.

Policies and procedures should be in place for appropriate action to be taken in a timely manner to safeguard and promote children's welfare. These should include:

◆ an effective child protection policy; and

◆ a staff behaviour policy (code of conduct) which should include acceptable use of technologies, staff/pupil relationships and communications including the use of social media.

These policies and procedures should be followed by all staff members, who must undergo safeguarding and child protection training as part of their induction. Training should be in line with guidance from the Local Safeguarding Children Board (LSCB). Staff should also receive safeguarding and child protection updates regularly and at least annually.

An appropriate senior member of staff must be appointed to the role of designated safeguarding lead to take responsibility for safeguarding and child protection. Academies may choose to have deputy safeguarding leads but they must be 'trained to the same standard as the designated safeguarding lead'. The responsibility, nevertheless, should not be delegated. Training for the designated safeguarding lead and any deputies must be updated every two years.

### 7.4  Safer recruitment

Trusts should have written recruitment and selection policies and procedures in place. To prevent people who pose a risk of harm from working with children, statutory responsibilities to check staff must be adhered to and proportionate decisions taken on whether to ask for any checks beyond what is required. Volunteers should be appropriately supervised.

Although there is no statutory requirement for trusts, *Staffing and Employment Advice for Schools: Departmental Advice for School Leaders, Governing Bodies, Academy Trusts and Local Authorities* (February 2017) recommends that it would be 'good practice for appointment panel members' to have undertaken training in how to take proper account of the need to safeguard and promote the welfare of children when recruiting staff (i.e. safer recruitment training).

Keeping *Children Safe in Education* explains that decisions about the suitability of a prospective employee must be based on 'checks and evidence including criminal record checks (DBS checks), barred list checks and prohibition checks together with references and interview information'. An enhanced DBS certificate including barred list information will be required where an individual:

◆ will be responsible, on a regular basis in a school or college, for teaching, training instructing, caring for or supervising children; or

◆ will carry out paid, or unsupervised unpaid, work regularly in a school or college where that work provides an opportunity for contact with children; or

◆ engages in intimate or personal care or overnight activity, even if this happens only once.

An additional check to ensure that they are not prohibited from teaching will be required for anyone appointed to carry out teaching work.

A check should be carried out on anyone engaged in a management role to ensure that they are not prohibited or restricted from participating in the management of a trust under the provisions of section128 of the Education and Skills Act 2008.

## 7.5 Complaints

Trusts are required to set out a formal, written complaints procedure under the Education (Independent Schools Standards) Regulations 2014 (SI 2014/3283), Schedule 1, Part 7. The complaints policy and procedure must be drawn up and effectively implemented. It should:

◆   be in writing;

◆   be made available to parents of pupils;

◆   set out clear time scales for the management of a complaint;

◆   set out a process for escalation of complaints, which should:

  –   allow for a complaint to be made and considered initially on an informal basis;

  –   establish a formal procedure for the complaint to be made in writing; and

  –   make provision for a hearing before a panel of at least three people who were not directly involved in the matters detailed in the complaint, one of whom is independent of the management and running of the school (i.e. not a member of the senior leadership team or a trustee).

Every school and academy will receive complaints and the majority will be dealt with informally to the satisfaction of all. However, the process should be followed where this is not possible and any lessons learned taken back to improve internal practices.

If a complainant has exhausted the internal complaints process but is still unsatisfied, their only recourse is to appeal direct to the Secretary of State for Education through ESFA.

Converter academies have specific clauses in their funding agreement in respect of any complaints that arose in whole or in part in the 12 months prior to conversion. In this case, the complaint must be investigated in accordance with the complaints procedures established as if it had taken place after the trust converted.

There is no legal requirement for trusts to have a complaints procedure for any parties other than parents of pupils.

Any complaints from trust employees will be dealt with under the grievance policy.

## 7.6 Reputational risk

The reputation of a trust or academy is extremely important; it will have a huge negative impact if the stakeholders and wider community have a poor perception. Unfortunately, reputation is also extremely vulnerable and at risk from a variety of sources.

Any school that has received a poor Ofsted judgment or experienced some very negative event will understand how long it can take to recover after any dent in reputation. Reputation can be lost in the blink of the eye, but communities have long memories which makes them difficult to rebuild. The opinions or beliefs of stakeholders or other members of a community are formed through their own expectations and experiences as well as messages and conversations that they participate in or are exposed to. The increased use of social media and improved communications can contribute to the very rapid spread of 'bad news' stories.

The loss of reputation is a massive risk to a trust or academy; it will lead to negative perceptions that could lead to pupils being removed from the academy or a drop in future new entrants. Any drop in pupil numbers results in a drop in funding which will cause significant financial damage.

Whilst reputational risk cannot be eradicated, a trust must have good policies in place around expectations of staff, excellent internal control mechanisms and ensure compliance with legal and regulatory requirements. Trustees could also give consideration to mitigation through a positive management of reputation, empowering spokespeople and carefully preparing press releases or other communications with stakeholders and the wider community.

# Chapter summary

◆ Trusts must ensure a robust risk management process is in place. All risks that potentially affect the trust must be identified. The board must have a clearly articulated risk appetite and set the risk tolerance in relation to the various risks that affect the organisation.

◆ Risks are analysed according to the expected potential loss as well as the likelihood of the risk occurring. They can then be prioritised with those judged to present the greatest probability of occurring as well as the greatest potential loss being highest and these should be managed first.

◆ Decisions must be taken about how to manage risks – one approach is SARA: Share, Avoid, Reduce, Accept. Risks must be kept under review and reflected in the risk register. Formal reporting on the principal risks must be included in the annual trustees' report.

◆ Business continuity and disaster recovery plans should set out a strategy in the event of a major disaster or event. Trusts are required to have insurance cover or opt into ESFA's risk protection arrangement.

◆ As an employer, every trust must ensure that premises are safe and employees and other people who enter the workplace are safe and without risks to health so far as practicable. All staff must get appropriate health and safety training and guidance and the HSE-approved law poster must be displayed. Certain serious workplace accidents, occupational diseases and specified dangerous occurrences must be reported under the provisions of RIDDOR (Reporting of Injuries, Diseases and Dangerous Occurrences Regulations 2013).

◆ Arrangements must be put in place to safeguard and promote the welfare of pupils with policies and procedures in place and followed by all staff. All staff must undergo safeguarding and child protection training as part of their induction which should be regularly updated. A senior member of staff must be appointed as designated safeguarding lead.

◆ There should be written recruitment and selection policies and procedures in place. Enhanced Disclosure and Barring Service checks and barred list checks must be undertaken for most individuals involved in a school setting.

◆ Trusts must have a formal, written complaints procedure which is made available to parents of pupils.

# Chapter eight
# Compliance and policies

**CONTENTS**

1. Introduction
2. Policies
3. Safeguarding and Disclosure and Barring Service (DBS) checks
4. Conflicts of interest and register
5. Whistleblowing

## 1. Introduction

This chapter outlines the policies that trusts must adopt and implement as well as other requirements with which they must comply. Trusts must take account of company and charity law and any guidance published by the DfE.

The chapter also looks at some of the requirements around trustees and local governors including checks undertaken on them and disclosures made on appointment and ongoing obligations regarding conflicts of interest.

## 2. Policies

While often grouped together, 'policies' are the overriding principles, rules and guidelines that are followed by an organisation and 'procedures' are the methods used to do so. They provide the framework which enables the smooth functioning of the trust or academy. They enable the organisation to operate within the agreed values and towards the vision embodied in the strategic plan.

Policies should be high-level documents which may be more strategically focused whereas procedures contain the detail around the steps to be taken.

### 2.1 Policy drafting

There are a number of statutory policies that all trusts/academies must have, but the trust will wish to consider various others which will help with the smooth operation of the organisation.

It is important that policies set the framework in which the strategic vision of the trust is to be realised. However, whilst the board is responsible for policy development, in practice the majority are delegated to a member of the executive, usually the headteacher/principal. A few of the statutory policies require formal approval by the board but the rest can be approved by an individual or a committee.

Policies relating to staffing, for example, will require consultation with those affected as well as their unions and this will need to be factored into the planning cycle. Care must be taken to ensure that changes to policies are permitted by law/regulation. As company directors the board members are expected to exercise reasonable care, skill and diligence and this can reasonably extend to taking professional advice where appropriate on the content and development of policies.

A MAT board will generally look to develop a consistency of approach across all academies. As well as being more practical to oversee, it also operates to foster a single vision. As policies are high-level documents, the MAT can choose the level of divergence in the practice and application of policies across academies, it can allow a diverse, individual approach by each academy or a take a more dictatorial line. All staff in a MAT are employed by the trust and so any employment or staffing policies must be consistent.

It is rarely necessary to draft a policy from scratch and precedent policies may be obtained from local authorities, corporate providers or member organisations, and tailored to the needs of the trust.

Policies do not need to follow an agreed format though it is usually helpful to develop a consistent 'trust-style'. Policies should avoid jargon or formal terminology where possible and be written in 'plain English' so that they can easily be read and understood. Any acronyms or abbreviations should be defined within the policy.

Detailed procedures can be drawn up to demonstrate the day-to-day implementation of the policy. These are operational documents and will often sit with the principal and executive team.

## 2.2  Access to policies

There are legal requirements to publish certain documents on the website or to make them available to parents of pupils.

It is also important that staff, trustees, governors and parents, as appropriate, are able to access policies that they may need. Access may be enabled through:

◆ website or virtual learning environment (VLE);

◆ inclusion in staff handbook or finance handbook;

◆ hard copies at the academy – including versions in community languages or for the visually impaired; and

◆ master file held in the academy/trust office.

## 2.3  Review

Relevant legislation/regulation sets out the review frequency necessary for some policies. However, it will be for the board to decide on frequency and the individual or committee to review and approve the majority of policies. Policies should be reviewed on a regular basis although not all need to be reviewed annually. Review will often involve the use of external advisors or reference to model policies which have been through consultations with stakeholders.

It is rare that policies need formal board approval and it is not a good use of board time to spend reviewing the detail of the policies. Therefore, responsibility for drafting and updating will normally be delegated to a member of the staff team with approval delegated either to the CEO/principal or a board committee. As with any delegation, they report back to the board once the authority has been exercised.

A process for managing policies must be established that identifies review dates and the party or committee responsible.

The board must also be assured that policies are embedded in practice. Monitoring will take place through consideration by the board of reports from the CEO/principal or other senior staff, the use of comparative data such as Analyse School Performance (ASP) and from processes such as external and internal audits.

Trustees and LGB governors will also undertake monitoring visits where they can witness the policy and procedure in action. It is good practice to have a trustee/governor visit policy which sets out clear protocols. Trustee/governor visits are not inspections and should never attempt to make judgements about the quality of teaching and learning. Consideration should be given to how visits will be arranged, the scope and nature of visits, who trustees/governors will meet and how visits will be reported back to the LGB/board; it can be useful to include a standard pro forma visit form for completion.

## 2.4  Statutory policies

On a practical level, trusts need to ensure that there are policies in place so that everyone has clarity around the operation of the organisation. However, there are only a small number of policies that are required by law. The DfE has provided advice on the policies and documents that boards are required to have by law in *Statutory Policies for Schools, September 2014*. It is important to recognise that this is not a comprehensive list of policies required and does not include all policies and procedures required on a practical level from the trustees' role as an employer and controller of premises.

## 2.5  Admissions arrangements

Every academy is its own admissions authority which means that it determines the criteria to be used if there are more applications than places. The admissions policy must be compliant with the *Schools Admissions Code* and must be reviewed and adopted annually, whether or not there are any changes. The board can delegate formal approval of the admissions policy to a committee (e.g. it could delegate to a local governing body to agree the particular arrangements that will apply to their academy).

The policy sets out order in which the criteria will be applied; there must be oversubscription criteria for each 'relevant age group'. Any child whose statement of special educational needs (SEN) or Education, Health and Care Plan (EHCP) names the school must be admitted first. Looked-after children (children in the care of the local authority) and previously looked-after children (children who ceased to be looked after because they were adopted) must be given the highest priority.

There are restrictions around selection by ability. Converter academies that were previously designated grammar schools or schools with partially selective arrangements are permitted to continue with selection by ability. However, other academies cannot introduce criteria which selects on the basis of high academic ability. It is possible to introduce pupil ability banding which ensures that the intake for an academy includes a proportionate spread of pupils of different abilities which is representative of:

◆ the full range of ability of applicants for the academy;

◆ the range of ability of children in the local area; or

◆ the national ability range.

The School Admission Code does offer the opportunity for selection on the basis of aptitude in a school specialism. Admission on this basis must not be more than 10% of the total admissions intake. The only specialist subjects on which selection by aptitude may apply are:

◆ physical education or sport, or one or more sports;

◆ the performing arts, or any one or more of those arts;

◆  the visual arts, or any one or more of those arts; and

◆ modern foreign languages, or any such language.

Schools which selected on aptitude in design and technology and information technology every year since 2007/08 may continue to do so.

In practice, it is tricky to ensure that testing looks simply for natural talent rather than general academic ability which is prohibited. The ability profile of those selected by aptitude must be examined to determine whether it is representative of all those applying and, if not, tests must be adjusted.

Whatever oversubscription criteria are adopted must be 'reasonable, clear, objective, procedurally fair, and comply with all relevant legislation'. There should be an effective, clear and fair tie-breaker to deal with a situation where two applications cannot otherwise be separated.

A consultation must take place where changes are proposed to the admission arrangements or if they have not been consulted on within the last seven years. A formal consultation must take place for a period of at least six weeks between 1 October and 31 January.

Academies do not have to consult on any proposal to increase or keep the same Published Admission Number (PAN).

## Stop and think 8.1

**Review a wide selection of admission policies from the websites of a diverse range of academies. What are the differences between the selection criteria? Do any have any selective elements? What impact are the different policies likely to have on the admission intake in the event of oversubscription?**

### 2.6 Allegations of abuse against staff

There should be a statement of the procedures in place to handle allegations against teachers, headteachers, principals, volunteers and other staff.

The board can delegate approval of the policy and can determine the frequency of review.

### 2.7 Behaviour policy

Every academy must have a behaviour policy (Education (Independent School Standards) (England) Regulations 2014 (SI 2014/3283). A written policy must be adopted, the aim of which is to 'promote good behaviour amongst pupils' but it must also set out 'sanctions to be adopted in the event of pupil misbehaviour'. An anti-bullying strategy must also be drawn up and implemented. Detailed DfE guidance is set out in *Behaviour and Discipline in Schools: Advice for Headteachers and School Staff* (January 2016).

There is no legal obligation to upload the behaviour policy to the website but information must be made available to parents on request.

### 2.8 Charging and remissions

The model funding agreement contains provisions requiring trusts to comply with the Education Act 1996 in relation to charging. Parents/carers and pupils cannot be charged for any activity unless there is a policy in place and there are restrictions around what charges may be made. DfE guidance, *Charging for School Activities: Departmental Advice for Governing Bodies, School Leaders, School Staff and Local Authorities* (October 2014) sets out the circumstances in which charges may be made and the restrictions that apply.

Generally, if activities take place during the normal school day, voluntary contributions may be requested and pupils must not be treated differently if they pay the contribution or not. However, the academy can charge for optional extras or where the pupil's parent wishes their child to own particular materials, books, instruments or equipment. A charge may not be made for education outside the school day if it is part of the national curriculum or part of the syllabus for a public examination that the pupil is being prepared for. No charges may be made for entry to a prescribed public examination which the pupil has been prepared for at the academy. No charges may be made as any part of the admissions process or towards education during normal school hours.

The board is free to decide the review frequency of the charging and remissions policy.

## 2.9  Child protection policy and procedures

Keeping children safe in education, September 2016, requires all schools and academies to have appropriate policies and procedures in place in order for 'appropriate action to be taken in a timely manner to safeguard and promote children's welfare'. This should include an effective child protection policy which includes details of procedures in accordance with government guidance and refer to locally agreed inter-agency procedures put in place by the LSCB. The policy should be reviewed and approved by the board annually and it should be made available publicly either via the website or other means.

## 2.10 Complaints procedure

The Education (Independent School Standards) (England) Regulations 2010 (SI 2010/1997), Schedule 1, Part 7 sets out the requirement to set out a complaints procedure which deals with handling complaints from parents of pupils. It must be in writing, setting out clear timescales for the management of any complaint. Initially a complaint should be dealt with on an informal basis by the teacher or headteacher. If a parent is not satisfied, a formal procedure should be established for a complaint to be made in writing and considered formally; if this fails to reach an amicable solution, the complaint should be heard before a panel of at least three people who were not directly involved in the matter, one of which is independent of the management and running of the academy. The policy should also set out the requirements around documentation and written records of complaints and meetings/hearings.

If the academy has boarding facilities, the complaints procedure must have due regard to Standard 5, of the Minimum Standards for Boarding Schools and, where appropriate, Standard 4 of the National Minimum Standards for Residential Special Schools, which relate to contact with parents/carers.

The complaints procedure must be made available to parents.

If a complainant does not feel that their complaint has been satisfactorily resolved despite following the complaints procedure, they may appeal directly to the Secretary of State via ESFA.

## 2.11 Data protection

Under the Data Protection Act 2018, academies are 'Data Controllers'. As such, they must 'Notify' (register with) the ICO annually.

The policy must be drafted with consideration to the six data protection principles:

1. Personal data shall be processed fairly and lawfully.

2. Personal data shall be obtained only for one or more specified, explicit and legitimate purposes, and shall not be further processed in any manner incompatible with that purpose or those purposes.

3. Personal data shall be adequate, relevant and not excessive in relation to the purpose or purposes for which they are processed.

4. Personal data shall be accurate and, where necessary, kept up to date. every reasonable step must be taken to ensure that personal data that is inaccurate, having regard to the law enforcement purpose for which it is processed, is erased or rectified without delay.

5. Personal data processed for any purpose or purposes shall not be kept for longer than is necessary for that purpose or those purposes. Appropriate time limits must be established for the periodic review of the need for the continued storage of personal data for any of the law enforcement purposes.

6. Personal data shall be processed in a manner that ensures appropriate security of the personal data, using appropriate technical or organisational measures (and, in this principle, 'appropriate security' includes protection against unauthorised or unlawful processing and against accidental loss, destruction or damage).

The board can delegate approval of the policy but review must take place at least every two years.

### 2.12 Early Years Foundation Stage (EYFS)

The statutory framework for the Early Years Foundation Stage requires a number of policies and procedures to be in place in relation to safeguarding and welfare and the administration of medicines. In practice, many of these requirements will be met by an academy or trust-wide policy.

The board can delegate approval of the policies, where necessary; the guidance should be considered in relation to review frequency.

### 2.13 Freedom of information

Academies fall within the definition of public bodies set out in the Freedom of Information Act 2000, Schedule 1, Part 4. This gives a right of access to the public to information held.

Academies must produce a Publication Scheme (Section 19) setting out the academy's 'commitment to make certain classes of information routinely available' (e.g. policies and procedures, minutes of meetings, annual reports and financial information). The ICO has developed a model publication scheme which can be adopted which consists of seven commitments and seven classes of information.

The board can delegate approval of the policy and can determine the frequency of review.

## 2.14 Equality information and objectives (public sector equality duty) statement

The Equality Act 2010 and The Equality Act 2010 (Specific Duties) Regulations 2011 (SI 2011/2260) require academies to draw up equality objectives and publish a statement annually demonstrating how they are meeting the aims of the equality duty.

The three aims of the general equality duty are to:

◆ Eliminate discrimination, harassment and victimisation and any other conduct that is prohibited by or under the Act.

◆ Advance equality of opportunity between people who share a relevant protected characteristic and people who do not share it.

◆ Foster good relations between people who share a relevant protected characteristic and those who do not share it.

The protected characteristics are:

◆ Age
◆ Disability
◆ Gender reassignment
◆ Marriage and civil partnership
◆ Pregnancy and maternity
◆ Race
◆ Religion or belief
◆ Sex
◆ Sexual orientation

The board can delegate approval; while the equality statement must be reviewed and published annually, the equality objectives must be drawn up and published every four years showing how they are meeting the aims of the public sector equality duty.

## 2.15 Health and safety

The Health and Safety at Work Act 1974 places a duty on all employers, including trusts, to take reasonable steps to ensure the health and safety of employees, pupils and visitors. The Management of Health and Safety at Work Regulations 1999: SI 1999/3242 also requires employers to produce a risk assessment.

The board can delegate approval of the policy and can determine the frequency of review.

### 2.16 Home-school agreement

The School Standards and Framework Act 1998: Part 4, Sections 110 and 111 requires every academy to adopt a home-school agreement together with a parental declaration. The home-school agreement must specify:

◆  the school's aims and values;

◆  the school's responsibilities in connection with the education of pupils;

◆  the parental responsibilities; and

◆  the school's expectations of its pupils regarding conduct expectations.

The parental declaration is simply a document used by parents to record their acknowledgement of the contents of the home-school agreement and accept the parental responsibilities and the school's expectations of its pupils.

The board can delegate approval of the policy and can determine the frequency of review.

### 2.17 Recruitment and selection

*Keeping children safe in education*, September 2016, requires all schools and academies to have written recruitment and selection policies and procedures in place. This is to prevent people who pose a risk of harm from working with children.

The board can delegate approval of the policies and can determine the frequency of review.

### 2.18 Sex and relationships education

The funding agreement requires trusts to have regard to the DfE's statutory guidance on sex and relationships education as well as the Education Act 1996. This includes the requirement to have an up-to-date policy which must:

◆  define sex and relationship education;

◆  describe how sex and relationship education is provided and who is responsible for providing it;

◆  say how sex and relationship education is monitored and evaluated; and

◆  include information about parents' right to withdrawal.

A copy of the policy must be provided to a parent of a registered pupil free of charge upon request.

The board can delegate approval of the policy and can determine the frequency of review.

### 2.19 Special educational needs

All academies must have regard to the *Special educational needs and disability code of practice: 0 to 25 years* which is published by the DfE and the Department of Health and Social Care as a result of provisions contained in the

Academies Act 2010. The code requires all schools and academies to set out their SEN policy information on their approach to supporting children and young people with SEN.

Academies are also required to provide a SEN Information Report under Section 69 Children and Families Act 2014 and The Special Educational Needs and Disability Regulations 2014, Part 3. The report must set out:

◆ arrangements for the admission of disabled persons as pupils at the school;

◆ steps taken to prevent disabled pupils from being treated less favourably than other pupils;

◆ facilities provided to assist access to the school by disabled pupils; and

◆ accessibility plan prepared in accordance with Schedule 10, paragraph 3, of the Equality Act 2010.

The Information Report must be approved by the board. It must be updated annually and as soon as possible during the year if any changes to the information occur.

## 2.20 Staff discipline, conduct and grievance procedures

All employers including trusts should have written procedures in place to deal with staff performance and conduct and to give them a route for complaints. The Advisory, Conciliation and Arbitration Service (ACAS) Statutory Code of Practice on discipline and grievance sets out basic practical guidance on handling disciplinary and grievance situations. While it is not compulsory to follow the Code, an employment tribunal could adjust any awards made in relevant cases by up to 25% for failure to comply with any provision.

## 2.21 Supporting pupils with medical conditions

Statutory guidance provides that boards should ensure that their academies develop a policy for supporting pupils with medical conditions in school. It is suggested that advice from relevant healthcare professionals may assist in the development of the policy.

Trust boards should ensure that the arrangements they set up include details on how the school's policy will be implemented effectively, including a named person who has overall responsibility for policy implementation

The policy should include:

◆ procedures to be followed whenever the academy is notified that a pupil has a medical condition;

◆ the role of individual healthcare plans and who is responsible for their development;

◆ roles and responsibilities of all those involved in the arrangements to support pupils with medical conditions including details of collaborative working arrangements;

- how staff will be supported in carrying out their role to support pupils with medical conditions and how this will be reviewed;
- how staff training needs are assessed, and how and by whom training will be commissioned and provided;
- arrangements for children who are competent to manage their own health needs and medicines;
- procedures to be followed for managing medicines;
- what should happen in an emergency situation;
- details of insurance arrangements which cover staff providing support to pupils with medical conditions; and
- how complaints may be made and will be handled concerning the support provided to pupils with medical conditions.

Consideration should also be given to whether to include references to home to school transport, defibrillators and/or asthma inhalers.

Although the guidance states that the policy must be reviewed regularly, it does not define a period and it is for the board to determine what is appropriate. The policy must be made readily accessible to parents and school staff.

### Test yourself 8.1

**Name any five statutory policies.**

### 2.22 Other statutory documents

There are a number of other documents that are required to be held.

#### Accessibility plan
Equality Act 2010: Schedule 10, Paragraph 3 and Disability Discrimination (prescribed Times and Periods for Accessibility Strategies and Plans for Schools) (England) Regulations 2005 require that a plan or strategy is put in place. The plan must be aimed at:

- increasing the extent to which disabled pupils can participate in the curriculum;
- improving the physical environment to enable disabled pupils to take better advantage of education, benefits, facilities and services provided; and
- improving the availability of accessible information to disabled pupils.

The board can delegate responsibility for the plan which does not need to follow a defined format. It must be reviewed every three years.

#### Central record of recruitment and vetting checks
This is a live document which records details of DBS checks carried out on members of staff (Independent School Standards Regulations 2010).

The articles of association also require enhanced DBS checks to be undertaken on trustees. Failure to undergo a DBS check or disclosure of information that would confirm their 'unsuitability to work with children' will result in that trustee being disqualified. Whilst the articles may not specify it, DBS checking should be carried out on all LGB governors as well.

The board can delegate responsibility for the record and, in practice, responsibility for maintenance lies with the headteacher/principal.

### Minutes of, and papers considered at, meetings of the board and its committees

The articles provide that minutes of any meeting of the board or a committee including any LGB, should be drawn up, formally approved at the next meeting and retained. Section 248 of the Companies Act 2006 requires that the minutes must be retained for at least 10 years. However, ICSA's recommendation is that they should be retained for the life of the company.

### Premises management documents

Trusts must ensure that all premises are managed and maintained to an acceptable standard of safety. Consideration must be given to health and safety, asbestos, fire safety, compliance with Disability Discrimination Act 1995, electrical testing and water hygiene. Documentation must be kept up-to-date and displayed as required.

The board may delegate responsibility for review and approval or all premises management documents to a trust committee, a trustee or the CEO/principal. In most MATs, responsibility will rest with a dedicated, specialist member of staff.

### Register of pupils' admission to school

The Education (Pupil Registration) (England) Regulations 2006: (SI 2006/1751, as subsequently amended) require that an admission register must be kept which contains an index of all pupils in alphabetical order together with the following details:

- name
- sex
- name of every parent of the pupil known to the school and details of the parent with whom the pupil normally resides
- day, month and year of birth
- day, month and year or admission or re-admission to the school
- name and address of the school last attended (if any)

The register is a live document and must be updated with any relevant new information received.

The board may delegate responsibility; in practice, responsibility is generally delegated to the CEO/principal who will direct appropriate staff to maintain the records.

### Register of pupils' attendance

The Education (Pupil Registration) (England) Regulations 2006 (SI 2006/1751, as subsequently amended) requires that an attendance register is kept. Records must be updated at the commencement of each morning session and once during the afternoon session stating whether each pupil is present, absent, attending an approved educational activity or unable to attend due to exceptional circumstances as set out within the Regulations.

In practice the responsibility for the register will be delegated to the headteacher/principal and the register updated daily by appropriate school staff.

# 3. Safeguarding and Disclosure and Barring Service (DBS) checks

The board are responsible for ensuring that all staff receive training that provides them with 'relevant skills and knowledge to safeguard children effectively' (Keeping Children Safe in Education). All staff must undergo safeguarding and child protection training in line with advice from the LSCB at induction and regular updates. They should also be provided with regular updates (e.g. via email, e-bulletins or staff meetings) at least annually.

The *Governance Handbook* states that it is 'helpful if everyone on the board has training about safeguarding, to make sure they have the knowledge and information needed to perform their functions and understand their responsibilities'.

The board should also ensure that pupils are taught about safeguarding through 'teaching and learning opportunities, as part of providing a broad and balanced curriculum' such as through personal, social, health and economic education (PSHE). Online safety training should be provided for both pupils and staff which is 'integrated, aligned and considered as part of the overarching safeguarding approach'.

The designated safeguarding lead and any deputies must undergo appropriate training to provide them with the knowledge and skills required to carry out the role which should be updated at least every two years.

Academies are also subject to the Prevent duty, as set out in the Counter-Terrorism and Security Act 2015, to have 'due regard to the need to prevent people from being drawn into terrorism'. All schools and academies must assess the risk of pupils being drawn into terrorism including support for extremist ideas that are part of terrorist ideology. Academies must have clear procedures in place for protecting children at risk of radicalisation which are usually included in the safeguarding policy.

Statutory guidance has been published on the Prevent duty which highlights the need for staff 'involved in the implementation of this duty' to receive appropriate training. In practice, this will be every member of staff. It would also be good practice for trustees to undergo training so that they recognise the requirements and can ensure that robust policies are in place. As a minimum, the designated safeguarding lead and any deputies must undertake Prevent awareness training so that they are able to provide advice and support to other members of staff. The Home Office has developed a core training product, Workshop to Raise Awareness of Prevent (WRAP).

The DfE has also published specific guidance on the Prevent duty in schools and academies.

Although not legally required, it is best practice for trustees and governors to undergo safeguarding and Prevent training. The *Governance Handbook 2017* provides that there a member of the board should 'take leadership responsibility for the organisation's wider safeguarding arrangements, which include the Prevent duty'. In practice, a member of each LGB is often delegated responsibility for oversight of safeguarding arrangements within their own academy. The model funding agreement requires that enhanced DBS certificates must be obtained for members of staff, supply staff, members and trustees. The requirement extends to include a member of any local governing body/advisory council, if relevant. An enhanced check shows spent and unspent convictions, cautions, reprimands and final warnings plus any information held by local police that's considered relevant to the role. Checking the barred lists will also show whether the applicant is on the list of people barred from doing the role.

For most trust appointments, an enhanced DBS certificate including barred list information will be required. Most staff will be engaged in regulated activity as a result of:

◆ responsibility, on a regular basis, for teaching, training instructing, caring for or supervising children;

◆ carrying out paid, or unsupervised unpaid, work regularly where that work provides an opportunity for contact with children; or

◆ engaging in intimate or personal care or overnight activity, even if this happens only once.

A charge is made for DBS checks for any paid positions. Disclosures for volunteers including trustees are technically free but will incur an administration charge.

There is no expiry date on a DBS check although the check represents a snapshot of the information accurate at the time that the check was carried out. DBS certificates from a previous role may be accepted by checking:

◆ the applicant's identity matches the details on the certificate

◆ the certificate is the right level and type for the role applied for

◆ if anything has changed via the update service

An individual can apply to register with the update service; the application must be received within 28 days of the DBS application or 30 days of the certificate being issued. There is a cost for registration and an ongoing annual fee (currently £13 per annum) unless it is for a volunteer, in which case there is no charge. The DBS certificate will then be portable from one job or voluntary role to the next unless:

◆ the employer requires a new certificate;

◆ a certificate for a different type of 'workforce' is required (e.g. a 'child workforce' certificate is required but an 'adult workforce' certificate is held); and

◆ a different level certificate is required (e.g. a standard DBS certificate is held and an enhanced one is required).

If a member of staff or trustee has been removed due to safeguarding concerns or would have been had they not resigned, the trust must have procedures in place to make a referral to DBS. It is an offence under the Safeguarding Vulnerable Groups Act 2006 not to provide this information which is punishable by a fine.

The articles provide that failure for a trustee to provide a DBS certificate, or if the certificate discloses information that the chairman, CEO or principal (depending on the terms of the articles) 'confirms their unsuitability to work with children' then they will be disqualified as a trustee.

### Test yourself 8.2

1. **In an academy settling, who is required to undertake safeguarding training?**

2. **For whom is an enhanced DBS check required?**

3. **Can the DBS certificate provided for a previous employer be accepted?**

# 4. Conflicts of interest and register

There have been numerous instances which have been picked up by the media, of academy bosses engaging members of their families to supply goods or services at great cost to the trusts that they run. The importance of having a fair and just process in place which is applied at all times is essential and obvious in these cases. Quite clearly, the individuals involved have a conflict of interest – their personal interests have influenced or, some cases, corrupted their motivation or decision making.

Financial or 'pecuniary' interests are easier to quantify objectively and are usually the primary focus. However, conflict can result from any personal interest even where the individual or their connection does not stand to gain financially.

The requirement is set out in section 175 of the Companies Act 2006:

> 'A director of a company must avoid a situation in which he has, or can have, a direct or indirect interest that conflicts, or possibly may conflict, with the interests of the company.'

An individual could have a 'direct' personal interest or an 'indirect' interest arising through a relative or another business that the individual is involved in to be regarded as a conflict. Trustees are, therefore, required by the Companies Act to avoid conflicts of interest and declare any interest in any transaction or arrangement or proposed transaction or arrangement prior to it taking effect.

The *Academies Financial Handbook* is very clear that trustees must understand and comply with their statutory duties as directors. In particular, trustees must avoid conflicts of interest. If any such interest arises, or may appear to arise, in any proposed transactions or arrangements, the trustee must declare their interest and it should be managed in accordance with the measures put in place to manage conflicts.

Trusts are the recipients of public funding and trustees must be mindful of this when dealing with trust resources. The *Handbook* sets out restrictions on related-party transactions which must be considered as a minimum. Not only should every potential conflict of interest should be identified and managed appropriately, but any situations where a trustee's interests or loyalties could be seen to potentially influence decision-making should be declared. This is sometimes known colloquially as the '*Daily Mail* test' – how would this look if it was reported by the press? If circumstances suggest that a decision could be influenced, then it should be disclosed. It is essential to ensure transparency.

It is good practice to have a policy on conflicts of interest which is publicly available and consistently applied.

When a trustee is absent from a meeting or part of a meeting due to a conflict of interest, they will not count towards the quorum.

Declarations of interest should be completed by all members, trustees, local governors (where applicable) and senior employees on first joining the trust and updated annually or as soon as possible following any changes. The declarations are used to complete a register of interests. The *Academies Financial Handbook* requires the 'relevant business and pecuniary interests of members, trustees, local governors and accounting officers' on their website; trusts have a discretion over publishing the interests of others (e.g. senior staff members) who may be named on the register of interests. Trustees should confirm whether the details contained in the register are accurate or provide updated information at each board meeting.

The *Academies Financial Handbook 2018* has detailed provisions relating to related party transactions due to the potential for conflict. Any such arrangements must be declared at the outset and managed appropriately. Related party transactions must be made at cost where the amount exceeds £2,500 cumulatively or individually in any financial year. From 1 April 2019, any related party transactions must be reported to ESFA and any above £20,000, either individually or cumulatively in a financial year, must have ESFA's prior approval.

In addition, trustees and LGB governors should be asked to declare any conflicts with any item on the agenda at the beginning of every meeting in which they are participating. The register should, theoretically at least, be presented to each board meeting and updated as necessary.

### Making it work 8.1

**In 2013, Al-Madinah school in Derby, the first Muslim free school in the country, was accused of conflicts of interest. A report by the DfE found that some of the trustees were 'closely involved' with suppliers either directly through their own supply company or through their family connections who supplied the school. Another trustee was providing human resource services to the school.**

# 5. Whistleblowing

The *Academies Financial Handbook 2018* states that trusts must have appropriate 'procedures in place for whistleblowing'. All staff must be made aware of who they can report their concerns to and the way that any concerns will be managed. It also requires that the trust 'must ensure that all concerns raised with them by whistleblowers are responded to properly and fairly'.

Whistleblowers can report their concerns to ESFA which will investigate any complaints raised. ESFA will respect the whistleblower's confidentiality when possible, though if an allegation is sufficiently serious it may reveal their identity without consent to take a case further.

Whistleblowing occurs when an individual raises concerns with an external body about wrongdoing, malpractice or risk that they have become aware of through their work. Generally, whistleblowers are protected by the provisions of the Public Interest Disclosure Act 1998 and should not be subjected to any detrimental treatment. Protected disclosures are those which tends to show that:

- a criminal offence has been committed, is being committed or is likely to be committed;
- a person has failed, is failing or is likely to fail to comply with any legal obligation to which he is subject;
- a miscarriage of justice has occurred, is occurring or is likely to occur;
- the health or safety of any individual has been, is being or is likely to be endangered;
- the environment has been, is being or is likely to be damaged; or
- information tending to show any matter falling within any one of the preceding paragraphs has been, is being or is likely to be deliberately concealed.

# Chapter summary

◆ Policies are high-level, strategically focused documents. While the board retains responsibility for policy development, most should be delegated to committees or the executive for review and approval.

◆ There are a number of statutory policies that all trusts/academies must have. Certain documents must be published on the website or made available to parents of pupils.

◆ The board must make sure that all staff undergo safeguarding and child protection and Prevent training and that pupils are taught about safeguarding. It is best practice that trustees and governors undertake safeguarding and Prevent training.

◆ An enhanced DBS certificate including barred list information must be obtained for members of staff, supply staff, members, trustees and any individual appointed to a local governing body/advisory council.

◆ Trustees must avoid conflicts of interest; where they do arise, they must be declared and managed appropriately. Declarations of interest should be completed by all members, trustees, local governors and senior employees on first joining the trust and at least updated annually. Declarations are used to complete a register of interests which should be published on the website.

◆ There is no legal requirement to have a whistleblowing policy but it is good practice to have one. Generally, whistleblowers have the benefit of legal protection.

# Chapter nine
# Information management

**CONTENTS**

## 1. Introduction

This chapter outlines the obligations and requirements placed on trusts both in dealing with information as well as in its interface with the outside world. We are living in a world where access to information is readily available for most people. The majority of secondary school students own smartphones, which they can use to view or download information or other media in milliseconds. The modern, digital age offers huge opportunities to everyone, but it needs to be carefully managed and relevant legislation and guidance followed.

## 2. Data protection and information sharing

In an increasingly digitised world, it is essential that the processing of data and sharing of information is carried out lawfully and fairly. A trust cannot carry out its functions without processing vast amounts of personal data. It is essential that this need is balanced against the rights and freedoms of individuals to ensure that information is collected and used fairly, stored securely and not disclosed unlawfully.

### 2.1  Freedom of Information Act 2000

Trusts are recipients of public funding and, therefore, under the obligations set out in the Freedom of Information Act 2000. They must provide public access to information so that there is transparency; this is achieved in two ways:

◆   by publishing certain information about activities; and

◆   by allowing members of the public to request information.

Any recorded information held is covered by the Act, including printed documents, computer files, letters, e-mails, photographs and sound or video recordings. It is not necessary to create documentation to respond to a request as the Act only relates to information already held in recorded form. It will, however, cover any documentation held on behalf of the trust by a third party even if it is physically held off-site.

Documentation which contains purely private or trade union information will not be covered by the Act, although individuals can make an application under the Data Protection Act 2018 if they wish to access their own personal data.

A Code of Practice, issued under the provisions of s. 46 of the Freedom of Information Act 2000, sets out good practice to:

◆   facilitate the disclosure of information under the Act by setting out good administrative practice to follow when handling requests for information, including, where appropriate, the transfer of a request to a different authority;

◆   protect the interests of applicants by setting out standards for the provision of advice which it would be good practice to make available to them and to encourage the development of effective means of complaining about decisions taken under the Act;

◆   facilitate consideration of the interests of third parties who may be affected by any decision to disclose information, by setting standards for consultation; and

◆   promote consideration of the implications for Freedom of Information before agreeing to confidentiality provisions in contracts and accepting information in confidence from a third party more generally.

### Publication of information

Trusts must adopt a publication scheme (essentially a policy) which sets out how it will meet its obligation to publish information including:

◆   the information that will be published;

◆   how and where that information is published; and

◆   whether the information is available free of charge.

In addition to the information that is published, a member of the public can make a request under the Act for further or more detailed information.

Trusts can adopt the model publication scheme produced by the ICO which states the information that it will make available to the public as part of normal business activities.

The publication scheme, a guide setting out the information that will be published and how it is available, as well as a schedule of fees should be displayed on the website, public notice board or by any other means that the trust normally communicates with the public. The information itself need not be published, though it is good practice to include it on a website if possible so that it can be accessed immediately. In any event, the information should be available 'promptly and automatically' to anyone who requests it.

### Requests for information

Members of the public can request information that is not listed in the publication scheme. It is not necessary for a request to mention the Freedom of Information Act or to direct it to a designated member of staff for it to fall under the remit of the Act. To be valid, a request must:

◆ Be in writing. A letter or e-mail are the most usual forms, though a request may be made via the web or a social networking site if this is a normal means of communication for the trust;

◆ Include the requester's real name. All requests should be treated equally and could be from an individual, a corporate body or by one person on behalf of another (e.g. a solicitor). Potential pseudonyms should be investigated as it may be possible to refuse a request if it is vexatious or repeated.

◆ Include an address for correspondence including a postal or e-mail address.

◆ Describe the information requested.

The requester does not need to give any reason for their request.

The Act requires the information to be provided within 20 school days or 60 working days if this is shorter. The time starts when the request is received, not when it has been passed to the designated officer or dealt with internally. Working days will apply if the time limit spans a holiday period and will relate to any day other than a Saturday, Sunday or public and bank holidays. Certain limited circumstances may allow extra time, but a written response must be provided within the time limit.

Charges may be made to cover costs of communication such as printing, photocopying and postage subject to specified limits. No charges may be levied for staff time spent in identifying or copying the information. A fees notice should be sent to the requester. Although the information need not be provided until the fee has been received, the time limit for complying with the request is not extended to take account for any delay in receipt. Information is often provided electronically removing the potential for any such charges.

A request can be refused entirely if:

◆ it would cost too much or take too much staff time to deal with the request;

◆ the request is vexatious; or

◆ the request is a repeat of a previous request from the same person.

The Act contains a number of exemptions which mean that information does not need to be released, but the majority of these are unlikely to apply to trusts. The most likely exemption will relate to any disclosure which would be 'likely to endanger the physical or mental health or the safety of any individual' complying with the request would be a breach of confidence or where someone requests their own personal data (which should be sought as a 'subject access request' under GDPR, incorporated in the Data Protection Act 2018).

Most exemptions require a 'public interest' test to be applied (i.e. whether the public interest considerations in favour of withholding the information outweigh the public interest considerations in disclosing it). Exempt information would include information:

◆   contravening the Data Protection Act;

◆   which could endanger the physical/mental health or safety of an individual;

◆   given in confidence;

◆   intended for publication in the future; and

◆   available by other means.

Any exempt elements of documents can be edited or erased/obliterated so that they are produced in a 'redacted' form.

## 2.2   Data protection

The Data Protection Act 2018 provides for the 'regulation of the processing of information relating to individuals, including the obtaining, holding, use or disclosure of such information'. It is based on six data protection principles which state that personal data must be:

**1.**   Processed fairly and lawfully.

**2.**   Processed only for the specified and legitimate purposes.

**3.**   Adequate, relevant and not excessive.

**4.**   Accurate and, where necessary, kept up to date.

**5.**   Not kept for longer than is necessary.

**6.**   Processed in a secure manner.

Trusts will be regarded as 'data controllers' and must, therefore, register with the Information Commissioner's Office. The Act regulates the use of 'personal data': any data which relates to a living individual who can be identified:

◆   from the data; or

◆   from the data and other information in the possession of, or which is likely to come into the possession of, the data controller.

It is necessary to show that one of the 'conditions for processing' is present to permit processing lawfully:

◆   The data subject has consented to the processing.

◆   The processing is necessary for the performance of a contract or to enter into a contract with the data subject.

◆ Processing is necessary because of a legal obligation.

◆ Processing is necessary to protect the data subject's, or another individuals' 'vital interests' (i.e. in the case of life or death).

◆ Processing is necessary for the administration of justice, for the exercise of any functions of either House of Parliament, for the exercise of any functions conferred on a person by an enactment or rule of law, for the exercise of any functions of the Crown, a Minister of the Crown or a government department, or for the exercise of any other functions of a public nature exercised in the public interest by a person.

◆ Processing is in accordance with the 'legitimate interests' condition.

The 'conditions' will apply more strictly where the information being processed is sensitive personal data.

### 2.3 Subject Access Request

Individuals can make a subject access request (SAR) to see any personal information that is held about them. The request must be made in writing setting out details of the information that is sought. A response should be provided within one month of receipt. Information can be withheld in very limited circumstances such as in connection with:

◆ the prevention, detection or investigation of a crime;

◆ national security or the armed forces;

◆ the assessment or collection of tax; and

◆ judicial or ministerial appointments.

A person with parental responsibility can obtain information relating to their child. However, it is the child who has the right of access to the information held on them and their best interests must always be considered; if the child is mature enough to understand their rights, the response should be made direct to them. Particular consideration should be given to:

◆ the child's level of maturity and ability to make decisions;

◆ the nature of the personal data;

◆ any court orders relating to parental access or responsibility that may apply;

◆ any duty of confidence owed to the child or young person;

◆ any consequences of allowing those with parental responsibility access to the child's or young person's information, especially if there have been allegations of abuse or ill treatment;

◆ any detriment to the child or young person if individuals with parental responsibility cannot access the information; and

◆ any views the child or young person has on whether their parents should have access to information about them.

## 2.4 General Data Protection Regulation (GDPR)

GDPR applies from 25 May 2018. According to the Information Commissioner's Office (ICO), GDPR has 'evolved from existing law' so that many of the concepts and principles are in line with those under the Data Protection Act albeit with some new elements and enhancements. GDPR applies to 'data controllers' as well as 'data processors' who process personal data on behalf of a controller.

GDPR applies to 'personal data' which is 'any information relating to an identifiable person who can be directly or indirectly identified by reference to an identifier'. There is a wide range of personal identifiers including name, photograph, audio/video recordings, identification number, location data or online identifier. Data can be automated or held in manual filing systems. Sensitive personal data is known as 'special categories of personal data' and includes information relating to:

◆ race
◆ ethnic origin
◆ politics
◆ religion
◆ trade union membership
◆ genetics
◆ biometrics (where used for identification purposes)
◆ health
◆ sex life
◆ sexual orientation

Article 6 sets out the lawful bases for processing which must apply whenever personal data is processed. Largely these require that processing is necessary to achieve the purpose. The lawful basis must be determined and documented before processing. The trust must provide a privacy notice which includes the lawful basis as well as the purposes for processing. It is necessary to identify a lawful basis for general processing and an additional condition for processing special category data or criminal conviction data. The lawful bases are:

◆ consent
◆ contract
◆ legal obligation
◆ vital interests
◆ public task
◆ legitimate interests

Article 5 of GDPR provides that personal information must be:

**(a)** processed lawfully, fairly and in a transparent manner in relation to the data subject ('lawfulness, fairness and transparency');

**(b)** collected for specified, explicit and legitimate purposes and not further processed in a manner that is incompatible with those purposes ('purpose limitation');

**(c)** adequate, relevant and limited to what is necessary in relation to the purposes for which it is processed ('data minimisation');

**(d)** accurate and, where necessary, kept up to date; every reasonable step must be taken to ensure that personal data that is inaccurate, having regard to the purposes for which it is processed, is erased or rectified without delay ('accuracy');

**(e)** kept in a form which permits identification of data subjects for no longer than is necessary for the purposes for which the personal data is processed ('storage limitation'); and

**(f)** processed in a manner that ensures appropriate security of the personal data, including protection against unauthorised or unlawful processing and against accidental loss, destruction or damage, using appropriate technical or organisational measures ('integrity and confidentiality').

GDPR grants a number of rights to individuals:

**(a)** The right to be informed about the collection and use of their personal data.

**(b)** The right of access to personal data and supplementary information to be aware of and verify the lawfulness of processing. A copy must be provided free of charge, normally within one month of receipt. A 'reasonable fee' may be charged where a request is manifestly unfounded or excessive or in respect of requests for further copies of the same information.

**(c)** The right to rectification of inaccurate personal data or completion if it is incomplete. A response must be given within one calendar month.

**(d)** The right to erasure, also known as 'the right to be forgotten'. A request may be made verbally or in writing and the controller has one month to respond.

**(e)** The right to restrict processing; personal data can be stored but not processed. A response must be given within one calendar month.

**(f)** The right to data portability so that individuals can obtain and reuse their personal data for their own purposes across different services.

**(g)** The right to object to:
- processing based on legitimate interests or the performance of a task in the public interest/exercise of official authority (including profiling);
- direct marketing (including profiling); and
- processing for purposes of scientific/historical research and statistics.

**(h)** Rights in relation to automated decision making and profiling.

Comprehensive but proportionate governance measures must be put in place to minimise the risk of breaches and uphold the protection of personal data.

Personal data must be processed by means of 'appropriate technical and organisational measures' – the 'security principle'.

Particular protection must be given when collecting and processing the personal data of children. Although consent is one possible lawful basis for processing, using an alternative basis may provide better protection for the child. Only children aged 13 or over are deemed able to give their own consent; under this age, consent must be obtained from the person with parental responsibility (with the exception of online preventative or counselling services).

Trusts are required to appoint a data protection officer (DPO) who can help to demonstrate compliance and are part of the enhanced focus on accountability. The DPO must be independent, an expert in data protection, adequately resourced and should report to the highest management level (i.e. CEO/principal). Article 39 GDPR defines the DPO's tasks as:

◆ to inform and advise about obligations to comply with the GDPR and other data protection laws;

◆ to monitor compliance with the GDPR and other data protection laws, and with data protection polices, including managing internal data protection activities; raising awareness of data protection issues, training staff and conducting internal audits;

◆ to advise on, and to monitor, data protection impact assessments (DPIA);

◆ to co-operate with the supervisory authority; and

◆ to be the first point of contact for supervisory authorities and for individuals whose data is processed (employees, customers etc).

The DPO is not personally liable for data protection compliance.

IT security must be fit for purpose and robust. There should be systems in place that protect data from accidental loss, destruction or damage as well as enabling the timely detection of any data breach. There should be agreed policies and procedures in place setting out how a data breach will be investigated and reported. Certain types of personal data breach must be reported to the ICO as the relevant supervisory authority within 72 hours of becoming aware of the breach. The breach should also be notified to any individual concerned without undue delay if it is likely to result in a high risk of adversely affecting their rights and freedoms.

There are massive penalties for non-compliance with GDPR with fines of up to €20 million or 4% of worldwide turnover as well as possible compensation claims from individuals.

## Test yourself 9.1

**What are the lawful bases for processing personal data out in GDPR?**

# 3. Website

All schools are required to upload information and documentation on their websites. Regular website reviews should be undertaken to make sure that it is compliant with requirements. The DfE has guidance on its website which details 'What academies, free schools and colleges should publish online'. It is not always entirely obvious as the requirements arise from a variety of sources.

The model funding agreement requires the following to be uploaded:

- funding agreement, memorandum and articles of association;
- the annual report and accounts;
- the names of the trustees; and
- the names of the members.

The current version of the articles adopted must be uploaded to the website – these may not be the version that was originally attached to the funding agreement but a subsequently adopted version. The articles may not reflect the provisions of the latest model version.

If requested, a paper copy of the information on the website must be provided to a parent free of charge.

## 3.1  Contact details

The website must include:

- The name of the academy
- Postal address
- Telephone number
- Name of the member of staff who deals with queries from parents and other members of the public
- Name of the headteacher or principal
- Name and address of the chair of the governing board
- Name and details of the special educational needs co-ordinator (SENCo) if it is a mainstream academy

## 3.2  Sponsor

If the trust is sponsored, the website should contain information about:

- the full name and contact details (address and a telephone number) where the sponsor is an individual; and
- the address and telephone number of the office where the sponsor is a group or organisation.

## 3.3  Admissions

The admission arrangements (which must be compliant with the School Admissions Code and School Admission Appeals Code) must be published and kept on the website for the full duration of the offer year (i.e. the school year in which offers for places are made). Alternatively, details should be provided of how the arrangements may be obtained through the local authority.

Information should set out ow applications are considered including:

◆ any arrangements in place for selecting the pupils who apply;

◆ oversubscription criteria (how places are offered if there are more applicants that places; and

◆ an explanation of the process parents need to follow if they want to apply for their child to attend.

The DfE also recommends that information about admission arrangements are published for 16 to 19 academies and colleges a year before the beginning of the academic year, including details of:

◆ open days that are planned;

◆ the process for applying for a place; and

◆ whether there is priority to applications from pupils enrolled at particular schools.

The admission appeals timetable setting out the dates by which appeals will be organised and heard must be published by 28 February each year.

## 3.4  Annual report and accounts

Financial information published should include:

◆ annual report;

◆ annual audited accounts;

◆ memorandum of association;

◆ articles of association;

◆ names of charity trustees and members; and

◆ funding agreement.

The *Academies Financial Handbook* provides that trusts must publish the annual accounts on their website no later than the end of January following the financial year to which the accounts relate.

The funding agreement permits the Secretary of State to publish the trust's annual reports and accounts, and the audit report.

### 3.5  Company information

Trusts are registered companies and must comply with the requirements of the Company, Limited Liability Partnership and Business (Names and Trading Disclosures) Regulations 2015 (SI 2015/17). The trust must state the full registered name of the trust company on its website(s) (including, in MATs, all individual academy school websites) as well as:

◆   the company registration number;

◆   place of registration (i.e. registered in England and Wales); and

◆   registered office address.

The information must be in legible characters and failure to publish it may result in a fine. It does not need to appear on every page.

This information should also be included on 'business letters' and electronic communications that could be considered to be business letters including all order forms, notices, official publications, bills of exchange, promissory notes, endorsements, cheques, invoices, receipts, letters of credit or orders for money or goods purporting to be signed by, or on behalf of, the trust.

### 3.6  Curriculum

Publication of information about the academy's curriculum on the website must include:

◆   the content of the curriculum in each academic year for every subject;

◆   its approach to the curriculum;

◆   where applicable, the names of any phonics or reading schemes in operation for Key Stage 1;

◆   where applicable, the GCSE options and other Key Stage 4 qualifications, or other future qualifications specified by the Secretary of State, offered by the academy;

◆   how the academy meets the 16 to 19 study programme requirements and the qualifications offered; and

◆   how parents (including parents of prospective pupils) can obtain more information about the academy's curriculum.

### 3.7  Equality objectives

Trusts are public bodies and must comply with the public-sector equality duty set out in the Equality Act 2010.

The trust must prepare equality objectives which show how the trust will meet the aims of the general equality duty.

The equality objectives (updated every four years) and information showing how the aims of the public-sector equality duty are being met (updated annually) must be published on the website under the requirements of the Equality Act 2010 (Specific Duties) Regulations 2011. The information must include information relating to persons who are employees or 'other persons affected by its policies and practices' such as pupils.

Details must be included about:

◆ eliminating discrimination;

◆ improving equality of opportunity for people with protected characteristics; and

◆ consulting and involving those affected by inequality in the decisions the trust or academy takes to promote equality and eliminate discrimination.

## 3.8 Examination and assessment results

Details about examination and assessment results must be uploaded in accordance with the relevant Key Stage (KS). It must be updated as soon as possible after it is available and at least annually.

### Key Stage 2
◆ Percentage of pupils who achieved the expected standard in reading, writing and maths.

◆ Average progress that pupils have made in reading between KS1 and KS2.

◆ Average progress that pupils have made in writing between KS1 and KS2.

◆ Average progress that pupils have made in maths between KS1 and KS2.

◆ Percentage of pupils who achieved a higher standard in reading, writing and maths.

◆ Pupils' average score in the reading test.

◆ Pupils' average score in the maths test.

### Key Stage 4
◆ Progress 8 score.

◆ Attainment 8 score.

◆ Percentage of students who achieved a strong pass (grade 5 or above) in English and maths.

◆ Percentage of pupils entering for the English Baccalaureate.

◆ Percentage of pupils who achieved the English Baccalaureate.

◆ Percentage of students staying in education or employment after KS4 (destinations).

GCSE grading has been moved onto a new 1–9 system. During the transition, the EBacc pass level will be based on grade 5 or above for reformed subjects and grade C and above for unformed subjects.

### Key Stage 5
◆ Progress students have made compared with students across the country, shown separately for A levels, academic, applied general and tech level qualifications.

◆ The average grade students got at KS5, shown separately for A levels, academic, applied general and tech level qualifications.

◆ Progress students made in English and maths.

◆ Retention (the proportion of students who get to the end of the main programme of study that they enrolled on) shown separately for A levels, academic, applied general and tech level qualifications.

◆ Destinations (percentage of students who continue in education or training, or move on to employment in the year after the end of KS4).

### 3.9 Exclusion arrangements

Details of the policy for excluding pupils must be published.

### 3.10 Gender pay gap reporting

Any trust with more than 250 employees must publish statutory calculations showing the pay gap is between their male and female employees (The Equality Act 2010 (Gender Pay Gap Information) Regulations 2017 (SI 2017/172). The trust must publish information annually on their own website as well as on a government website:

◆ average gender pay gap (both mean and median averages);

◆ average bonus gender pay gap (both mean and median averages);

◆ proportion of males and females receiving a bonus payment; and

◆ proportion of male and female full-pay relevant employees in lower, lower middle, upper middle and upper quartile pay bands.

A wide definition of 'employee' is used so that not only those employees on the normal payroll will be included, but also workers such as some self-employed people.

It is not compulsory to provide any narrative or explanation with calculations, but it may be helpful to provide some reasoning for any gender gap identified and details of actions that are being taken to reduce or eliminate it.

### 3.11 Governance

The *Academies Financial Handbook* requires that details of the governance arrangements must be published on the trust's website in a 'readily accessible format' including:

◆ the structure and remit of the members, board of trustees, its committees and local governing bodies (the trust's scheme of delegation for governance functions), and the full names of the chair of each (where applicable);

◆ for each member who has served at any point over the past 12 months, their full names, date of appointment, date they stepped down (where applicable), and relevant business and pecuniary interests including governance roles in other educational institutions;

- for each trustee and local governor who has served at any point over the past 12 months, their full names, date of appointment, term of office, date they stepped down (where applicable), who appointed them (in accordance with the trust's articles), and relevant business and pecuniary interests including governance roles in other educational institutions. If the trust's accounting officer is not a trustee their relevant business and pecuniary interests must still be published;

- for each trustee their attendance records at board and committee meetings over the last academic year;

- for each local governor their attendance records at local governing body meetings over the last academic year; and

- the board of trustees must prepare an annual governance statement; this is published within the annual accounts and published on the website. For new trusts producing audited accounts for the first time, this includes 'what they have done to review and develop their governance structure' as well as the composition of the board. Established trusts should also include an 'assessment of the trust's governance, including a review of the composition of the board in terms of skills, effectiveness, leadership and impact'.

### 3.12 Ofsted reports

The website must either:

- publish a copy of the academy's most recent Ofsted report; or
- publish a link to the most recent Ofsted report.

### 3.13 Performance tables

A link to the school and college performance tables must be published.

### 3.14 PE and sport premium for primary schools

The premium is given to primary schools to make 'additional and sustainable improvements to the quality of PE and sport' that is offered to pupils. The premium should be used to:

- develop or add to the PE and sport activities that is already offered; and
- build capacity and capability within the academy to ensure that improvements made now will benefit pupils joining the school in future years.

The grant funding agreement provides that the following must be published:

- how much PE and sport premium funding was received for the current academic year;
- a full breakdown of how the funding was spent or will be spent in the current year;

◆ the effect of the premium on pupils' PE and sport participation and attainment; and

◆ how the academy will make sure that the improvements are sustainable.

## 3.15 Policies

Certain policies should be available on the website:

◆ Behaviour policy, including discipline, exclusions and anti-bullying strategy which complies with section 89 of the Education and Inspections Act 2006.

◆ Charging and remissions policy including details of activities/cases where a charge will be made to parents and the circumstances where an exception will be made on a payment normally expected under the policy.

◆ Procedure for handling complaints from parents of children with special educational needs about the support provided by the school (SEND Code of Practice, January 2015).

◆ Safeguarding including child protection policy.

Whilst not legally obligatory, the DfE recommends publication of:

◆ Complaints policy

◆ Whistleblowing policy

## 3.16 Pupil Premium (PP)

Pupil Premium funding is additional funding given to 'raise the attainment of disadvantaged pupils of all abilities and to close the gaps between them and their peers'. An amount is received in respect of each pupil registered as eligible for free school meals (FSM) at any point in the last six years.

The funding agreement requires publication of information about PP:

◆ the amount of PP allocation during the current financial year;

◆ what the PP will be spent on;

◆ what the PP allocation was spent on in the previous financial year; and

◆ the impact of the previous year's PP allocation on educational attainment.

In addition, the DfE recommends publication of:

◆ details of the PP strategy;

◆ details of the main barriers to educational achievement that the disadvantaged children in the academy face;

◆ how PP funding will be spent to overcome these barriers and the reasons for the approach chosen;

◆ how the effect of PP will be measured; and

◆ the date of the next PP strategy review.

School performance tables also report on the performance of disadvantaged pupils compared with their peers.

### 3.17 Register of interests

Whilst the register of business and pecuniary interests must include details relating to members, trustees, local governors and the accounting officers. Trusts have a discretion over who else should be included but consideration should be given to including the senior leadership team, business manager and anyone else with any purchasing authority.

### 3.18 Slavery

Commercial organisations that supply goods or services in the UK and with an annual turnover of £36 million or more (including any subsidiaries, wherever based) are required to publish a slavery and human trafficking statement. This requirement, imposed by the Modern Slavery Act 2015, must be updated annually. Government guidance suggests that any incorporated organisation meeting the criteria will be caught by the provisions irrespective of whether it pursues primarily charitable or educational aims. Legislation has now been extended to specifically include 'public bodies'.

The statement must set out the steps it has taken during the financial year to ensure that slavery and human trafficking is not taking place in any part of the trust or academies. It must be formally approved by the board and signed by a trustee.

### 3.19 Special educational needs and disabilities (SEND)

A special educational needs (SEN) information report must be published which sets out the policy for pupils or students with SEN and how this policy is put into effect. The information must be updated annually and, if there are changes during the year, as soon as possible. The report must comply with:

◆ Section 69 of the Children and Families Act 2014 including:
  – arrangements for the admission of disabled pupils
  – steps that have been taken to prevent disabled pupils from being treated less favourably than other pupils
  – facilities provided to help disabled pupils to access the academy
  – the accessibility plan.
◆ Regulation 51 and Schedule 1 to the Special Educational Needs and Disability Regulations 2014.
◆ Section 6 of the Special Educational Needs and Disability Code of Practice: 0–25 years.

The report must include details of:

◆ admission arrangements for pupils with SEND;
◆ steps taken to prevent pupils with SEND from treated less favourably than other pupils;

- access facilities for pupils with SEND; and
- an accessibility plan.

### Accessibility plan for disabled pupils

Accessibility planning must be carried out for disabled pupils under the requirements of the Equality Act 2010 (Schedule 10, paragraph 3). The accessibility plan must be published which should include details of how the academy will:

- increase disabled pupils' ability to participate in the curriculum;
- improve the physical environment so disabled pupils can take better advantage of the education, benefits, facilities and services offered; and
- improve the availability of accessible information to disabled pupils.

The accessibility plan need not be a freestanding document but could be incorporated into another document such as the school development plan.

### 3.20 Values and ethos

A statement of the values and ethos should be published.

### 3.21 Year 7 literacy and numeracy catch up premium grant

The funding agreement requires publication of information about the Year 7 literacy and numeracy catch up premium grant on the website:

- the amount of catch-up premium grant that it will be received during the current financial year;
- what the catch-up grant will be spent on;
- what the catch-up grant was spent on in the previous financial year; and
- the impact of the previous year's catch-up grant on educational attainment and how that effect was assessed.

### Stop and think 9.1

**Why might it be good to ensure that all requirements for uploading information to the website have been complied with? Are there positives apart from purely compliance?**

# 4. Social media

Social media is part of the world we now live in. It is routinely used in classrooms to encourage pupil engagement and independent learning – the majority of pupils, certainly at secondary level, will already own a smartphone and be active on social media networks. Many teachers and educationalists use social media for blogging, engaging in debates or gaining valuable continuing professional development (CPD). Many trusts and individual academies use social media as a rapid and accessible form of communication as well as a platform for promoting the school.

All trusts must consider the use of social media, recognising any risks that may arise. There should be comprehensive policies and procedures in place which establish good working practices. There are clear links between the potential misuse of social media and the board's safeguarding responsibilities including child protection issues, grooming and cyber-bullying.

The permanent nature of social media should not be ignored. People's movements and comments can be used as evidence in courtrooms. Particular care should be taken when uploading photos or videos on social media to ensure that appropriate consent has been given where necessary. There should be detailed guidelines in place around what is acceptable for comment or content; certain subjects such as politics or religion may be specifically banned. Trust/academy accounts should not follow or link to other content, accounts or pages that are inappropriate.

There should also be a policy on the use of social media by staff. There must be very clear guidelines around connecting with pupils on social media – in most cases it will be unacceptable for staff to connect with pupils. Staff should also ensure that they have rigorous privacy settings on social network sites to avoid photographs taken in social settings or exchanges of comments with friends from becoming more widely available and causing embarrassment.

Trustees, governors and other volunteers should also be required to adopt a code of conduct and agree to comply with relevant guidelines relating to social media.

## Making it work 9.1

**There are regularly stories in the press of teachers who have been suspended from their posts following inappropriate posts on social media. Although these are generally extreme cases, staff can easily find themselves in a difficult or embarrassing situation if they post photos or content that may offend or bring their school or the profession into disrepute. Social media is not the place to boast of a terrible hangover or sexual conquest!**

# 5. Get Information About Schools (GIAS)

**GIAS** is a register of schools and colleges in England. Information is held on establishments (academies), establishment groups (MATs) and governors and trustees. GIAS replaces and expands the DfE's EduBase.

Details of the individuals involved in the leadership and management of the trust must be updated through the GIAS service. Information is stored on:

**Get information about schools**
An online register of schools and colleges in England which holds information on establishments, establishment groups (e.g. MATs) and governors/ trustees (replaces EduBase).

- members (including any who left in the last 12 months) and who they were appointed by and appointment date;
- trustees (including any who left in the last 12 months), who they were appointed by and term of office;
- chair of trustees;
- members of any local governing body (including any who left in the last 12 months); and
- chair of the local governing body.

Details are kept on the names of the individuals, who they were appointed by and the start and end of their term of office.

Trusts can update their records via Secure Access. Accounts are managed by an approver within the trust, which means that local authorities or clerking services are unable to update governance details.

# Chapter summary

- As recipients of public funding, trusts must comply with the obligations set out in the Freedom of Information Act 2000. Public access to information enables transparency by publishing certain information about activities as well as obligations to respond to requests for information from members of the public.
- Information relating to individuals is protected by the Data Protection Act 1998. Trusts are 'data controllers' and must register with the Information Commissioner's Office. Individuals can make a subject access request (SAR) to see any personal information that is held about them.
- The General Data Protection Regulation (GDPR) applies from 25 May 2018 expanding and enhancing previous data protection legislation. 'Data controllers' and 'data processors' must process personal data in accordance with GDPR. Individuals are granted a number of rights. Trusts must appoint a data protection officer (DPO).
- All schools are required to upload information and documentation on their websites. They must also ensure that information on Get Information About Schools (GIAS) is kept up-to-date including information about individuals involved in the leadership and management of the trust.
- The use of social media should be considered and comprehensive policies and procedures adopted.

# Chapter ten
# Performance management and reviews

**CONTENTS**

## 1. Introduction

This chapter outlines the ways in which performance management and reviews can help to inform the leadership and management of a trust, enabling an effective planning cycle – assess, plan, do, review. This cycle supports a self-improving system based on planning and analysis. It is a simple system which can be used for the trust organisation, governance or individuals within the trust – albeit the actual processes involved will differ.

The chapter also looks at the way that strategic objectives are set, both on an organisational and individual level and how these shape the performance management and evaluation processes. Objectives must be clear, with the wording carefully drafted: it is essential that the individual is involved in framing the objective which will enable them to embrace it and work towards achieving it.

There is also a place for external reviews of governance. Sometimes recommended by Ofsted, ERGs allow for an independent perspective on the trust's governance structures and the ability of the board to facilitate effective, long term improvements.

## 2. Setting strategic objectives and key indicators

The *Governance Handbook* states that the purpose of governance is to 'provide confident, strategic leadership'. One of the core functions of the trust board is strategic leadership: setting the 'overall strategic framework, including its vision and strategic priorities'. The board leave the operational aspects of running the trust to the CEO that it has appointed.

Strategic leadership is the first of the six key features of effective governance identified in the *Governance Handbook* that sets and champions vision, ethos and strategy through:

- a clear and explicit vision for the future set by the board, in collaboration with executive leaders, which has pupil progress and achievement at its heart and is communicated to the whole organisation;

- strong and clear values and ethos which are defined and modelled by the board, embedded across the organisation and adhered to by all that work in it, or on behalf of it;

- strategic planning that defines medium to long-term strategic goals, and development and improvement priorities which are understood by all in the organisation;

- processes to monitor and review progress against agreed strategic goals and to refresh the vision and goals periodically and as necessary including at key growth stages or if performance of the organisation drops;

- mechanisms for enabling the board to listen, understand and respond to the voices of parents/carers, pupils, staff, local communities and employers;

- determination to initiate and lead strategic change when this is in the best interests of children, young people and the organisation, and to champion the reasons for, and benefits of, change to all stakeholders;

- procedures for the board to set and manage risk appetite and tolerance; ensuring that risks are aligned with strategic priorities and improvement plans and that appropriate intervention strategies are in place and embedding risk management at every level of governance; and

- an informed decision on whether to form, join or grow a group of schools which is underpinned by robust due diligence and an awareness of the need to review the effectiveness of governance structures and processes if and when the size, scale and complexity of the organisation changes.

The board must ensure that the framework is robust with clear accountability and monitoring of progress against the vision. The board should set clear key performance indicators (KPIs) that are a quantifiable measure which can be used to determine how well the strategic objectives have been met. Each trust will set their own KPIs to reflect their criteria, priorities or current strength as an organisation. KPIs are:

- Quantitative: they can be presented in the form of numbers or based on some other measurement.
- Practical: they integrate well with current processes.
- Directional: they help to determine if there has been improvement.
- Actionable: they can be put into practice to effect desired change.

Section 414 of the Companies Act 2006 requires companies, including trusts, to include an analysis using financial KPIs as well as analysis using other KPIs including information relating to environmental and employee matters in the annually produced strategic report. KPIs could include:

◆ Ofsted inspection outcome
◆ SATs/KS4/KS5 results
◆ Pupil attendance data
◆ Surplus funds at year end
◆ Unrestricted funds to be in surplus
◆ Pupil numbers
◆ Percentage of income spent on staffing costs
◆ Staff performance reviews

The *Academies Financial Handbook 2018* specifically requires trusts to select financial KPIs. The board must measure performance against these financial KPIs regularly with an analysis included in the annual trustees' report.

The board must recognise its strategic role and not step over the line into operational matters which are the remit of the CEO and executive team. Trustees must also ensure that they act in the best interests of all children and young people within the trust; defining the framework for strategic development and against which progress is measured, will ensure that an objective approach is adopted across the trust.

## Test yourself 10.1

1. **What factors should be included in key performance indicators to make them effective?**

2. **Give some examples of types of KPIs that could be set.**

## 2.1 Self-evaluation

To establish meaningful KPIs, it is essential to have a realistic view of the current position of the trust and/or academy. Trustees must be confident that they have an up-to-date and accurate picture of performance and other aspects within their academy or academies.

Ofsted previously required schools to complete a standard self-evaluation form (SEF) which informed inspection and was intended to be part of the ongoing school self-improvement process. The rationale was that thorough and rigorous self-evaluation provided the best means for identifying strengths, weaknesses and areas for improvement; schools could achieve this by asking two key questions: How well are we doing? How can we do better?

The standard SEF was criticised for being time-consuming and bureaucratic and was subsequently withdrawn. However, although there is no longer any expectation for schools and academies to complete a centrally designed SEF, they are expected to evaluate themselves rigorously and Ofsted expect a summary of any self-evaluation to be available at the start of any inspection. This should focus on the academy's specific priorities and risks. In making their decision relating to the effectiveness of leadership and management, Ofsted inspectors will consider 'the rigour and accuracy of self-evaluation and how well it leads to planning that secures continual improvement'. *The Ofsted School Inspection Handbook* specifically states: 'Ofsted does not require self-evaluation to be graded or provided in a specific format. Any assessment that is provided should be part of the school's business processes and not generated solely for inspection purposes.'

Self-evaluation will be undertaken by the executive, who reflect on the practice in the academy, identifying areas of progress and aspects which require further improvement. The evaluation will be dependent on gathering a variety of data, both internal and external. The self-evaluation should be recorded in some format that remains a live document: it is common practice for it to be RAG-rated and highlighted red, amber, green according to the progress in each priority area.

Self-evaluation is a continuous process that informs the planning and reporting schedule of the academy. The leadership, executive and trustees/governors, must be able to refer to convincing evidence of successes and have a clear plan of action to demonstrate how improvements will be made. Trustees, governors and the executive are better able to carry out their responsibilities effectively where there is a robust, open and honest process of self-evaluation.

Responsibility for conducting and updating the self-evaluation rests with the leadership and management of the trust and/or academy and must, therefore, have the full input of trustees/governors. The *Competency Framework for Governance* specifies that everyone on the board should participate in the trust's 'self-evaluation of activities relating to financial performance, efficiency and control'. However, the board should have an involvement in all aspects of the self-evaluation, challenging and questioning the decisions taken on the basis of information and data available. The priorities in the self-evaluation should be drawn directly from the strategic priorities set by the board.

### 2.2  SWOT and PESTLE analysis

Boards often use a SWOT analysis to conduct a formal examination of strengths, weaknesses, opportunities and threats faced by the trust:

◆ *Strengths*. Factors or characteristics that give the trust an advantage and are likely to have a positive effect in achieving objectives.

◆ *Weaknesses*. Factors or characteristics that place the trust at a disadvantage or are likely to have a negative effect or be a barrier.

◆ *Opportunities*. Elements that are likely to have a positive effect on the trust/academy or that could be exploited to the trust's advantage.

◆ *Threats*. Elements or conditions that could cause upset or cause difficulties for the trust or make the objectives unachievable.

Both internal and external aspects should be considered and typically strengths and weaknesses will identify those internal characteristics whilst opportunities and threats will consider external aspects.

The SWOT analysis is a useful tool in auditing the current position and form the basis of future planning. It is most effective when conducted in a brainstorming type session and will enable a comprehensive analysis.

Trusts may occasionally also use PESTLE analysis which looks specifically at the external, macro-environmental factors. This can be particularly useful in the context of MAT growth and consideration of expansion plans:

◆ *Political*. The extent to which the government may influence policy or the economy more widely e.g. tax or educational policy, etc.

◆ *Economic*. The economic factors that could directly impact a trust e.g. a rise in inflation, interest rates, etc.

◆ *Socio-cultural*. The environment in which the trust operates e.g. cultural trends, demographics, populations analytics, etc.

◆ *Technological*. Innovations that may affect the sector e.g. the impact of technological awareness, etc.

◆ *Legal*. The legal and regulatory environment in which the trust operates as well as the internal policies and schemes of delegation e.g. DfE regulation, employment law, etc.

◆ *Environmental*. Any factors that are determined by the surrounding environment (e.g. geographical location, etc). The importance of each category will vary from trust to trust according to individual circumstances.

The SWOT and PESTLE analysis are simple yet effective tools which can be used to assess the current and future situation of a trust. They can be used to effectively underpin strategic planning, giving a rounded picture of the trust's current position and looking to identify outside factors that could impact on performance or development. However, neither analysis is of value without a plan to take forward the ideas generated.

# 3. Performance management

Trusts rely on staff to operate. The quality of staff and their effectiveness will make or break trusts and their academies. The Chartered Institute of Personnel and Development defines performance management as the 'activity and set of processes that aim to maintain and improve employee performance in line with an organisation's objectives'. Good performance management will take a holistic approach and will use various tools such as objective setting, appraisals and feedback, training and development and performance-related pay.

The *Academies Financial Handbook 2018* states that one of the core functions of governance that trustees should focus on is 'holding executive leaders to account for the educational performance of the organisation and its pupils, and the performance management of staff'. It is through effective performance management processes that the trustees can ensure that their strategic vision is being progressed and work undertaken to realise the objectives. Although in practice trustees will not be responsible for the performance management of all staff, they must ensure that processes are robust, fair and transparent and that objective setting and appraisals are being carried out in accordance with agreed policy.

The trust should use performance management to enable all staff to perform to the best of their abilities. Performance management policies normally provide for individuals to agree objectives with their line manager which tie in to the overall school and/or trust development plan as well as reflecting their job description and ambition. Regular reviews should take place to ensure that the individual is on track; support, coaching or training should be available as appropriate. *The School Teachers' Pay and Conditions* document applies to maintained schools and is adopted, or the approach followed, by many trusts. The document has been through a rigorous consultation process with the teaching unions who set clear expectations regarding the application of appraisal policies. Furthermore, the teaching unions have model policies which are based on the concept of the appraisal process as 'developmental and supportive' and intended to 'foster professional dialogue between colleagues'.

*The School Teachers' Pay and Conditions* is structured around performance related pay; the premise is that ongoing contributions and good performance will be recognised and rewarded through the pay system. In theory, it is an incentive for continuous improvement in performance. The *Governance Handbook* states: 'Boards must assure themselves that the arrangements proposed for linking appraisal to pay progression are robust and can be applied consistently.'

Performance management is not simply to ensure the success of the trust in meeting its objectives. Staff need to know what is expected of them in terms of performance and behaviour and understand that this will lead to proper recognition and reward in return. A good performance management process will treat all staff fairly, encouraging excellent employee relations and high levels of productivity and staff well-being. The process will measure performance, but it should also support training and development.

Performance management should apply to all employees although there may need to be different approaches within a policy for the executive team, teaching colleagues and the various categories of support staff. The trust board will be responsible for approving the performance management policy and for the performance management of the CEO of a MAT or principal of a SAT. Performance management for the rest of the staff body is normally delegated to the executive, albeit in many community MATs, members of the local governing board may be involved in the performance management of the headteacher/head of school for their academy. Of course, the exact processes for performance management will differ hugely across trusts: large trusts are likely to have the benefit of employment specialists on whom they can rely for advice and support on any employment or performance issues.

The clerk/company secretary should also have a process for a performance review irrespective of how they are employed or engaged. At the very least, there should be an annual review of performance against the job description or service level agreement/external contract to establish strengths and weaknesses and to identify areas for future development or training. In an employee setting, the clerk/company secretary should be involved in setting their own formal objectives in accordance with the trust's policy. Where a clerk is engaged through a third party, such as a local authority governance service, performance management may well be undertaken as part of their employment contract. Nevertheless, a review should be carried out to establish whether clerking services meet requirements. Support including training, coaching or other CPD should be made available to the clerk/company secretary as appropriate.

## 3.1  Objective setting

The performance management process relies on the setting of objectives. It is important that there is clarity around objectives and exactly what is expected of all staff in terms of their performance. Care in setting objectives will avoid issues later around a lack of understanding or differences in expectation. Although objectives may be agreed verbally, these should always be finalised by clear, written communications which fit within the overall performance management policy.

Objective setting can, however, be very challenging to ensure that they are precise, appropriate, offering the relevant level of challenge whilst managing the school's progress; objectives must be ambitious but achievable. Objectives provide clarity around expectations and should link with the trust or academy's strategic objectives. Objectives are also important because they form the basis on which that individual's performance will be judged.

The performance management process should be constructed in a way that allows all individuals to be involved in setting objectives, they should be agreed rather than imposed. Research has found that staff are more motivated to achieve objectives that they have been involved in setting.

It is now generally agreed that objectives should be SMART: specific, measurable, achievable, relevant and time bound. This ensures that objectives can be set that are meaningful and against which progress can be measured.

◆ Specific. The objective should be precise and clear with no ambiguous statements. The desired outcome or result should be defined and identified.

◆ Measurable. It should be possible to demonstrate achievement of the objective by means of some indicators or quantification. Consideration should be given to whether external data will be available or whether evaluation or assessment will be required internally and who will be responsible.

◆ Achievable. It must be within the individual's capabilities to achieve the objective and should not be reliant on circumstances that the individual has no control over. Objectives should be challenging and offer an opportunity for self-development, but they should not be impossible to achieve. Consideration should be given to the resources available to the individual and whether lack of availability or funding may render an objective impossible.

◆   Relevant. Objectives should relate to the most important, identified priorities and these should link to the overall strategic objectives of the trust/academy.

◆   Time-framed. A date should be set for the completion of each objective. Some objectives may be long-term and may span several years. In these cases, a series of phased milestones should be agreed against which progress can be reviewed and achievement measured.

## Making it work 10.1

◆   **Objective 1: To work with all stakeholders to ensure a smooth process to achieve academy status**

   **This objective may not be achievable as it relies on external parties and processes.**

◆   **Objective 2: To achieve an Outstanding Ofsted grading**

   **It may not be possible to meet this objective within a normal one-year performance cycle as it is dependent on Ofsted conducting a full visit!**

◆   **Objective 3: All pupils to meet age-related expectations and to be making expected progress**

   **This is a SMART target and may be appropriate for a teacher with a full-time classroom commitment. The context would need to be considered to establish whether the objective was achievable.**

### 3.2   CEO/principal performance management

Although there is no specific legal requirement for a performance management process for the CEO/principal, it will generally be the route by which the board ensures progress is made towards the strategic objectives – the CEO/principal is formally held to account for the progress made and tasked with carrying forward the key priorities for the coming year.

A report, *Effectively Managing Headteacher Performance*, produced by the National College for Teaching and Leadership in 2014 makes clear that 'one size does not fit all' in terms of performance management and trusts can take steps to 'improve and refine their processes for their own needs, as well as for meeting external demands'. However, the report identifies ten features of effective headteacher performance management:

1.   Integrated with the school development plan.

2.   Has a secure annual cycle of objective-setting and review together with interim monitoring.

3.   Underpinned by sound relationships, characterised by openness, trust and integrity, among all those involved.

4. Involves the setting of meaningful and challenging but achievable objectives for the headteacher.

5. Strikes an appropriate balance among internal and external accountability, development and reward.

6. Makes use of a wide variety of data from a range of sources to inform and underpin decision-making.

7. Evaluated and adapted over time to meet evolving requirements of individual circumstances and shifting organisational needs within a dynamic context of governance.

8. Appropriate for the stage of development of the school and the headteacher.

9. Viewed as part of an ongoing and wider process of working with the headteacher and all members of staff to ensure high levels of performance.

10. Integral to the development of overall governing body capacity to meet the needs of the school.

Trustees should remember that preparation is important. This might be the only time the CEO has an opportunity to talk about themselves and their own aspirations. As their employer it is the duty of trustees to give them the opportunity to reflect on their own performance. It is also an opportunity to discuss their professional development and for trustees to assess if succession planning is going to be necessary during the following year. The CEO has a responsibility to remind trustees about the process, but it is trustees' responsibility to make the arrangements.

Trustees will often appoint an external adviser to support them. They will make themselves familiar with the data and be able to discuss appropriate objectives. Trustees can ask them to draft up the appraisal report and it can be useful to ask them to lead the meeting so that the trustees can focus on the content of the discussion rather than trying to manage the process. Trustees should remember it is their meeting. The adviser is there to assist and they will provide useful professional insight but trustees should not let them take over the meeting.

At least one week before the appraisal meeting, the CEO should circulate the evidence that they wish to use to demonstrate that they have met their objectives making clear how the information provided relates to them.

Objectives should be reviewed at least once during the academic year in a formal meeting. If the trust context has significantly changed, it is appropriate to amend an objective if it is genuinely no longer achievable or has been superseded by a new priority. Where trustees have any concerns about the CEO's performance, an earlier or additional review meeting can be arranged to raise those concerns.

Trustees should also consider whether there is anything that can be done to improve the CEO's well-being or work–life balance. Trustees may not be able to reduce the work for which the CEO is accountable, but there may be some small ways in which pressure can be reduced and, at the very least, trustees will be demonstrating their awareness that it can be a difficult and lonely job and trustees are there to support as well as to challenge. The remit of the CEO's role will differ hugely between trusts; trustees should recognise this and the demands on them, both physically and emotionally.

The performance management of academy headteachers will differ according to the MAT's particular approach and resources. Some MATs will treat the process in the same way as performance management of any other member of staff and it will be conducted by either the CEO or an executive team. However, some MATs, particularly those community MATs that have built from a local group of schools, will delegate the responsibility to the local governing body, sometimes with a trustee on the panel. The local governing body should be informed of the objectives set.

ESFA has written to trusts paying CEOs above £150,000pa to warn about excessive salaries. It is, therefore, essential that the performance management processes that link to pay decisions are clear and robust. The *Academies Financial Handbook 2018* states that boards must ensure that 'decisions about executive pay follow a robust evidence-based process reflective of the individual's role and responsibilities, and that the board's approach to pay is transparent, proportionate and justifiable, in line with the handbook'.

### Making it work 10.2

**The Kemnal Academies Trust is one of the largest MATs in the South of England with over 40 primary and secondary academies. The board is responsible for the performance management of the chief executive. TKAT uses an 'earned autonomy' model of governance and although it does not delegate responsibility, the local governing bodies take an active part in the performance management of the headteacher which is undertaken by the chief executive officer or her delegate. The appraisal and performance management of all other staff will be undertaken by the relevant headteacher, with the support of the local governing body and/or chief executive officer as appropriate.**

### 3.3   360° reviews of the chair of the board

In the same way that the executive undertake performance management to make sure that they are on track and as a mechanism to sustain and improve performance, the chair of the board should be subject to a regular a review of their effectiveness.

The *Governance Handbook* explains that good chairs 'ask for regular feedback from their board to improve their own effectiveness'. As the chair does not have a line manager, a 360° review is commonly used which seeks feedback from the CEO/Principal, other trustees and any others with whom the chair regularly works or interacts. The review will focus on the skills and contributions made by the chair and will typically cover aspects such as leadership, teamwork, communication skills, accountability and vision.

The review should identify areas of strength in the chair's current performance but also any aspects where improvement could be made.

The *Competency Framework for Governance* sets out the skills and behaviours that help the chair to reflect on how they personally are 'demonstrating the agreed values and culture of the organisation and what impact their individual contribution' is making to effective governance as well as to 'assist in building relationships and improving accountability', ensuring that there is a 'clear distinction between strategic and operational leadership and 'in setting the tone and culture of the board'. The chair:

◆ actively invites feedback on their own performance as chair;

◆ puts the needs of the board and organisation ahead of their own personal ambition and is willing to step down or move on at the appropriate time;

◆ knowledge of different leadership styles and applies these appropriately to enhance their personal effectiveness;

◆ sets challenging development goals and works effectively with the board to meet them;

◆ leads performance review of the board and its committees;

◆ undertakes open and honest conversations with board members about their performance and development needs, and if appropriate, commitment or tenure;

◆ recognises and develops talent in board members and ensures they are provided with opportunities to realise their potential;

◆ creates a culture in which board members are encouraged to take ownership of their own development;

◆ promotes and facilitates coaching, development, mentoring and support for all members of the board; and

◆ is open to providing peer support to other chairs and takes opportunities to share good practice and learning.

# 4. Skills audits

The *Academies Financial Handbook 2018* requires that the board should 'identify the skills and experience that it needs, and address any gaps through recruitment, and/or induction, training and other development activities'. It highlights that this skills review is 'particularly important as key transition points' though fails to define what these points might be. In any event, the skills make-up of the board should be re-evaluated and appropriate action taken if the governance structure changes significantly such as SAT to MAT or SAT/MAT mergers, or if the chair or several other trustees cease to sit on the board.

The trust board of a MAT should also identify the skills and experience needed on any local governing bodies and address any gaps found. Similarly, this will need to be reviewed regularly and when there is significant change such as the development of regional hubs.

The *Governance Handbook* also indicates that regular skills audits aligned to the trust's strategic plan are an element of the evaluation process to 'monitor and improve the quality and impact of governance'. The *Governance Competency Framework* considers that reflection by the individual trustees/governors will help to 'create a stronger and more motivated board'.

The audit or review should take account of skills and competencies needed by the board to fulfil its role in alignment to the trust's strategic plan. The *Academies Financial Handbook* highlights the *Competency Framework* for Governance to which trusts should refer. The National Governance Association (NGA) has developed a skills audit and matrix which is structured around the six features of effective governance set out in the *Competency Framework*. There are different versions that can be used by SATs and MATs to help identify the knowledge, experience, skills and behaviours that are needed. No individual, not even the chair, is expected to have all the skills listed in the audit and set out in the *Competency Framework*. However, they should all be met by the board.

Identifying skills gaps on the board highlights weakness in governance; one of the six key features of effective governance is having 'people with the right skills, experience, qualities and capacity'.

The *Governance Handbook* explains that identifying skill and knowledge gaps will 'define recruitment needs and inform a planned cycle of CPD activity including appropriate induction for those new to governance or to the board' and it identifies a range of training material to help trustees to develop.

The board should develop skills-based recruitment criteria which can also be used to inform elections.

# 5. Review of governance

The *Governance Handbook* states that processes should be adopted for 'regular self-evaluation and review of individuals' contribution to the board as well of the board's overall operation and effectiveness'.

Reviews of the board and governance of the trust will normally be undertaken as part of an annual review to ensure effectiveness. The *Competency Framework for Governance* explains that evaluation is important and a key element of good governance: 'The board needs to assess its effectiveness and efficiency and ensure ongoing compliance with its statutory and legal duties under review.' The *Framework* suggests that everyone on the board:

◆   recognises their own strengths and areas for development and seeks support and training to improve knowledge and skills where necessary;

◆   is outward facing and focused on learning from others to improve practice;

◆   maintains a personal development plan to improve his/her effectiveness and links this to the strategic aims of the organisation;

◆   is open to taking up opportunities, when appropriate, to attend training and any other opportunities to develop knowledge, skills and behaviours;

◆ obtains feedback from a diverse range of colleagues and stakeholders to inform their own development;

◆ undertakes self-review, reflecting on their personal contributions to the board, demonstrating and developing their commitment to improvement, identifying areas for development and building on existing knowledge and skills;

◆ evaluates the impact of the board's decisions on pupil/student outcomes;

◆ utilises inspection feedback fully to inform decisions about board development; and

◆ contributes to self-evaluation processes to identify strengths and areas for board development.

There are various tools that can be used as part of this process including skills audits for board members, a 360° review for the chair and other practices drawn from the corporate sector. The All-Party Parliamentary Group for Education Governance and Leadership has published 21 *Questions for Multi Academy Trust Boards*. This is a series of questions for governing bodies which can be used for self-review. The questions cover:

◆ Vision, ethos and strategy

◆ Governance structures

◆ Trustee board effectiveness and conduct

◆ Engagement

◆ Effective accountability of the executive leadership

◆ Impact on outcomes for pupils

Part of the regular review should encompass a committee self-evaluation, including local governing boards/academy councils in a MAT. This should follow the same processes as the board including skills audits and 360° reviews for committee chairs. The results from the committee self-evaluation should feed into the overall review to give a complete picture of the governance across the trust.

As part of a self-assessment, the board can refer to the ICSA Maturity Matrix which will highlight 'factors that would indicate an academy having fledgling governance arrangements to those leading good practice and being sought out as "best in class"'.

The annual report must include a governance statement which sets out details of the trust's governance arrangements including its scheme of delegation. The *Academies Financial Handbook* 2018 provides that for new trusts it must include 'what they have done to review and develop their governance structure and composition of the board' and established trusts must also include an 'annual assessment, including a review of the composition of the board in terms of skills, effectiveness, leadership and impact'. The review should refer to the six key features of effective governance set out in the *Governance Handbook* (strategic leadership, accountability, people, structures, compliance and evaluation).

### Stop and think 10.1

**How could a review of governance be built into the annual schedule of work for the board, what might it include and how might results inform future planning and strategic leadership?**

### 5.1   External review of governance

An external review of governance (ERG) can be carried out to establish the effectiveness of governance arrangements. ERGs are sometimes recommended by Ofsted, particularly where a school has been found to be 'requires improvement' or 'inadequate' and there are identified weaknesses in leadership and management. An ERG can highlight issues in governance that need to be resolved to become 'good'. Where Ofsted recommends a review, the monitoring inspector will expect it to have been undertaken in a timely way and the impact assessed for the next monitoring visit.

The *Governance Handbook*, in fact, states that, to grow successfully, a board 'should commission a robust independent review of its effectiveness and readiness for growth' or, in fact, prior to transitioning to academy status in the first place! An ERG can be a useful tool for any academy that wishes to further develop its governance and improve the effectiveness of the board. It can help the board to identify the priorities for improvement and development of governance.

According to the DfE, the aim of an ERG is to help the board to:

◆   be more skilled, focused and effective;

◆   be more aware of the freedoms that it has to work in different ways;

◆   be clear in its vision for the trust and how, together with the executive leadership team, it can achieve this;

◆   be confident that it has a clear delineation of roles and responsibilities;

◆   have the right number of skilled and committed trustees to meet the needs of the trust;

◆   hold school leaders to account for improving outcomes for all pupils, including those who are disadvantaged; and

◆   be clear about how it ensures that its young people are well prepared to be responsible citizens in Britain.

It will generally be led by a system leader or governance professional such as a NLG; that individual should have:

◆   experience of outstanding governance;

◆   a good understanding of governance, including different contexts and governance structures;

◆   a clear understanding of Ofsted expectations;

◆  successful experience of leading governors and school improvement; and

◆  excellent inter-personal skills.

There may be other options in terms of providers of ERGs such as local providers of school improvement and governor services, members of National Coordinators of Governor Services Group or the National Governance Association.

However, templates and tools are available on the DfE website that set out the process, a framework and report template which are available to anyone. The expectations of the review should be discussed and agreed prior to commencement.

The review will follow a series of steps:

◆  Initial discussion between the reviewer, chair of the board and the CEO/ principal to:

  –  discuss the context and needs of the trust/academy;

  –  explain the principles and process of the review;

  –  discuss the self-review process; and

  –  agree dates for receiving information from the trust/academy and for the initial face-to-face meeting.

◆  Gather documentation for the reviewer.

◆  First meeting between the reviewer, chair of the board and CEO/Principal to

  –  discuss the self-review process;

  –  assess the capacity of the board, its strengths and areas for development; and

  –  agree how to run the self-review meeting with the board.

◆  Reviewer will meet with as many trustees as possible to assess the capacity of the board, its strengths and areas for development.

◆  Board self-review session conducted by the reviewer. The format and logistics will be agreed with the chair. The reviewer will confirm the main areas for development and the action required with the board during the self-review process.

◆  Areas for improvement will be agreed. The reviewer will produce a report setting out strengths and covering areas for improvement. The reviewer will either produce an action plan or work with the board to create one.

◆  Any actions identified should be embraced by the board and measures introduced to implement them. The board can draw on external support where appropriate which can be provided by the reviewer.

Where an ERG has been recommended by Ofsted following a 'requires improvement' judgement, the effectiveness of the review and evidence of impact on the quality of governance will be considered during monitoring visits.

# Chapter summary

◆ The board is responsible for setting strategic objectives and clear key performance indicators (KPIs) by which progress can be measured. An analysis of KPIs should be included in the annual strategic report. Self-evaluation should inform the setting of objectives and KPIs; there should be an ongoing internal self-evaluation process and SWOT/PESTLE analyses where appropriate.

◆ Performance management should be used to enable all staff, including the clerk/company secretary, to perform to the best of their abilities. The board is responsible for the performance management of the CEO/principal. The chair of the board should be subject to a regular review of their effectiveness (e.g. through a 360° review. Objectives should be SMART: Specific, Measurable, Achievable, Relevant and Time-framed.

◆ Boards must carry out regular audits of the skills they possess taking account of the Competency Framework for Governance. Any skills gaps can be identified and addressed through recruitment, and/or induction, training and other development activities.

◆ The annual report must include a governance statement with details of governance and a review of the board' skills, effectiveness, leadership and impact. An external review of governance (ERG) can be carried out to give an objective view: ERGs are sometimes recommended by Ofsted.

# Part four

# Financial management

**Overview**

This part explores the main sources of income for academies as well as the legal and governance issues that relate to the proper application and management of funds. It also examines the need for financial compliance to legal requirements as well as the need for robust financial controls.

Students will gain a broad understanding of the key principles affecting financial management in an academy and how they affect the trustees and office holders as they seek to discharge their legal duties and responsibilities in practice.

## Learning outcomes

In this module you will:

◆ Understand the main sources of income for academies and restrictions imposed on their management.

- ◆ Understand regulatory and legal requirements for financial planning, reporting and control.
- ◆ Understand the importance of financial planning and how it relates to strategic planning.

# Chapter eleven
# **Funding**

**CONTENTS**

## 1. Introduction

This chapter outlines the main sources of funding for trusts and their academies in respect of both revenue and capital. It also considers the potential to pool funding across MATs and how central services can be funded.

This chapter also considers the impact of tax schemes such as Gift Aid and tax relief that enable a larger proportion of funding to reach the trust. There are now many more trusts that are looking to alternative means of raising money such as through fundraising, trading subsidiaries and loans or leasing arrangements.

With the move towards a National Funding Formula, there is an increasingly consistent approach to funding across local authorities. The Education and Skills Funding Agency (ESFA) funds trusts on the same basis as maintained schools, though allocations and payments are made to trusts on the basis of an academic year rather than the financial year used for maintained schools.

# 2. Funding agreement

The funding agreement is the key contract between the Secretary of State and the trust: the trust agrees to provide educational services in accordance with the terms set out and, in return, funding will be provided by the DfE.

Trusts normally adopt the model funding agreement in place at the time of creation or conversion. The DfE does not expect trusts to deviate from the model versions of the funding agreement unless there are exceptional circumstances that can be justified. The models have, however, differed over time as DfE policy has adapted.

# 3. Sources of income

Funding comes from a variety of different sources depending on the type of funding and the size of the trust. There is an increasing need for trusts to bid for funding.

## 3.1  Revenue

### GAG income
The biggest source of funding for mainstream academies and free schools comes from the **general annual grant** (GAG) which is intended to cover the normal running costs of the trust. It is calculated on the same basis as for maintained schools within the local authority; ESFA uses the local funding model which is calculated by the local authority to calculate allocations for academies. Detailed guidance on GAG for 2018–2019 is available on the DfE website.

**general annual grant**
Funding paid to cover the normal running costs of the academy (e.g. salary and administration costs).

A new national funding formula (NFF) is being introduced which aims to remove discrepancies in funding allocations across the country. Previously local authorities decided how to distribute the funds within guidelines which meant that there were huge differences in school funding between one local authority and another.

NFF will take account of various factors including the proportion of disadvantaged pupils and schools/academies with high levels of in-year pupil mobility. Although the move to NFF takes effect from the 2018–2019 financial year, there will be a transitional period. For 2018–2019 and 2019–2020 notional school-level allocations will be calculated which set the total funding available for schools in each local authority area; local authorities will, for that year, continue to set a local distribution formula to determine individual budgets.

NFF is made up of four blocks which are used to calculate each school's funding allocation:

◆   *Per pupil costs*. This accounts for the largest factor in the formula making up some 72.9% of the total schools block. All pupils attract a basic funding, the 'age-weighted pupil unit' (AWPU). The next two years will be a transition period during which there will be a minimum per-pupil funding level in the formula. If after applying factors in relation to AWPU, deprivation, low prior attainment, English as an additional language (EAL), lump sum, sparsity and area cost adjustment, the per pupil funding falls below the minimum amount, the allocation is topped up.

◆ *Additional needs*. There are four additional needs factors, deprivation which is indicated by a student's eligibility for free school meals, eligibility for free school meals over the last six years and the level of deprivation in the area where the pupil lives as measured by the Income Deprivation Affecting Children Index (IDACI); low prior attainment where a student did not achieve expected level in the Early Years Foundation Stage Profile or who did not achieve expected level at KS2.

◆ *School-led funding*. Every school is allocated a lump sum of £110,000 and the smallest, most remote schools will receive additional sparsity funding. Funding will be allocated based on historic spend in respect of premises costs for business rates, split sites and exceptional premises factors as well as private finance initiative (PFI) costs and funding for growth and mobility.

◆ *Geographic costs*. An area cost adjustment will be applied to take account of variation in costs between different parts of the country.

There will also be a minimum funding guarantee so that no school/academy should lose more than 1.5% for two years or 3% in total. The minimum funding guarantee does not include funding for sixth forms or places in special units.

A newly opened academy or free school may attract a larger GAG for the 'start-up period' to help it operate effectively.

GAG for mainstream academies is calculated annually based on pupil numbers recorded in the autumn census return done in the previous October or on an agreed estimate of pupil numbers (although academies funding on estimates may fall under the **pupil number adjustment** process). Funding allocation statements will be uploaded to Secure Access by 31 March prior to the commencement of the financial year.

**pupil number adjustment**
Adjustment to funding based on estimated pupil numbers calculated using census data.

GAG is paid in equal instalments across the year with monthly payments via BACS to the academy's nominated bank account to arrive on the first working day of the month.

There are no limits on the amount of GAG funding that could be carried forward from year-to-year. However, the Academies Financial Handbook makes clear that trusts 'should use their allocated GAG funding for the full benefit of their current pupils'. Any trust contemplating a substantial surplus should have a clear plan for how it will be used to benefit their pupils, such as a long-term capital project.

## GAG

The *Academies Financial Handbook* permits MATs to amalgamate a proportion of GAG for its academies to form one central fund. This means that the funding can be applied across any of the constituent academies in the trust.

Used to meet the normal running costs at any of its constituent academies within the trust. In accordance with its funding agreement a MAT must not pool PFI funding. The funding can be used to alleviate financial pressure in an individual academy, allowing funding to be spread across the MAT's academies in accordance with need.

The MAT must, however, consider the 'funding needs and allocations of each constituent academy' to avoid a situation where one academy is losing out on its funding whilst another academy gains.

The MAT must put in place an appeals mechanism so that an academy principal can appeal to the trust if they feel that their academy has been unfairly treated. If the grievance is not resolved, the principal can 'appeal to the Secretary of State, via ESFA, whose decision will be final and who can dis-apply the provisions for pooling'.

Lord Agnew, Parliamentary Under-Secretary of State for the School System, wrote to auditors in June 2018:

> 'GAG pooling. This is one of the greatest freedoms a MAT has. The opportunity to pool GAG is particularly valuable, in particular to simplify the provision of support to weaker schools in a MAT until they can grow their pupil numbers. It is worth remembering that a MAT is a single financial entity.'

### Education services grant (ESG)
The ESG general funding rate was removed in September 2017. Prior to that time, it offered a per-pupil amount intended to enable education services previously provided by the local authority. New academies or free schools and schools which convert to academy status from September 2017 will not qualify for any ESG payments.

Protection arrangements were put in place to ensure that no academy would experience losses of more than 3% of their overall budget due to the withdrawal of ESG.

### Special and Alternative Provision Academies
The move to a national funding formula also has an impact on the way high needs funding is provided to local authorities and this has a direct impact on the funding for special schools. There is funding beyond the GAG for elements such as pupil premium in line with provision for mainstream schools. For special and alternative provision academies, there is provision for high-needs top-up funding and/or funding for commissioned SEN or AP services from local authorities and/or commissioning schools.

### 3.2  Capital

### Formula funding
MATs with five or more academies and at least 3,000 pupils (qualifying MATs) receive a School Condition Allocation (SCA). Trusts must deploy this formulaic allocation of capital funding strategically across their academies to

address priority maintenance needs. The DfE requires trusts in receipt of SCA to 'keep buildings safe and in good working order by tackling poor building condition, building compliance, energy efficiency and health and safety issues'. Trusts must:

◆ carry out their duties under the Health and Safety at Work Act 1974 and comply with all relevant building regulations, including the management of asbestos where relevant;

◆ understand in detail the data relating to the current condition of the trust's estate and develop a long-term asset management strategy; and

◆ maintain the estate for the long-term by renewing and modernising key building elements through preventative works and replacement when they are beyond economic repair.

### Condition Improvement Fund (CIF)

Single academies and academies that are not part of a qualifying MAT or opted-in chain and sixth-form colleges can apply for CIF funding to improve the condition of school buildings or expand facilities. The core priority of the scheme is to support condition projects with a focus of keeping 'buildings safe and in good working order'. It will generally aim to address issues with significant consequences including 'poor building condition, building compliance, energy efficiency or health and safety': compliance and health and safety will have highest priority. The highest priorities identified for CIF funding in 2017–2018 were emergency asbestos removal, gas safety, electrical safety, lift safety, legionella, fire safety and safeguarding. However, the priorities may change over time and care should be taken to make sure that any application is aligned to the priorities to maximise chances of a successful bid.

A small proportion of expansion projects for academies with an Ofsted grading of Good or Outstanding may also attract CIF funding where expansion of existing facilities and/or floor space is required to:

◆ increase the number of admissions in the main year of entry; or

◆ address overcrowding, including cases of recently approved age-range expansion and sixth-form expansions.

However, the DfE also states that consideration should be given to opening a free school as an alternative to expansion.

CIF is an annual bidding process and an application must be made within specific timescales and the window for submission is tight. There are detailed requirements relating to the programme priorities and assessment criteria that must be taken into account in preparing a bid and applications are generally supported by reports from technical advisors or other specialists. Applications are made via the CIF online portal.

A submission may be made for up to two projects each of which falls within project thresholds: primary and special schools can apply for funding for between £20,000 and £4 million for each project and secondary schools, all-through schools and sixth-form colleges between £50,000 and £4 million. Any capital projects valued below these limits must be funded from revenue funding.

Although the DfE states 'We do not expect you to spend significant time and resources preparing bids for CIF beyond that required to carry out your responsibilities for managing your site effectively', CIF is consistently oversubscribed. Successful applications will demonstrate a 'high project need', be supported with evidence and align closely with the priorities of CIF.

The bid-writing process is time consuming and reliant on specialist expertise. While bids can be developed in-house, many trusts choose to commission specialist support to help them to do this. A number of consultancy organisations work on a 'no win, no fee' basis whereby they commit to undertake to support the bid process and will attain a fee, albeit with an uplift on what otherwise would have been paid, only if the bid succeeds. Consultants will be able to advise trusts on the best strategy for submission and the priority works to focus on based on their previous experience. They may also be able to provide the technical know-how to write a winning bid. Trusts are expected to make a contribution towards the cost of works. Loans are available to cover all or part of the 'project costs to demonstrate commitment to the proposed scheme'. Application for both Energy Efficiency Salix Loans and CIF Loans are made using the normal CIF application form. Loans are offered at Public Works Loan Board rates of interest and repayments made through abatement of revenue funding paid to the trust.

### Healthy Pupils Capital Fund (HPCF)
For the financial year 2018–2019, there is an additional Healthy Pupils Capital Fund (HPCF), which uses revenue generated from the Soft Drinks Industry Levy. It is intended to improve pupils' physical and mental health by improving access to facilities for physical activity, healthy eating, mental health and wellbeing and medical conditions (such as kitchens, dining facilities, changing rooms, playgrounds and sports facilities).

Trusts in receipt of SCA, receive an additional direct allocation from HPCF. Trusts eligible to bid for CIF are also able to bid for HPCF.

### Test yourself 11.1

**What are the main sources of income for trusts?**

### Private Finance Initiative (PFI) academies
Generally, condition and maintenance work will be covered by the contract with the PFI provider, which will also set out details regarding payment terms.

Trusts must negotiate with the PFI provider regarding any expansion plans to establish agreement for the provider to take on the project or to allow a third party to do so. Unfortunately, PFI contracts often leave little option for the trust regarding choice of works contractor or opportunity to obtain best value.

### Strategic School Improvement Fund

Trusts can apply for a Strategic School Improvement Fund grant. The fund is intended to support the development of a school-led system and 'aims to target resources at the schools most in need to improve school performance and pupil attainment'. It is hoped that the fund will help academies and schools to 'use their resources most effectively and to deliver more good school places'.

It is anticipated that there will be further rounds of funding but the application process is expected to be highly over-subscribed. Details are on the DfE website.

The fund is intended to support a broad range of school improvement activities including:

◆ improving leadership

◆ governance

◆ teaching methods and approaches

◆ financial health and efficiency.

The fund supports 'medium- to long-term sustainable activities across groups of schools' and there is a preference towards school-led provision (i.e. where there is school-to-school support).

### 16-to-19 funding

Funding for 16-to-19-year olds is allocated by ESFA through separate arrangements. A national funding formula is used to calculate the allocation which applies to all institutions providing 16-to-19 education. Special schools/academies are funded on place numbers only and not based on the national funding formula.

The basic funding is based on the numbers of students enrolled in the previous academic year irrespective of the type of institution or what subjects or courses are studied. Students must meet the published eligibility criteria including residency requirements and they must stay on their study programmes for a certain amount of time to attract funding.

Other formula factors are also applied to produce additional uplifts to fund support for disadvantaged young people (including those with special educational needs and difficulties), to reflect more expensive programmes, and to reflect more expensive areas of the country. The elements used in the formula are:

◆ student numbers, split into bands by size of programme;

◆ national funding rate per student;

◆ retention factor;

◆ programme cost weighting;

◆ disadvantage funding;

◆ large programme uplift; and

◆ area cost allowance.

*Pupil premium*

Pupil premium is additional funding aimed at raising the attainment of disadvantaged pupils of all abilities and 'to close the gaps between them and their peers'.

Academies and schools receive funding for each pupil registered as eligible and there are different rates available according to eligibility:

◆ Primary pupils in year groups reception to year 6 recorded as Ever 6 FSM (i.e. who are known to have been eligible for free school meals (FSM) at any time over the last six years).

◆ Secondary pupils in year 7 to year 11 recorded as Ever 6 FSM.

◆ Looked-after children (LAC) defined in the Children Act 1989 as one who is in the care of, or provided with accommodation by, an English local authority for one day or more.

◆ Pupils who have left local authority care as a result of adoption, a special guardianship order, a child arrangements order or a residence order (known as post-LAC).

A lower rate of pupil premium is payable in respect of any pupil aged 4 and over in year groups reception to year 11 who is either an Ever 6 service child or in receipt of pensions from the Ministry of Defence under the Armed Forces Compensation Scheme (AFCS) and the War Pensions Scheme (WPS).

Pupil premium is payable in respect of a financial year beginning 1 April (i.e. it does not align with the trust's financial year) and is based on pupils recorded in the January school census.

The Education Endowment Foundation (EEF) has analysed pupil premium spending and produced a teaching and learning toolkit which can be used to inform decisions about pupil premium spending. This identifies the cost, impact and evidence base for various strategies used to support disadvantaged pupils. The EEF has also produced an evaluation tool which can be used to measure the impact of measures taken.

Academies will generally be required to publish details of the pupil premium strategy and a report on the previous year. For the current academic year, the DfE recommends that information should be published on the amount of pupil premium funding received, details of the main barriers to educational achievement faced by disadvantaged pupils in the school, how pupil premium funding will be spent to overcome these barriers and the reasons for the approach, how impact will be measured and the date of the next pupil premium strategy review. Details on how pupil premium funding was spent and the impact on pupils should be published for the previous academic year.

Guidance for schools on developing and presenting a pupil premium strategy together with a template that can be used has been produced by the Teaching Schools Council.

## PE and sport premium

Most schools and academies with primary-age pupils receive PE and sport premium. Generally, funding is based on the number of pupils in years 1 to 6. However, where schools do not follow year groups, such as in some special schools, the funding is based on the number of pupils aged 5 to 10 years. The number is determined on the basis of pupil details included in the January school census.

Funding is allocated in two separate payments in November and May.

The PE and Sport Premium funding must be used to make 'additional and sustainable improvements to the quality of PE and sport' offered. The DfE explains that this means it should be used to:

◆ develop or add to the PE and sport activities already offered; and

◆ build capacity and capability within the school to ensure that improvements made now will benefit pupils joining the school in future years.

Schools should expect to see improvement across five key indicators:

◆ the engagement of all pupils in regular physical activity – the Chief Medical Officer guidelines recommend that all children and young people aged 5 to 18 engage in at least 60 minutes of physical activity a day, of which 30 minutes should be in school;

◆ the profile of PE and sport is raised across the school as a tool for whole-school improvement;

◆ increased confidence, knowledge and skills of all staff in teaching PE and sport;

◆ broader experience of a range of sports and activities offered to all pupils; and

◆ increased participation in competitive sport.

Funding should not be used to employ coaches or specialist teachers to cover planning, preparation and assessment (PPA) arrangements or to teach the minimum requirements of the national curriculum.

Information should be published on the website about the amount of funding received for the current year, how it has been spent or will be spent, the effect on pupils' PE and sport participation and attainment and how improvements will be made sustainable.

## Universal Infant Free School Meals (UIFSM)

Funding is granted to enable all government-funded schools/academies to offer free school meals to every pupil in reception, year 1 and year 2. Final allocations of funding are based on the average number of meals recorded in the October and January school census. At the present time, schools/academies receive £2.30 per meal. However, the funding is specifically to enable the provision of a free meal to every eligible pupil which means that it should be cost-neutral.

### Year 7 catch-up funding

The literacy and numeracy catch-up premium is additional funding to support year 7 pupils who did not achieve the expected standard in reading or maths at the end of key stage 2 (KS2). Funding is calculated based on the same overall amount to the previous year, adjusted to reflect the percentage change in the size of the year 7 cohort, based on the October census. Academies receive the funding on 1 March.

The funding should be used to provide extra support from those year 7 pupils identified as needing support. Funding must be used to pay for programmes and approaches that are known to be effective and the DfE suggests that this could be:

◆ individual tuition;

◆ intensive small-group tuition;

◆ external services and materials; and

◆ summer schools that help students catch up over a short period of time.

Details of how the year 7 catch-up premium funding is spent must be published on the website. This should include how much funding was received for the current financial year and how it will be spent, details of how funding was spent in the last financial year and how it made a difference to the attainment of the pupils who attracted the funding and how the impact was assessed.

# 4. Funding central services in a MAT

It is necessary to have a CEO within any MAT. There is normally a central administrative team, although some MATs perform these functions from one school with cross-charges to others. The size and remit of the MAT will depend on various factors including the number of academies within the MAT and their pupil sizes, the attitude of the trust to delegation of power and the maturity of the MAT.

Originally, most MATs used top-slicing of academies' funding to create a central fund from which these costs were met. Typically, between 3–5% of income was 'charged' from each academy in the MAT. It is, however, impossible to compare or benchmark the top-slice amounts as the level of leadership, services or administrative support provided will differ between MATs.

Some MATs adapt the top-slice model to differentiate between those academies that need the most support and those that do not (i.e. they 'charge' academies for the greater need and use of central services). This can lead to concerns and friction from individual academies over the level of top-slicing, particularly in relation to other academies within the MAT.

There is now an increasing tendency for MATs to formally pool GAG income across the trust; the *Academies Financial Handbook* allows the amalgamation of GAG to form one central fund. PFI funding cannot be pooled.

While GAG income is normally calculated with reference to academy pupil numbers, a MAT can decide on the size of allocations required for each academy based on its 'funding needs'. There must be a mechanism in place for appeals if an academy principal feels that the academy has been 'unfairly treated'; the principal may appeal to the Secretary of State, by means of ESFA, if they remain unsatisfied after the internal appeal process has been exhausted.

Not only does pooling of GAG allow funds to be applied where most needed across the MAT, but it removes the need to top-slice.

## Stop and think 11.1

**Consider why a MAT would decide to pool GAG and then distribute funding to meet need rather than employ a top-slice arrangement. Do you think that the governance structure and maturity of the organisation might influence decisions made?**

# 5. Gift Aid

The model funding agreement provides that a trust will 'establish an appropriate mechanism for the receipt and management of donations and shall use reasonable endeavours to procure donations through that mechanism'. Trusts are expected to encourage donations.

Gifts and financial donations can be maximised by way of 'Gift Aid' which is a form of tax relief. It is not necessary for the trust to register with HMRC for Gift Aid but it must formally apply for recognition as a charity. Tax can be reclaimed on the 'gross' equivalent of any donation (i.e. the value before basic rate tax was deducted).

Gift Aid of 25% can also be claimed on 'bucket collections' through the Gift Aid Small Donations Scheme (GASDS). Donations must have been made in cash of £20 or less (i.e. in bank notes or coins) or contactless card donations of £20 or less (collected on or after 6 April 2017). Claims can be made up to a maximum total of £2,000 in a single tax year, i.e. on donations of £8,000 (£1,250/£5,000 for years prior to 6 April 2016).

Claims can be made only on donations and not on membership fees. Donations made by cheque, text message or direct debit will not fall under the scheme.

To claim under GASDS, the trust must have:

◆ claimed Gift Aid in the same tax year as the GASDS claim;

◆ not incurred a penalty in the last two tax years; and

◆ for claims on donations made before 6 April 2017, made a successful Gift Aid claim in at least two out of the last four tax years, without a gap of two or more tax years between those Gift Aid claims or since the last claim made.

The GASDS claim cannot be more than 10 times the Gift Aid claim in the same tax year.

Records must be retained of:

◆    total cash donations collected;

◆    date of the collection/s;

◆    date it was paid into a bank account; and

◆    records of any contactless card donations (e.g. receipts from the card machine).

# 6. Tax relief

Trusts are charitable companies, therefore they do not need to pay tax on income that is used for charitable purposes. Where a trust has formally applied to HMRC for recognition as a charity, it may present its letter of recognition from HMRC to the bank or building society and will then receive interest received without tax deducted.

Tax can be reclaimed by making a claim to the bank or building society for the present tax year or by claiming direct from HMRC for previous tax years.

### Test yourself 11.2

1.   **What is GASDS and when could a trust use the scheme?**

2.   **How can a trust claim tax relief?**

# 7. Raising money and trading subsidiaries

As charitable companies, trusts may engage in some types of trading (i.e. the sale of goods or services). However, the trading must be in 'furtherance' of the objects which are the 'establishing, maintaining, carrying on, managing and developing' of schools or educational institutions; this is known as 'primary purpose trading'.

Furthermore, consideration must be given to the tax implications of trading. If it is primary purpose trading, it will generally be exempt from tax.

However, charities are not permitted to engage in trades which pose a significant risk to assets. Therefore, consideration should be given to trading through a subsidiary company which would safeguard the assets of the trust. The subsidiary company would also be free to undertake activities that do not fall under the objects.

Trading subsidiaries can Gift Aid donations to the parent trust which will reduce or eliminate the profits which are liable to tax.

Professional advice should be sought on the appropriateness of establishing a trading subsidiary. Setting up a separate company will also involve additional management and administrative time and costs. Particular care should be exercised on the treatment and application of VAT in catering operations and in lettings and especially where facilities may have been created with grant or capital funding.

Trustees must also be aware of their responsibilities and ensure that the interests of the trust are paramount and are never be overshadowed by the work of any subsidiary companies.

The trustees' report, which is part of the annual report and financial statement must include information on fundraising practices to comply with the provisions of the Charities (Protection and Social Investment) Act 2016. This must include:

◆ approach to fundraising;

◆ work with, and oversight of, any commercial participators/professional fundraisers;

◆ fundraising conforming to recognised standards;

◆ monitoring of fundraising carried out on its behalf;

◆ fundraising complaints; and

◆ protection of the public, including vulnerable people, from unreasonably intrusive or persistent fundraising approaches, and undue pressure to donate.

The financial statements must include details of all expenditure incurred by the trust on raising funds. This will include:

◆ the costs of: all fundraising activities, events and non-charitable trading;

◆ costs of fundraising, other than through charitable trading (e.g. advertising and marketing);

◆ costs incurred by trading for a fundraising purpose (e.g. costs of goods sold or services provided). In consolidated accounts, this will include the costs incurred by a trading subsidiary; and

◆ costs of investment management (if applicable).

## Making it work 11.1

**Cabot Learning Federation is a MAT based in the south-west. The leasehold granted from the foundation included a number of houses which are rented out and produce income. A trading company, John Cabot Ventures, receives the rental income and any other commercial income such as fees for consultancy work or training.**

# 8. Loans and leasing agreements

The model funding agreement provides that trusts 'must not borrow against Publicly Funded Assets, or so as to put Publicly Funded Assets at risk' without the Secretary of State's consent or as permitted in the *Academies Financial Handbook* and is subject to ESFA's prior approval.

Although short-term borrowing is not generally permitted, credit cards can be used but the *Academies Financial Handbook* provides that they must only be used for business expenditure and balances cleared before interest accrues.

CIF and the Salix Energy Efficiency Fund are available to trusts as an acceptable form of borrowing.

Salix provides funding to cover up-front capital cost of energy efficient technology, which will reduce energy costs for trusts. Interest-free loans are repaid through the predicted savings on energy use.

Trusts must bid for Salix funds in a similar way to CIF. To qualify, a project must pay for itself within eight years through predicted annual energy savings and the project must not exceed a maximum cost of £200 per tonne of carbon dioxide saved. Loan repayments are made for between four and eight years by direct debit every March and September.

# Chapter summary

- The funding agreement is the contract between the Secretary of State and the trust in which the trust agrees to provide educational services in return for funding provided by the Department for Education.
- The main source of revenue funding is the general annual grant (GAG) which is calculated annually based on pupil numbers recorded in the autumn census. The Education Services Grant (ESG) was removed from September 2017 though some protection arrangements are still in place.
- Capital funding is either provided through the School Condition Allocation (SCA) formula funding for MATs with five or more academies and at least 3,000 pupils (qualifying MATs). Single academies and academies that are not part of a qualifying MAT or opted-in chain and sixth-form colleges must apply for condition improvement fund (CIF) funding to fund capital works. For the financial year 2018 to 2019, there is an additional Healthy Pupils Capital Fund (HPCF).
- Private finance initiative (PFI) academies will be bound by the terms of the contract with the PFI provider regarding capital works and maintenance.
- MATs must make provision to fund central services. Originally this was primarily done through top-slicing of academies' funding but there are now various models including pooling of GAG income to form one central fund. PFI funding cannot be pooled.
- Trusts should take advantage of Gift Aid and other tax reliefs. Consideration should be given to the use of trading subsidiaries where appropriate.
- Borrowing is not normally permitted by trusts but loans are available through CIF and the Salix Energy Efficiency Fund.

# Chapter twelve
# Financial management

**CONTENTS**

# 1. Introduction

This chapter outlines the way in which funds must be managed and reported. Trusts are charitable companies so they are required to comply with the Companies Act 2006 as well as the Charities Act 2011. They are also classified as 'central government public sector bodies' by the Office for National Statistics; as a result, they are subject to public standards of accountability which importantly includes a higher level of transparency. Although there is no formal reason why a qualified accountant needs to be involved in preparation of the financial statements by the trust, the complexity involved will require the appointment of someone with suitably robust experience to comply!

This chapter also outlines the specific guidance with which trusts must operate. The *Academies Financial Handbook* which sets out the financial management, control and reporting requirements that apply to trusts and the *Academies Accounts Direction* which is the guidance pack to use when preparing annual reports and financial statements.

# 2. Accounting reference date

The Accounting Reference Date (ARD) is the date to which company accounts are prepared (i.e. the financial year-end). When the company is first formed, Companies House automatically generates an ARD which corresponds to the date of incorporation.

The model funding agreement defines the trust financial year as the year from 1 September to 31 August, in line with the academic year. This means that trusts must ensure that the ARD is set to 31 August.

The ARD also determines the date by which accounts must be delivered to Companies House.

# 3. Accounting officer

The funding agreement requires every trust to appoint an accounting officer and to notify the Secretary of State of that appointment. The *Academies Financial Handbook* also requires the board to appoint in writing a senior executive leader, removing the potential for any non-hierarchical or collaborative structure or for the role to rotate between postholders – one individual must be identified as being accountable for the trust. In a SAT this will be the principal, in a MAT it will be the CEO (or equivalent positions). They are not automatically appointed as a trustee under current provisions.

The *Academies Financial Handbook* sets out the remit of the accounting officer role. They have a personal responsibility to Parliament and ESFA's accounting officer for the 'financial resources under the trust's control'. They are responsible for 'high standards of probity in the management of public funds', particularly:

- *Value for money.* The economic, efficient and effective use of resources to achieve the best possible educational outcomes
- *Regularity.* Ensuring that income and expenditure is dealt with in accordance with legislation, the funding agreement and the Academies Financial Handbook and complies with internal procedures
- *Propriety.* Income and expenditure are dealt with in accordance with Parliament's intentions (including standards of conduct, behaviour and corporate governance)

Each year, a statement on regularity, propriety and compliance must be completed and signed by the accounting officer and submitted to ESFA with the audited accounts. The accounts also contain a governance statement in which the accounting officer must demonstrate how the trust has secured value for money.

The accounting officer must have oversight of financial transactions by:

◆ ensuring that property and assets are under the control of the board and measures exist to prevent losses or misuse;

◆ ensuring that bank accounts, financial systems and financial records are operated by more than one person; and

◆ keeping full and accurate accounting records to support the annual accounts.

However, although the accounting officer retains accountability, the practical aspect of ensuring that detailed accounting processes are followed will be delegated to the chief financial officer (CFO) who performs the role of finance director/business manager. Nevertheless, the accounting officer cannot delegate their personal responsibility for assuring the board that there is compliance with the *Academies Financial Handbook* and funding agreement and must notify it in writing 'if any action it is considering is incompatible with the articles, funding agreement or handbook' or if 'the board fails to act where required by the funding agreement or handbook'. If the board is proposing to proceed in acting in contravention of the requirements despite advice from the accounting officer, they must notify ESFA's accounting officer immediately in writing.

The accounting officer must also follow the guidance contained in HM Treasury's publication *Managing Public Money*.

# 4. Chief financial officer

In practice, it is essential that all trusts appoint someone who can take on the responsibility for day-to-day oversight of the trust's financial affairs and to whom responsibility for the 'detailed financial procedures' is delegated. The *Academies Financial Handbook* requires all trust boards to appoint a CFO who is the finance director, business manager or equivalent to 'lead on financial matters'.

The CFO has a 'technical' role making sure that the proper processes are in place and also a 'leadership role' in ensuring that the financial systems are robust and in place.

The CFO may delegate their duties to staff or contractors. However, any finance staff employed must be 'appropriately qualified and/or experienced'. The trust should establish whether the CFO or other finance personnel should have a formal business or accountancy qualification together with membership of a relevant professional body; this will be dependent on the 'risk, scale and complexity of financial operations'. Although a formal accountancy qualification may 'serve as a proxy for the necessary skills and experience required for the role', there is no presumption.

# 5. Financial planning

Not only is financial planning a requirement of the *Academies Financial Handbook 2018*, it is also a necessary ongoing process that ensures the continued viability of the trust. In addition, resources must be used efficiently to maximise outcomes for pupils. The *Handbook* requires the board and any committees to meet regularly enough to 'discharge their responsibilities and ensure robust governance and effective financial management arrangements'. Board meetings should generally be held six times a year or more. If the board meets less than six times in a year it must include a description of how it 'maintained effective oversight of funds with fewer meetings' in the governance statement accompanying the annual accounts.

## 5.1  Budgeting and forecasting

The *Academies Financial Handbook 2018* requires the board of trustees to approve a balanced budget for each financial year; approval must be formally noted in the board minutes or passed by written resolution.

The trust must submit budget forecast information to ESFA using the online return form:

◆ a budget forecast return outturn by 21 May

◆ a three-year budget forecast return by 30 July.

These budget forecasts must be formally approved by the board prior to submission. The board and any separate finance committee must 'ensure rigour and scrutiny in budget management'.

◆ *Budget setting.* The board must ensure that budget forecasts are compiled accurately, based on realistic assumptions and are reflective of lessons learned from previous years. Boards should challenge pupil number estimates which are the basis of revenue projections.

**management accounts**
Accounts produced by an academy for internal decision- making and monitoring purposes.

◆ *Budget monitoring.* Monthly **management accounts** must be prepared which set out the trust's financial performance and position. They should comprise budget variance reports and cash flow forecasts. These must be shared with the chair of the board every month and with the other trustees at least six times a year. Management accounts must be considered by the board when it meets and it must ensure that appropriate action is taken to maintain financial viability.

The trust can draw on unspent funds brought forward from previous years to enable the budget to balance in-year. Trusts must not go into a cumulative deficit position and there are strict guidelines around loans, including short-term financing such as overdrafts. If a trust is intending to set a deficit revenue budget 'which it cannot address after unspent funds from previous years are taken into account', the board must notify ESFA within 14 days of its meeting.

## 5.2 Executive pay

The *Academies Financial Handbook 2018* contains a specific provision regarding the setting of executive pay levels. Any such decisions must be made following a 'robust evidence-based process' and must be 'reflective of the individuals role and responsibilities'.

The approach to pay must be 'transparent, proportionate and justifiable' and include:

◆ Process – agreed in advance and documented.

◆ Independence – conflicts of interest must be avoided. The executive member cannot be involved in deciding their remuneration.

◆ Decision-making – factors to be taken into account are clear and taken into account.

◆ Proportionality – pay is defensible relative to the public-sector market.

◆ Documentation – the process and rationale must be recorded and retained.

◆ Basic presumption that non-teaching pay should not increase at a faster rate to that of teachers.

◆ Understanding that inappropriate pay can be challenged by ESFA especially if there is poor financial management of the trust

## Making it work 12.1

**UHY's 2018 academies benchmarking report found that almost one-third of MAT CEOs were paid more than £150,000 in 2016/2017. Some were significantly above this level, with Harris Federation's Sir Daniel Moynihan paid over £440,000. With the Prime Minister paid a salary of £150,402 for the same period, these high salaries have attracted much criticism.**

## 5.3 Investment policy

The articles give the board of trustees the power to invest funds subject to ensuring that the investment risk is properly managed. The *Academies Financial Handbook* requires all trusts to have an investment policy to 'manage and track its financial exposure, and ensure value for money'. Therefore, trustees must set out their investment strategy in a formal investment policy which is reviewed 'regularly', taking advice from a professional adviser where appropriate. The policy should set out the attitude towards risk, return and liquidity challenges. Trustees must 'exercise care and skill' in all their investment decisions and must make sure that 'exposure to investment products is tightly controlled so that security of funds takes precedence over revenue maximisation'. For any investment transactions with are 'novel, contentious and/or repercussive' the prior approval of ESFA is required.

In addition, the board should have regard to the Charity Commission's guidance: *CC14 Charities and Investment Matters: A Guide for Trustees*.

# 6. Value added tax

Value added tax (VAT) is charged on the supply of goods and services and, therefore, applies to most business transactions. Any company, including trusts, can register for VAT purposes which means that they can reclaim any VAT they have paid on business-related goods or services but must also charge VAT on the goods or services they sell.

There are currently three different rates of VAT depending on the goods or services concerned: standard rate; reduced rate; zero rate. There are also limited exemptions.

If the company's VAT taxable turnover exceeds the threshold set (currently £85,000), it is compulsory to register with HM Revenue and Customs (HMRC). Below that, it is possible to voluntarily register. Registration is via a formal application to HMRC and subsequently VAT reclaimed by completing and submitting VAT returns to HMRC. A return must be submitted either monthly or quarterly irrespective of whether there is VAT to pay or reclaim. The return must set out:

◆ total sales and purchases;

◆ the amount of VAT owed;

◆ the amount of VAT to be reclaimed; and

◆ the VAT refund from HMRC.

Trusts that are not VAT registered are able to reclaim VAT paid on goods and services by completing and submitting Form VAT126. Form 126 claims can be submitted monthly, quarterly or in respect of any number of whole months.

Records must be maintained to support reclaims.

# 7. Financial monitoring

Trusts have an obligation to ensure that there is sound financial management in operation. The accounting officer has a personal responsibility to ensure value for money, regularity and propriety.

The board and finance committee (if there is one) have particular responsibilities set out by the *Academies Financial Handbook* whereby they must ensure effective financial management and maintain robust oversight.

This means that the board must take an active role in ensuring that financial affairs are properly conducted. Trustees must be confident that accounts are correct on an ongoing basis and that internal controls ensure that funds are spent wisely and fraud avoided. The board must meet regularly to discharge their responsibilities; in practice, a dedicated finance committee is required which focuses on financial scrutiny and oversight.

Monitoring should include:

◆ the current and forecast financial position;

◆ regular reconciliation of bank and control accounts; and

◆ regular financial report to the board.

The board must ensure that budget monitoring takes place, tracking and controlling all expenditure within established limits and identifying where corrective action is required.

Forecasting cash flow is also important to ensure that the trust does not run out of cash! According to the *Academies Financial Handbook 2018*, 'The trust must manage its cash position robustly'. It must avoid going overdrawn and may be required to report the cash position to ESFA if there are concerns about financial management.

Trusts are not permitted to take out loan funding (except in limited circumstances such as SALIX). This means that the trust cannot resort to an overdraft or a short-term loan if it does run out of cash.

Cash flow problems may lead to ESFA issuing a Financial Notice to Improve (FNtl) setting out what the trust must do to address the concerns about financial management or governance. The trust is bound to comply with the FNtl and the delegated authorities relating to special payments, write-offs, acquisition and disposal of fixed assets, leasing and managing GAG are revoked and must be approved by ESFA in advance.

Trusts must provide ESFA with various information. In accordance with timescales and format advised by ESFA. If the trust fails to provide the required information or if is not of acceptable quality, ESFA may 'conduct investigations to collect it'. Any costs of the investigations that have been occasioned can we deducted from the trust's recurrent funding. ESFA can take further actions deemed necessary to enforce compliance, such as publication of the names of late returners.

## 7.1 Financial management and governance self-assessment

Any new trusts or trusts joining a MAT must complete a short Financial Management and Governance Self-Assessment (FMGS). It is submitted to ESFA using an online form within four months of opening or joining the MAT. As the name suggests, trusts must self-assess their financial management and governance arrangements to provide assurance as to their adequacy. For trusts joining existing MATs which have previously prepared audited accounts, FMGS must confirm that the same financial management and governance arrangements will be adopted.

The *Academies Financial Handbook* outlines that ESFA will conduct financial management reviews which will examine whether the systems and control mechanisms in place meet the requirements of the *Handbook*.

## 7.2 Internal financial controls

The *Academies Financial Handbook* 2018 requires that trusts must have in place 'sound internal control, risk management and assurance processes'.

The trust must establish a control framework which includes:

◆ ensuring delegated financial authorities are complied with;

◆ maintaining appropriate segregation of duties;

◆ co-ordinating the planning and budgeting processes;

◆ applying discipline in financial management, including managing debtors, creditors, cash flow and monthly bank reconciliations;

◆ planning and oversight of any capital projects;

◆ management and oversight of assets;

◆ regularity, propriety and value for money in the organisation's activities ;

◆ reducing the risk of fraud and theft; and

◆ independent checking of financial controls, systems, transactions and risks.

The board can manage the programme of risk review and checking of financial controls to suit their circumstances. The *Academies Financial Handbook* offers the following options:

◆ use of an internal audit service (either in-house, bought-in or provided by a sponsor);

◆ a supplementary programme of work by the trust's external auditors;

◆ appointment of a non-employed trustee with an appropriate level of qualifications and/or experience who neither charges nor is paid by the trust for their work; or

◆ peer review.

The board could decide to commission a programme of work combining a variety of these options. The governance statement accompanying the annual accounts should include details regarding which of these options has applied and why. The outcome of the programme should also inform the accounting officer's statement of regularity.

The findings from the programme of work must be 'made available to all trustees promptly' and, on request, may be required by ESFA.

### Test yourself 12.1

**How can the programme on internal risk review be carried out?**

### 7.3 Audit committee

The *Academies Financial Handbook* provides that the board must establish a committee 'to provide assurance to the board over the suitability of, and compliance with, its financial systems and operational controls, and to ensure that risks are being adequately identified and managed'. Only those trusts with an annual income over £50 million are required by the provisions of the *Academies Financial Handbook* to have a dedicated audit committee; all other trusts have the flexibility to decide whether to have a committee or whether the functions of the audit committee function should fall under the remit of another committee (usually the finance/resources committee).

Trust staff must not be members of any audit committee. In the absence of a separate audit committee, trust staff should not participate as a member when audit matters are discussed by the finance committee. Trust staff may remain in attendance at any audit committee meetings, irrespective of whether it is a separate committee or not, to provide information and to participate in relevant discussions and the accounting officer and other relevant senior staff should routinely attend.

The audit committee or other committee carrying out that function, must agree 'a programme of work to provides its assurance on financial controls and risks' including at any constituent academies where relevant.

# 8. Regularity, propriety and compliance

The accounting officer is required to complete and sign an annual statement on 'regularity, propriety and compliance' which is submitted to ESFA with the audited accounts.

◆ *Regularity*. The requirement to deal with all items of income and expenditure in accordance with legislation, the terms of the trust's funding agreement and this handbook, and compliance with internal trust procedures. This includes spending public money for the purpose intended by Parliament.

◆ *Propriety*. The requirement to deal with expenditure and receipts in accordance with Parliament's intentions and the principles of parliamentary control. This covers standards of conduct, behaviour and corporate governance.

◆ *Compliance*. The requirement to deal with all income and expenditure in accordance with legislation, the funding agreement and any other statutory guidance or regulation.

# 9. Procurement

Trusts must ensure that all spending is for the 'purpose intended' and represent 'value for money' (i.e. all funds must be used economically, efficiently and effectively). Trusts can make financial savings by the use of good procurement. There are a number of procurement consortiums offering access to national contracts and frameworks for commonly purchased categories of goods and services. The *Academies Financial Handbook 2018* specifically highlights the DfE's recommendation of Deals for Schools, which are national deals that are available to schools and academies 'to help them save money on some of the things they buy regularly' such as energy and water supplies, printers, photocopiers or scanners, software licensing and ICT. Individuals within trusts may have delegated authority to spend on behalf of the trust. These should be minimised as far as possible, not only to enable robust internal controls, but also to enable the opportunity to achieve economies and efficiencies in purchasing decisions.

The *Academies Financial Handbook 2018* specifies that trusts must have 'a competitive tendering policy' applied and in place. Trusts are regarded as a 'contracting authority' for EU public procurement purposes and must observe Official Journal of the European Union (OJEU) procurement thresholds. There are detailed rules that apply for higher-value contracts above a threshold which is revised every two years. From January 2018, the thresholds are €221,000 (around £181,302) for supply and service contracts and €5,548,000 (around £4,551,413) for works contracts. If the thresholds are exceeded, trusts must follow the EU procurement process which contains onerous obligations. Specialist advice should be sought as appropriate.

There are some 'Part B' services which will not be caught within the procurement rules. These include catering, education services, health and legal services.

Some transactions have delegated authority limits so trusts must obtain prior approval of ESFA.

### 9.1 Irregular expenditure

There may be other circumstances which should be taken into consideration by accounting officers and chief financial officers. The *Academies Accounts Direction 2017–2018* highlights some common themes in relation to irregularity identified in trusts' accounts from previous years:

- lack of prior approval for finance leases (which constitute borrowing);
- no statement of assurance for related party transactions;
- related party transactions not at cost;
- non-contractual severance payments made without the required approvals; and
- weak internal controls.

The *Accounts Direction* also highlights irregular expenditure not for the purpose intended (e.g. excessive gifts and alcohol). The *Academies Financial Handbook* also states that the value of gifts must be 'reasonable' and regard is given to 'propriety and regularity in the use of public funds'. However, there is a grey area around the purchase of alcohol on which the *Handbook* is silent – is the *Accounts Direction* intending a blanket ban on the purchase of alcohol or is the occasional purchase of a bottle of wine as a gift acceptable?

# 10. Related party transactions

Section 175 of the Companies Act 2006 states that a 'director of a company must avoid a situation in which he has, or can have, a direct or indirect interest that conflicts, or possibly may conflict, with the interests of the company'. The *Academies Financial Handbook* also refers to trustees' duty 'not to accept benefits from third parties, and to declare interest in proposed transactions or arrangements'.

Consequently, all trustees must ensure that they avoid any such situation and declare any interests that they, a relative or a related party, might have that could conflict or be seen to conflict. Not only will a conflict of interest arise from a 'direct' personal interest, but it could also arise from an 'indirect' interest through a relative or another business that the trustee is involved in.

Charity law sets out strict rules regarding the benefits that can be received by trustees. They cannot be employed by, or receive remuneration, from the trust in their capacity as a trustee.

The model articles contain provisions allowing trustees' dealings with the trust relating to contracts 'for the supply of goods or services', interest on money lent and rent on premises. The board must be satisfied that it is in the interests of the trust to contract with that trustee rather than with someone who is not a trustee. However, there have been various examples of trusts contracting via related party transactions where trustees or the senior executive have benefited either directly or indirectly. As a result, the articles are rather superseded by the provisions of the *Academies Financial Handbook*.

Any related party transactions must comply with the 'at cost' requirements whereby the trust 'must pay no more than 'cost' for goods or services provided to it' agreed on or after 7 November 2013 by related persons, i.e. someone who is:

◆ a member or trustee;

◆ an individual or organisation related/connected to a member or trustee including: relatives; persons carrying on business in partnership with the member or trustee or one of their relatives; a company in which the member or trustee or one of their relatives holds more than 20% of share capital or voting power; or an organisation controlled by a member or trustee or one of their relatives;

◆ an individual or organisation that has the right to appoint a member or trustee; or

◆ an individual or organisation recognised as a sponsor of the trust.

There is a *de minimis* level of £2,500 below which the 'at cost' requirements need not apply to related party transactions. Where the cumulative annual total with the related party exceeds £2,500, the element above this level must be at no more than cost.

There is an assumption that contributions made to a diocese for services that the trust receives 'associated with securing the academy trust's religious character and ethos, that only the diocese can provide' meet the 'at cost' requirement. How this will operate in practice remains to be seen.

The 2018 version of the *Academies Financial Handbook* has significantly increased the restrictions on related party transactions. All transactions with related parties made on or after 1 April 2019 will needed to be reported to ESFA in advance of the transaction taking place.

Trusts must obtain approval for any proposed 'novel, contentious and/or repercussive' transactions with related parties from ESFA. In addition, ESFA's prior approval must be obtained for any related party contracts for the supply of goods or services agreed on or after 1 April 2019 where:

◆ the contract exceeds £20,000;
◆ the contract takes the total value of contracts with the related party beyond £20,000 in the same financial year; and
◆ there have been contracts with the related party exceeding £20,000 individually or cumulatively in the same financial year.

The *Academies Financial Handbook 2018* specifically notes that the rules around related party transactions do not relate to 'salaries and other payments made by the trust to a person under a contract of employment through the trust's payroll'. However, as the *Handbook* also notes the DfE's 'strong preference' for no employees other than the CEO to be appointed as trustees, so there should be less and less of such situations going forward.

Some relationships with related parties are likely to attract greater public scrutiny and must be recognised as such by the board. In particular:

◆ transactions with individuals in a position of control or influence, including the chair of the board and the accounting officer;
◆ payments to organisations with a profit motive, as opposed to those in the public or voluntary sectors; and
◆ relationships with external auditors beyond their duty to deliver a statutory audit.

Trusts must keep records and make disclosures in their annual accounts showing that any transactions with related parties including these, have been 'conducted in accordance with the high standards of accountability and transparency required within the public sector'.

The *Academies Financial Handbook 2018* requires that the board must ensure that 'requirements for managing related party transactions are applied across the trust'. The board chair and accounting officer must ensure that 'their capacity to control and influence does not conflict' with the requirements around managing related party transactions.

Trustees should take care to ensure that all potential conflicts of interest, whether real or perceived, are declared and managed appropriately, 'promoting integrity and openness in accordance with the seven principles of public life'.

The *Academies Accounts Direction 2017–2018* states that notes in the financial statements regarding related party transactions must distinguish between income and expenditure related party transactions. Confirmation must be included that any element above the *de minimis* level of £2,500 is provided at no more than cost and it must be supported by a statement of assurance confirming this from the related party.

## Stop and think 12.1

**From what you know of duties enshrined in company law, charity law and the restrictions in the *Academies Financial Handbook 2018*, think of an example where a related party transaction would be of clear benefit to the trust. Assuming that the transaction complies with the requirements for reporting and approval, how can the trust ensure that the public perception of such a transaction did not pose a reputational risk?**

# 11. Annual report and accounts

The funding agreement requires trusts to produce accounts for the 12-month accounting period to 31 August each year. Detailed guidance is provided by ESFA's *Academies Accounts Direction*, published annually by the end of May prior to the end of the financial year to which it relates. It contains model versions of the reports and financial statements that trusts can refer to when preparing their own.

Accounts must be prepared under the Charities' Statement of Recommended Practice (SORP) and in line with the guidance contained in the relevant *Academies Financial Handbook*.

The annual report and financial statements consist of:

*Reports*:

◆ Trustees' report – signed by a trustee (usually the chair).
◆ Governance statement – signed by a trustee (usually the chair) and the accounting officer and which includes a review of value for money.
◆ Statement on regularity, propriety and compliance – signed by the accounting officer.
◆ Statement of trustees' responsibilities – signed by a trustee (usually the chair).
◆ Independent auditor's report on the financial statements – signed by the auditor.
◆ Independent reporting accountant's assurance report on regularity – signed by the reporting accountant who must be the same person as the external auditor of the financial statements.

The *Academies Accounts Direction 2017–2018* introduced a number of additional requirements for inclusion in the financial statements. Trusts must include a section about fundraising practices to comply with the Charities (Protection and Social Investment) Act 2016. This covers:

◆ The trust's approach to fundraising.

◆ Details of any work with, and oversight of, any commercial participators/ professional fundraisers.

◆ Confirmation that fundraising is conforming to recognised standards.

◆ Details of the monitoring of fundraising carried out on its behalf.

◆ Any complaints.

◆ Protection of the public, including vulnerable people, from unreasonably intrusive or persistent fundraising approaches, and undue pressure to donate.

Trusts with more than 49 full-time equivalent employees throughout any seven months during the reporting period must include information on trade union facility time to comply with the Trade Union (Facility Time Publication Requirements) Regulations 2017 (SI 2017/328). The financial statements must include information on:

◆ The number of employees who were relevant union officials during the period.

◆ The number of employees and their percentage of time spent on facility time.

◆ The percentage of pay bill spent on facility time.

◆ Details of paid trade union activities.

*Financial statements:*

◆ Statement of financial activities (SOFA).

◆ Balance sheet – signed by a trustee (usually the chair).

◆ Cash-flow statement.

◆ Notes which expand on the financial statements.

The trustees' report supports the financial statements and is in accordance with section 415 to 419 of the Companies Act 2006 regarding a directors' report. It provides further information allowing for a full appreciation of the trust's activities by describing the objectives for the trust, progress made during the year and plans for the future. It must contain:

◆ reference and administrative details;

◆ opening section;

◆ structure, governance and management; and

◆ objectives and activities.

A strategic report is included in the trustees' report which contains a fair review of the trust's business and a description of the principal risks and uncertainties it faces, including:

- achievements and performance;
- financial review;
- plans for future periods;
- funds held as custodian trustee on behalf of others; and
- auditor.

A governance statement is required by HM Treasury for all public bodies to provide assurance that the trust is appropriately managed and is controlling the resources for which it is responsible. Information on the governance framework and confirmation that trustees have carried out their responsibility for ensuring that effective systems have been put in place.

The annual report and accounts must be submitted to ESFA by 31 December and filed with Companies House by 31 May. The *Academies Accounts Direction 2017–2018* clarifies that accounts may be submitted before the deadline of 31 December where 'all academies have been transferred or trust closed'.

A copy must be provided to anyone who requests them. They should be published on the trust website no later than the end of January following the financial year to which the accounts relate.

## 11.1 Academies Accounts Direction

The *Academies Accounts Direction* is issued annually and supplements the *Academies Financial Handbook*. It sets out in detail the technical requirements to:

- prepare an annual report and financial statements to 31 August;
- have the 'accounts' audited by an independent registered auditor;
- submit the audited accounts to ESFA by 31 December;
- file the accounts with Companies House as required under the Companies Act 2006; and
- arrange an independent audit of regularity at the trust and include an independent reporting accountant's report on regularity as part of the trust's accounts.

The guidance contained within the *Academies Accounts Direction* is in line with the Charities' SORP issued by the Charity Commission. The SORP, which provides a 'comprehensive framework of recommended practice for charity accounting and reporting' must be followed by trusts due to their structure as charitable companies.

## 11.2 Multi-academy trusts

MATs must prepare a single set of accounts which covers all academies within the trust with additional disclosures to:

- Identify the share of funds attributable to each academy at the end of the current and comparative period.

- Provide a narrative describing the action being taken by any academy in respect of which the total of the funds is a deficit.
- Identify the amounts spent during the period by each academy on:
  - teaching and educational support staff;
  - other support staff;
  - educational supplies; and
  - other costs.

Details of central services provided by the trust to academies during the year must be disclosed; the *Academies Accounts Direction* includes an illustrative format. A note must describe:

- the types of central services provided;
- the trust's policy for charging for those central services; and
- the actual charges placed on each academy for the services during the year.

# 12. Audit

Part 16 of the Companies Act 2006 requires all companies including trusts to have their annual accounts audited unless they fall under an exemption, none of which apply in the case of trusts. This is further confirmed by a provision in the funding agreement which requires the accounts to be 'audited annually by independent auditors' who provide an 'audit report stating whether, in the auditors' opinion, the accounts show a true and fair view of the Academy Trust's affairs'. The *Academies Financial Handbook* sets out the DfE's expectations relating to the statutory audit. Trusts must appoint an auditor to certify whether the trust's annual accounts 'present a true and fair view of the trust's financial performance and position'. The audit contract must be made in writing with the letter of engagement covering only the external audit and no additional services that may have been engaged.

The auditor must hold a current audit-practising certificate issued by a recognised supervisory body and be completely independent of the trust. The audit should be carried out in accordance with International Standards on Auditing.

The auditor is appointed by the members. They may also remove the auditor from office at any time during their term of office. Twenty-eight days' notice of the intention to remove the auditor must be given prior to a resolution at a members' general meeting with a copy of the notice for the meeting sent to the auditor. The auditor has the right to provide a written response which should be circulated to all members and can attend and speak at the meeting. Removal of an auditor requires an 'ordinary resolution' passed by simple majority (i.e. at least half plus one of all the votes cast). The written resolution procedure may not be used for removal of an auditor. The removal of the auditor must be notified to Companies House within 14 days of the resolution.

Auditors must produce a statement setting out any circumstances that they consider should be brought to the attention of the members and ESFA when they cease to hold office for whatever reason, which must be deposited at the trust's registered office. In addition, where they resign or are removed, the auditor and the trust must notify the 'appropriate audit authority' (i.e. ESFA) immediately (CA 2006, ss 522–525). Reasons for removal of the auditor or a statement of explanation where the auditor has resigned must also be provided. Notification to ESFA is not required where the auditor is changed at the end of the agreed term of office.

The trust must provide a copy to all members within 21 days of the day it was deposited or apply to the court to avoid having to do so. If, after 21 days, the auditor does not receive notice of an application to the court, they must send a copy to Companies House within the next seven days.

The *Academies Financial Handbook 2018* contains specific obligations on the board to ensure that there is an 'appropriate, reasonable and timely response' to any findings of the auditors which will give an opportunity to 'strengthen the trust's systems of financial management and control'.

# 13. Reserves

The DfE previously imposed limits on the amount of surplus GAG income that could be carried forward to the next financial year, in the same way as has applied to maintained schools. However, most trusts now (with the exception of those on estimates-based GAG funding) do not have to balance income and expenditure in each year and can carry forward unspent GAG without any limit. However, the *Academies Financial Handbook 2018* states:

> 'ESFA will report to DfE any trusts where it has serious concerns about a long-term substantial surplus with no clear plans for its use.'

However, trusts should have a reserves policy which sets out the level of carry forward that will be retained and the justification for the figure. Particularly in the current climate where funding is tight and trusts are not generating surpluses, the reserves figure may be aspirational with a plan to build over a number of years.

## Stop and think 12.2

**What considerations do you think should be taken into account when developing reserves and investment policies? Do you think reference should be made to total income, staffing salaries, age and condition of property, etc?**

# 14. Asset register

The *Academies Financial Handbook 2018* provides that the accounting officer must ensure that trust property and assets are 'under the control of the trustees' and that measures are in place to 'prevent losses or misuse. Previous versions of the Handbook specifically required the accounting officer to maintain fixed asset registers. Although this is no longer formally defined as a responsibility, a fixed asset register is a simple way of logging all fixed assets owned by the trust, i.e. capital assets which are capable of being owned or controlled and from which a trust can expect to derive a benefit for more than one year. Typical fixed assets are land, buildings, vehicles and information technology which are not for sale in the ordinary course of the trust's operations. The register should show the value of the asset, date of acquisition and any other details required to enable a calculation of depreciation for tax purposes.

The *Handbook* also requires trusts to obtain approval from ESFA for transactions involving:

◆ acquiring a freehold of land or buildings;

◆ disposing of a freehold of land or buildings; and

◆ disposing of heritage assets, as defined in financial reporting standards, beyond any limits set out in the funding agreement for disposal of assets.

Trusts can dispose of any other fixed asset without approval of ESFA though it must ensure that disposal 'achieves the best price that can reasonably be obtained, and maintains the principles of regularity, propriety and value for money'.

# Chapter summary

◆ Every trust must appoint an accounting officer who is the 'senior executive leader' (i.e. the CEO/principal). They have a personal responsibility for financial resources, particularly value for money, regularity and propriety. In practice, day-to-day oversight is delegated to a chief financial officer (CFO).

◆ The trust board is responsible for good financial management and effective monitoring and internal controls. It must approve a balanced budget for each financial year and use an evidence-based approach to executive pay. The board may invest funds in accordance with an agreed investment policy.

◆ Trusts can register for VAT purposes so that they can reclaim any VAT they have paid on business-related goods or services and charge VAT on the goods or services they sell. If a trust is not VAT registered, it may reclaim VAT by completing and submitting a claim.

◆ Trusts with an annual income over £50 million must have a dedicated audit committee. Other trusts have the flexibility to decide whether to have an audit committee or whether it should fall under the remit of the finance committee. Trust staff must not be members of an audit committee.

◆ All spending must be for the 'purpose intended' and represent 'value for money'. There should be a competitive tendering policy in place and trusts must follow the EU procurement process where appropriate.

◆ Trustees and members must avoid any conflict of interest, direct or indirect. Goods and services provided to the trust by a related person must be provided at cost unless it falls under the *de minimis* level. All connected party transactions must be reported to ESFA and must seek prior approval where they exceed £20,000 either individually or cumulatively.

◆ Accounts for the 12-month accounting period to 31 August each year must be prepared under the Charities' Statement of Recommended Practice (SORP) and following guidance contained in the *Academies Financial Handbook* and *Academies Accounts Direction* and must be audited by an independent auditor.

# Test yourself answers

## Chapter 1

### Test yourself 1.1

**1. Why were the Nolan Principles introduced?**

The Seven Principles of Public Life, the 'Nolan Principles', were introduced to ensure the highest standards of propriety in public life following scandals involving the House of Commons. They apply to anyone who works in education.

**2. What are the Seven Principles?**

The Seven Principles are:

◆ Selflessness
◆ Integrity
◆ Objectivity
◆ Accountability
◆ Openness
◆ Honesty
◆ Leadership

## Chapter 2

### Test yourself 2.1

**What are the six features of effective governance identified in the Competency Framework for Governance?**

The six features of effective governance identified in the Competency Framework for Governance are:

◆ Strategic leadership
◆ Accountability

- People
- Structures
- Compliance
- Evaluation

## Test yourself 2.2

### What are the four key competencies set out in the Clerking Competency Framework?

The four key competencies set out in the Clerking Competency Framework are:

- Understanding governance
- Administration
- Advice and guidance
- People and relationships

# Chapter 3

## Test yourself 3.1

### 1. What would a school need to show to be approved to convert as a SAT?

The school would need to show that it has the capacity to be successful and sustainable as a SAT. The DfE will consider applications on a case-by-case basis but will look at:

- exam results from the last three years
- pupil progress over the last three years
- most recent Ofsted inspections
- the school's finances
- plans to work with other schools.

### 2. Why might a school consider setting up as a MAT?

The DfE's preference is currently for maintained schools converting to academy status to join an existing MAT. Alternatively, if it can show capacity, it can establish an 'empty MAT' in expectation that other schools will join.

### 3. What is a MAT and what is the legal status of its academies?

A MAT is a single legal entity which is responsible for running each of the individual academies or schools within the trust. The individual academies/schools do not have a separate legal identity and any governing body attached to it has the standing of a MAT committee.

4. **What should church schools consider if looking to join with non-church schools in a MAT?**

Church schools need to ensure that the governance structure of the MAT will fit their governance arrangements (i.e. 25% foundation trustee positions on the board for Voluntary Controlled schools and 75% for Voluntary Aided schools).

# Chapter 4

## Test yourself 4.1

### Why is it practical to have more than three members even though the model articles provide for only three as a minimum?

Decisions requiring a special resolution (e.g. appointment of a new member, require a voting majority of 75% which is impossible without unanimity if there are only three members).

If there are only three members and one wished to leave immediately and would not cooperate in appointing a replacement, the resignation would not be effective as the articles require there to be three members remaining after any resignation.

It is not possible to have 25% diocesan representation unless there are four members in a Church of England Voluntary Controlled MAT or mixed MAT.

## Test yourself 4.2

### 1. What routes are there for trustees to be appointed/elected to the board?

The articles will determine the number and category of trustee from:

- member appointments;
- foundation/sponsor appointments;
- parent appointments/elections (MATs do not have to have parent trustees if there are at least two parent governors on each LGB);
- co-opted trustees limitation on number set out in the articles;
- CEO/principal;
- staff trustees (this no longer favoured by the DfE);
- nominees of the employer and university sponsors form the majority on the board in a UTC; and
- n older articles, LGB chairs and principals may be ex officio (subject to particular number).

### 2. What issues are there with appointing the Chief Executive Officer/Principal to the board?

The members can appoint the CEO/principal as a trustee if that individual 'agrees so to act'. (Earlier versions of the articles provide that the CEO is *ex officio* trustee.) There is an inherent conflict if they are there to present plans, give advice and provide information to a board which they are a member of.

## Test yourself 4.3

### What limitations are there on appointing Local Authority Associated Persons?

The number of votes exercisable by Local Authority Associated Persons must not exceed 19.9% of the total number of votes exercisable by members.

LAAPs must make up less than 20% of the total number of trustees with the number of votes exercisable by LAAPs on any resolution not exceeding 19.9% of the total number of votes exercisable by trustees. In practice, this means that no LAAP can be appointed as a member unless there are at least six members (the current DfE preferred model allows for five). The articles allow for the votes of the other members 'having a right to vote at the meeting' to be increased on a pro-rata basis.

# Chapter 5

## Test yourself 5.1

1. **What are the 'statutory registers' that trusts are required to keep under the Companies Act 2006?**

Trusts are required to keep the following under the provisions of the Companies Act 2006:

◆ register of members;
◆ register of directors/trustees;
◆ register of secretaries;
◆ register of directors'/trustees' residential addresses; and
◆ register of people with significant control (PSC).

2. **What registers must be kept under provisions contained in the Academies Financial Handbook 2018?**

Register of interests and register of gifts, hospitality and entertainments.

3. **What registers are open to inspection and who by?**

Certain registers can be inspected by trust members free of charge or by others on payment of the necessary fee and subject to the correct notice period:

◆ register of members;
◆ register of directors; and
◆ register of secretaries.

## Test yourself 5.2

1. **What filings must a trust make to Companies House?**

Trusts must submit the following to Companies House:

- change of registered office
- notification of single alternative inspection location
- appointment of trustees
- resignation of trustees (their term will not automatically expire)
- any change in trustees' details
- change of secretary
- change of articles
- confirmation statement
- annual report and accounts
- copy of any members' special resolution.</BL>

**2. What are the advantages and disadvantages of WebFiling?**

Advantages:

(a) WebFiling online is quick.

(b) An e-mail confirmation is automatically sent when a change has been made and when it has been accepted or rejected.

(c) The charge for filing the confirmation statement via WebFiling is lower than that for submission in hard copy.

(d) An 'eReminders' service sent to up to four addresses that the accounts and the confirmation statement are due.

(e) Companies can opt into the PROOF (PROtected Online Filing) and Monitor services.

Disadvantages:

(a) The trust must register with Companies House and must await an authentication to be sent through the post before it can start.

(b) WebFiling can only be used for:

 - changes of trustees, secretary, company name or address; and
 - the confirmation statement.

Any other changes must be filed in hard copy.

# Chapter 6

### Test yourself 6.1

**1. How many members are required for a general meeting to be quorate?**

A special resolution is required for decisions relating to the constitution or future of the trust:

- changes to the articles
- change of name of the trust

- any resolution required by the articles to be a special resolution
- the appointment of members.

Special resolutions require a 75% majority of the votes cast in person or by proxy.

**2.  What majority is required to pass a special resolution and when might it be used?**

The model articles provide that the quorum is two members. A representative of a corporate member (e.g. a diocese which is represented by one of its advisors) or a validly appointed proxy will count towards the quorum.

**3.  What could prevent someone who is present at a general meeting from voting?**

Members cannot vote if they owe any money to the trust or if there is a perceived or actual conflict.

Trustees are entitled to attend and speak at general meetings but do not have a vote.

Any other persons invited to a general meeting, such as members of the executive, do not have a vote.

## Test yourself 6.2

**1.  What is the quorum for a board meeting and what happens if it is not met?**

The quorum is the greater of:

- three trustees; or
- one-third (rounded up to a whole number) of the total number of trustees holding office at the date of the meeting.

If the quorum is not met, the meeting must be closed immediately. If there is further business that has not been conducted, another meeting must be called within seven days.

**2.  How are decisions made in a board meeting?**

Decisions or 'resolutions' are passed by a majority of the votes cast by the trustees' present. Each trustee has one vote except where there is an equal division of votes cast for and against a resolution in which case the chair will have an additional 'casting vote'. Voting is normally conducted on a show of hands although trustees can use any mechanism they choose.

## Test yourself 6.3

**What is a written resolution?**

A written resolution is one that is proposed by the trustees or by the members in writing (i.e. without the requirement for a meeting to be held). It is not necessary for all the members of the company to sign the written resolution to pass it, though a trustees' written resolution does need to be unanimous.

# Chapter 7

## Test yourself 7.1

**1.    What are the main steps in a risk management process?**

- Risk identification
- Risk estimation (assessing likelihood and impact)
- Risk prioritisation
- Risk mitigation
- Risk monitoring
- Risk reporting

**2.    What risk treatment or strategies should be considered?**

- **S**hare risk – outsource the activity or transfer the risk through insurance.
- **A**void risk – change the plan or the activity so that the problem is not encountered.
- **R**educe risk – make changes that mitigate or control the risk.
- **A**ccept risk – note the risk and take the chance that it, or part of it, might arise.

## Test yourself 7.2

### What is the RPA and how does it work?

RPA is the 'risk protection arrangement' organised by ESFA. It is a voluntary risk scheme by which losses are reimbursed from a pooling arrangement underwritten by government funds. Trusts 'opt in' to the RPA scheme and pay a per pupil sum deducted from GAG at source.

## Test yourself 7.3

**1.    What do the HSE and Institute of Directors suggest are the three essential principles of effective leadership in health and safety?**

*Guidance to Directors* identified three essential principles of effective leadership in health and safety:

- Strong and active leadership from the top
- Worker involvement
- Assessment and review.

**2.    Give an example of a typical injury that will not be reportable under RIDDOR.**

Examples of injuries that will not normally be reportable under RIDDOR (Reporting of Injuries, Diseases and Dangerous Occurrences Regulations 2013):

- Accidents to pupils sustained in PE lessons (unless the pupil is killed or taken to hospital for treatment or was work-related).
- Sporting injuries (unless they arise out of or in connection with a work activity).
- Injuries sustained in a road traffic accident on the way to school in the school bus.
- Injuries sustained on a school trip abroad.

# Chapter 8

## Test yourself 8.1

### Name any five statutory policies.

- Accessibility plan
- Admissions arrangements
- Allegations of abuse against staff
- Behaviour policy
- Charging and remissions
- Child protection policy and procedures
- Complaints procedure
- Data protection
- Early Years Foundation Stage (EYFS)
- Freedom of Information
- Equality information and objectives (public sector equality duty) statement
- Health and Safety
- Home-school agreement
- Recruitment and selection
- Sex and relationships education
- Special Educational Needs
- Staff discipline, conduct and grievance procedures
- Supporting Pupils with Medical Conditions

## Test yourself 8.2

### 1. In an academy setting, who is required to undertake safeguarding training?

All staff must undergo safeguarding, child protection and Prevent training. Pupils must be taught about safeguarding. It is best practice that trustees and governors undertake safeguarding and Prevent training. The designated safeguarding lead and any deputies must undergo appropriate training at least every two years.

**2. For whom is an enhanced DBS check required?**

Enhanced DBS certificates must be obtained for members of staff, supply staff, members, trustees and members of local governing bodies/advisory councils if relevant.

**3. Can the DBS certificate provided for a previous employer be accepted?**

A DBS certificate issued in relation to a previous employer will only be acceptable if the individual is registered with the update service.

# Chapter 9

## Test yourself 9.1

**1. What are the lawful bases for processing personal data out in GDPR?**

Article 6 of GDPR sets out six lawful bases for processing which must apply whenever personal data is processed:

(a)   Consent

(b)   Contract

(c)   Legal obligation

(d)   Vital interests

(e)   Public task

(f)   Legitimate interests.

# Chapter 10

## Test yourself 10.1

**1. What factors should be included in key performance indicators to make them effective?**

Key performance indicators should be:

◆   *Quantitative*: They can be presented in numbers or other form of measurement.

◆   *Practical*: They integrate well with current processes.

◆   *Directional*: They help to determine if there has been improvement.

◆   *Actionable*: They can be put into practice to effect desired change.

**2. Give some examples of types of KPIs that could be set.**

Typical KPIs include:

◆   Ofsted inspection outcome

◆   SATs/KS4/KS5 results

- ◆ Pupil attendance data
- ◆ Surplus funds at year end
- ◆ Unrestricted funds to be in surplus
- ◆ Pupil numbers
- ◆ Percentage of income spent on staffing costs
- ◆ Staff performance reviews.

# Chapter 11

## Test yourself 11.1

### What are the main sources of income for trusts?

The main sources of revenue income:

- ◆ GAG income
- ◆ Education services grant (ESG)
- ◆ Capital funding:
  - – Formula funding – School Condition Allocation (SCA)
  - – Condition Improvement Fund (CIF)
- ◆ Healthy Pupils Capital Fund (HPCF) - for the financial year 2018–2019 only.

## Test yourself 11.2

### 1. What is GASDS and when could a trust use the scheme?

GASDS is the Gift Aid Small Donations Scheme. It can be used in respect of donations of £20 or less in cash or contactless card donations up to a maximum total of £2,000 in a single tax year (i.e. on donations of £8,000).

The trust must have:

- ◆ Claimed Gift Aid in the same tax year as the GASDS claim
- ◆ Not incurred a penalty in the last two tax years
- ◆ For claims on donations made before 6 April 2017, made a successful Gift Aid claim in at least two out of the last four tax years, without a gap of two or more tax years between those Gift Aid claims or since the last claim made.

The GASDS claim cannot be more than 10 times the Gift Aid claim in the same tax year.

### 2. How can a trust claim tax relief?

A trust may present the letter of recognition as a charity from HMRC to a bank or building society to receive interest without tax deducted. Tax paid may be reclaimed directly from the bank or building society for the current year or from HMRC for previous tax years.

# Chapter 12

## Test yourself 12.1

### How can the programme on internal risk review be carried out?

The board can adapt recommendations to suit their circumstances and could combine a variety of the options:

- Use of an internal audit service (either in-house, bought-in or provided by a sponsor).
- A supplementary programme of work by the trusts external auditors.
- Appointment of a non-employed trustee with an appropriate level of qualifications and/or experience who neither charges nor is paid by the trust for their work.
- Peer review.

# Directory of web resources

DfE guidance on Schools Causing Concern: **https://assets.publishing. service.gov.uk/government/uploads/system/uploads/attachment_data/ file/680559/Schools_causing_concern_guidance_-_February_2018.pdf**

UK Corporate Governance Code 2018: **https://www.frc.org.uk/ getattachment/88bd8c45-50ea-4841-95b0-d2f4f48069a2/2018-UK-Corporate-Governance-Code-FINAL.PDF**

DfE Governance Handbook: **https://assets.publishing.service.gov.uk/ government/uploads/system/uploads/attachment_data/file/582868/ Governance_Handbook_-_January_2017.pdf**

DfE Competency Framework for Governance: **https://assets.publishing. service.gov.uk/government/uploads/system/uploads/attachment_data/ file/583733/Competency_framework_for_governance_.pdf**

The Seven Principles of Public Life – the Nolan Principles: **https://www.gov.uk/ government/publications/the-7-principles-of-public-life/the-7-principles-of-public-life--2**

Charity Governance Code: **https://www.charitygovernancecode.org/en/pdf**

DfE Academies Financial Handbook 2018: **https://assets.publishing.service. gov.uk/government/uploads/system/uploads/attachment_data/ file/714474/Academies_Financial_Handbook_2018.pdf**

DfE Clerking Competency Framework: **https://assets.publishing.service.gov. uk/government/uploads/system/uploads/attachment_data/file/609971/ Clerking_competency_framework.pdf**

DfE Statutory Policies for Schools 2014: **https://assets.publishing.service.gov. uk/government/uploads/system/uploads/attachment_data/file/357068/ statutory_schools_policies_Sept_14_FINAL.pdf**

DfE School Admissions Code: **https://assets.publishing.service.gov.uk/ government/uploads/system/uploads/attachment_data/file/389388/ School_Admissions_Code_2014_-_19_Dec.pdf**

Freedom of Information Code of Practice: **https://assets.publishing.service. gov.uk/government/uploads/system/uploads/attachment_data/ file/722165/FOI-Code-of-Practice-July-2018.pdf**

External reviews of governance: a guide for schools: **https://www.gov.uk/ guidance/reviews-of-school-governance**

Condition Improvement Fund guidance: **https://www.gov.uk/guidance/ condition-improvement-fund**

Academies accounts direction 2017 to 2018: **https://assets.publishing. service.gov.uk/government/uploads/system/uploads/attachment_data/ file/712372/Academies_Accounts_Direction_2017_to_2018.pdf**

# Glossary

**Academy** – state-funded schools, independent of local authority control.

**Academy chain** – any collaboration between academies whether that is done through a legal structure (i.e. MAT or umbrella) or a more informal approach (e.g. collaborative agreement).

**Accounting reference date** – the date that marks the end of a company's accounting year end for the purposes of preparation and filing of statutory accounts.

**Accounts** – a statement of the academy's financial affairs which can refer to published accounts or internal management accounts.

**Annual return** – a return of information that all companies must make to the registrar of companies within every 12-month period providing a snapshot of the company including its directors, principal business activities and registered office.

**Articles of association** – the academy's main constitutional document which sets out the rules regarding internal management, decision making and the running of the trust as well as its liabilities.

**Board meeting** – a formal meeting of the board of directors.

**Board of directors** – the collective term for the academy's directors acting together as the governing body of the company, having the powers and authorities that are bestowed upon it by the company's constitution.

**Board resolution** – a formal resolution or decision of the board of directors.

**Charitable company** – a company set up and run solely for non-profit making purposes with the proceeds only to be used for the purpose of the charity.

**Companies House** – an executive agency of the Department for Business Innovation and Skills, Companies House is the registry for companies incorporated in the UK.

**Company limited by guarantee** – a company where the liability of the members is limited to a fixed amount that each member agrees to contribute to the assets of the company in the event of a winding up.

**Company secretary** – an officer of a company with no legally defined role but who generally has responsibilities with regard to the administrative, governance and compliance aspects of a company's affairs.

**Connected person** – persons who are considered to be connected with a director such as a spouse or civil partner, any other person with whom the director lives with in an enduring family relationship, the director's children and stepchildren, the director's parents and a body corporate in which the director has an interest in at least 20% of the share capital.

**Corporate director** – a company which acts as a director of another company.

**Corporate governance** – principles and best practice concerning the way in which companies are run and directed. There is no one definition of what corporate governance is, in the broader view it also encompasses issues relating to corporate social responsibility and business ethics.

**Date of incorporation** – the date on which a company was formed.

*De facto* **director** – a person acting as a director who has not been formally or validly appointed.

**Derivative claim** – a claim brought by a member of a company against a director on the academy's behalf in accordance with the procedure set out in the Companies Act 2006.

**Directors' general duties** – seven general duties of directors which are set out in the Companies Act 2006.

**Disqualification order** – a court order preventing a person from, among others, acting as a director of a company without the consent of the court for the period of time specified in the order. Breach of a disqualification order is a criminal offence.

**Earmarked Annual Grant** – a grant paid in respect of either recurrent expenditure or capital expenditure for specific purposes agreed between the Secretary of State and the academy.

**Education & and Skills Funding Agency** – an executive agency of the DfE (formerly EFA, Education Funding Agency)

**Electronic filing** – a form or document filed with Companies House in electronic format using either approved software or the Companies House WebFiling service.

**Executive director** – a director who is a full-time employee with management responsibility within the academy.

**Freedom and Autonomy for Schools – National Association** – a national forum for self-governing primary, secondary and special schools and academies.

**Free school** – an academy set up by a 'proposer group' such as parents, teachers, charities or other groups.

**General annual grant** – funding paid to cover the normal running costs of the academy (e.g. salary and administration costs).

**General meeting** – a formal meeting of an academy's members.

**Get information about schools** – an online register of schools and colleges in England which holds information on establishments, establishment groups (e.g. MATs) and governors/trustees (replaces EduBase).

**Incorporation** – the process by which a company is created, also referred to as 'formation' and 'registration'.

**Independent Academies Association** – a membership organisation dedicated to supporting leaders of academies.

**Lagged funding** – funding based on the previous year's census (i.e. funding is received in the following academic year).

**Maintained school** – a school funded by central government via the local authority.

**Management accounts** – accounts produced by an academy for internal decision-making and monitoring purposes.

**Member** – a person or corporate body whose name is entered in the academy's register of members.

**Memorandum of Association** – document confirming the three 'subscribers' who wish to form the academy and become its members. The memorandum has no ongoing significance once an academy has been incorporated.

**Minutes** – a formal record of the proceedings of a meeting and the decisions made.

**Model articles** – the standard form articles for academies prescribed by the Secretary of State under powers granted by the Companies Act.

**Multi-academy trust** – a single legal entity formed by a number of schools combining to form a single academy.

**Natural director** – a director who is a real person.

**Non-executive director** – a director who is not a full-time employee involved in the management of the academy.

**Officer** – a director, manager or secretary of an academy (under CA 2006, s. 1173 of the Companies Act 2006). In the case of an 'officer in default' this is broadened to include any person who is to be treated as an officer of the company for the purposes of the provision of the Companies Act in question.

**Ordinary resolution** – a decision/resolution requiring approval by a majority of an academy's members.

**Principal regulator** – responsible for overseeing the compliance of exempt charities with charity law. For academies, the principal regulator is the Secretary of State for Education.

**Protected online filing** – an agreement between an academy and Companies House that the academy will always file certain information electronically.

**Pupil number adjustment** – adjustment to funding based on estimated pupil numbers calculated using census data.

**Pupil premium grant** – additional funding provided to support disadvantaged pupils and pupils with parents in the armed forces.

**Quorum** – in relation to a board meeting or a members' meeting, the minimum number of directors or members respectively who must be present in order for the meeting to be validly constituted.

**Registered office** – an academy's official address at which legal and other documents can be validly served and at which certain company records must be kept if not kept at a SAIL. For a single academy this is likely to be the school itself.

**Remuneration** – payments and benefits that an employee is entitled to in respect of services provided by the employee to an academy.

**Risk assessment** – the process of identifying risks, the persons affected by them, the severity of the likely injuries or loss that might result from them, whether the control measures in place are adequate and any further measures needed to control them.

**Service address** – an address for correspondence that directors must provide to Companies House which can, and ideally should, be different from their residential address. Generally, this is the academy's registered office address.

**Shadow director** – a person who has not been appointed as a director but who directs or gives instructions to an academy's true directors.

**Single alternative inspection location** – a location that is not the registered office, at which certain company records are held.

**Special resolution** – a members' resolution requiring a majority in favour of 75% or over.

**Sponsor** – a body responsible for the performance and finances of an academy.

**Stakeholder** – a person or group of persons with an interest in an academy or who are in some way affected by an academy's activities.

**Statutory registers** – books/registers containing information relating to an academy's directors, members etc, which academies must maintain in accordance with the Companies Act.

**Umbrella trust** – an academy chain whereby the over-arching academy, or umbrella, is a charitable trust in its own right and each of the individual schools is a single academy.

**Voluntary aided** – a maintained school with a majority of the board of governors appointed by a foundation or trust, usually a religious body, which may also own the land and contribute financially.

**Voluntary controlled** – a maintained school with a quarter of the board of directors appointed by a foundation or trust, usually a religious body. The foundation may own the land, but will have less direct influence than in a VA school.

**Written resolution** – a document setting out one or more proposed resolutions that is circulated to an academy's members for approval as an alternative to holding a general meeting.

# Index

Lightning Source UK Ltd.
Milton Keynes UK
UKHW03f1838210918
329308UK00005B/266/P